Life Force Logic

Don Alexander

September 2014

I had a long conversation with myself and it changed forever my concept of who and what I am and why I believe as I do.

Don Alexander

This book is dedicated to my wife, Elaine, who has patiently tolerated my random exercises in logic for more than forty years.

AUTHOR'S NOTE:

The scientific references in my reasoning with myself will probably be somewhat unfamiliar to those readers who have not been exposed to a formal edu-cation in Earth Sciences including chemistry, physics, biology, and astronomy plus basic genetics. However, all such references have been gleaned from scientifically established facts which are undisputed in the hallowed but vain halls of higher education. What is very much in dispute is the mixing of such facts with unbridled imagination that is both unscientific and in most cases totally moronic.

Nevertheless, it will be rather simple for the

reader to decide which reasoning herein makes sense and which reasoning does not comport with logic nor mathematical possibilities. Few individuals (even those with Phd behind their names) will deny the premise that for any event or happening to actually take place the description thereof must comply with a reasonable degree of believability and mathematical possibility.

Throughout this book, as indicated by context, the masculine pronoun covers both sexes.

Bibliography Notes

Where a number appears in brackets such as [3], the bracketed number corresponds with an entry in the usual bibliography following the last chapter in this book. The bibliography herein is limited because whenever practical a quote is noted next to the spot where quote is located in the text. Pronouns that refer to Deity are capitalized in both quotations and overall text.

Scientific references are drawn from many years of study at various universities combined with extensive personal research. All Biblical quotes are taken from the King James Version of the Holy Bible which is now public domain. In some cases the quote is paraphrased to make the Scripture more understandable and a note appears to identify such paraphrasing. When portions of a quote are omitted to conserve text, a line of dots or a short broken line will indicate a partial quote.

The author's educational credentials are a Bachelor of Science degree with a triple major in business, psychology and political science coupled with a Juris Doctor degree issued by Missouri University in December, 1990. Previous publications include 13 books and 2 screenplays.

Chapter outline

1. Molecular structure of matter, energy and motion and why big bang and Darwinian evolution are highly suspect

2. Why evolution from lower life forms is scientifically impossible

3. Reasons why big bang and evolution of bacteria into higher life forms are intellectually dishonest

4. Why big bang and evolutionary theory violate every law of physics

5. Summary of the logical and scientifically compatible record of the origin of human life

6. When and how humans populated Planet Earth

7. through 13.
Synopsis covering what is recorded within all sixty-six books making up the Holy Bible

Foreword

Human intelligence exceeds that of lower living creatures by the distance of infinity. All the beasts of the field and those of the forest together with all lower ranked organisms move feed and reproduce thereby exhibiting that qualitative state which scientists have dubbed "life." Within the three dimensional universe described in terms of space, distance and time, humans stand alone in the ability to think, meditate, sculpture opinions and beliefs; to argue, debate and ponder that which lies beyond the scope of sensory perceptions. A common characteristic of humanity is to deny that which conflicts with preconceived opinions, beliefs and religious orientation regardless of where actual truth leads an unbiased mind.

The purpose underlying this literary effort is to pursue truth regardless of where reality ultimately leads both the author the reader. "What is truth?" This question has been raised through the centuries and answers have been leavened with ignorance, bias and disinterest. The question was raised nearly two thousand years before this writing by a Roman governor seeking to release a prisoner known to be innocent but beset by a religious mob screaming for blood in the interest of truth.

The author will endeavor within limited abilities to rely upon logical reasoning, tested and proven scientific facts, rational comparisons, direct evidence plus eye witness testimony to present a coherent and unbiased explanation of that simple truth which the overwhelming majority of humanity rejects.

Chapter one

If you are reading this, the chances are excellent that you are alive. Okay. That seems fairly logical. I think, therefore I am (Rene Decartes). I am what? I am a human being. Great. What exactly is a human being? Well, I have a physical body. I move. I feed. I can probably reproduce (although I could become sterile). Therefore, by definition written by those esteemed to know, I am alive.

Well, is my life quality the same as my physical body, or could my life and the body be separable? How about if my heart stops beating and my lungs stop functioning and my brain no longer absorbs oxygen........an hour later, can I still move, feed and reproduce? No. I am most certainly dead.

I are dead in the sense that there is no life present in my physical body even though my body is intact in that I still have my heart, lungs, brain and other vital organs although my blood is certainly no longer circulating. I must assume in such case that I would no longer be alive. Because I can no longer move, feed and reproduce? Yes. Is it fair to conclude that physical death is the absence of the ability to move, feed and reproduce? Yes, it appears so. That fits the scientific definition of an inorganic state of being.

Doesn't it then logically follow that if physical

death is the absence of life, then the physical body and life are not the same and thus are divisible? That does seem logical but I never thought of my physical body and my life in those dimensions. I mean within three dimensions of space, distance and time. Okay. What fills space, distance and time? Most probably light, darkness, energy, matter and motion. [21]

Physical structures are divided into two classes: (1) living or (2) non-living. A physical structure classified as living must have the abilities to move, feed and reproduce. Thus, a dog, a flea, a bacterium, and an elephant have life. Grass, trees, flowers, cabbage, strawberries, and various other forms of plant life exist along with a vast variety of bacterial, insect, marine, mammal and human life.

Plant life is very limited in abilities. Plants send roots into the soil, take in water, soil nutrients and sunlight. Plants reproduce through pollination but do not bark, chase cars, roar in the jungle, chase down and eat other living creatures, etc. Bacteria move, take in nutrients, and reproduce but do not build nests, exhibit maternal instincts, dig worms, protect offspring, etc. Insects do not fish, hunt grizzlies, or build skyscrapers; but rather just move, feed, reproduce and make humans quite miserable. Fish, frogs, birds, reptiles, mammals, and other animal life forms exhibit instinctual, adaptive and fixed behavior patterns but do not pave roads, build motor vehicles, write books, design spaceships, build and fly jetliners, fashion nuclear weapons, perform brain surgery, write poetry, meditate, imagine events, etc.

Humans are virtually unlimited in thought, reason, logic, design, engineering, imagination, communicat-ions, ingenuity, cruelty, jealousy, love, hate, exploiting their environment and other living creatures, etc, etc. Consequently, it is patently obvious that there exists a hierarchy of life forms possessing abilities that vary drastically between levels of existence. The concept of life forms with abilities and powers far beyond humans is not a moronic premise.

Okay. So, how is light created? Generally speaking, by the burning of combustible plasma, solids, liquids and gases. Is darkness a word to describe the absence of light? No. Darkness is the inability to perceive light. A blind person sees darkness in the presence of light. Light is always present because light is created by atomic particles known as electrons jumping orbits between quantum states during changes in each electron's temperature, then cooling and falling back to ground state nearer the nucleus of individual atoms.

A more definitive understanding of light is achieved by considering the micro universe in the form of the sub-atomic particles which make up both the micro and macro masses including both inorganic matter and living organisms. All matter within the universe is composed of what scientists call elements. The known elements total 112 of which 91 predate the appearance in space of our solar system. Currently, 84 of the 112 are considered "primordial" because they appear naturally and do not involve any laboratory synthesis.

The other 21 elements resulted from transmutation of some of the original elements through the process of radioactive decay, nuclear fission or nuclear fusion. A significant number of the elements are found in all organic and inorganic masses and are essential to the very existence of the physical structure of bacteria, plants, insects, animals and humans.

The known elements, including the nuclear elements resulting from nuclear fission and nuclear fusion, are: hydrogen, beryllium, sodium, magnesium, lithium, potassium, calcium, scandium, titanium, vanadium, chromium, manganese, iron, cobalt, nickel, copper, zinc, boron, carbon, nitrogen, oxygen, fluorine, neon, aluminum, silicon, phosphorus, sulfur, chlorine, argon, gallium, germanium, arsenic, selenium, bromine, krypton, rubidium, strontium, yttrium, zirconium, niobium, molybdenum, technetium, ruthenium, rhodium, palladium, silver, cadmium, indium, tin, antimony, tellurium, iodine, xenon, caesium, barium, hafnium, tantalum, tungsten, rhenium, osmium, iridium, platinum, gold, mercury, thallium, lead, bismuth, polonium, astatine, radon, francium, radium, rutherfordum, dubnium, seaborgium, bothrium, hassium, meitnreium, ununhexium, damstadium, roentgerium, copemicium, ununtrium, ununquadum, ununpentium, ununsepium, ununoctium, lanthanum, actinium, cerium, thorium, protactinium, praseodymium, neodymium, uranium, promethium, neptunium, samarium, plutonium, europium, americium, gadolinium, curium, terbium, berkelium, dysprosium, californium, holmium, einsteinium, erbium, fermium, thulium, mendelevium, ytterbium, nobelium, lutetium, and lawrencium.

The physical molecular structure comprising the bodies of all life forms ranging from a single-celled bacterium to humans consists of the primordial elements (non-nuclear elements). The thirty-seven trillion or so single cells the human body is composed of contain nothing but oxygen, carbon, hydrogen, nitrogen, calcium, phosphorus, potassium, sulfur, chlorine, sodium, magnesium, iron, cobalt, copper, zinc, iodine, selenium and fluorine, plus a few trace elements.

Life itself is by far the strangest phenomenon of all. It does not consist of the primordial elements nor any of the non-primordial elements and therefore could never have originated from any energy, matter or momentum within the entire universe. Therefore, life is not part of the physical body and thus is not dependent upon a physical manifestation. Yet, the body cannot move, feed nor reproduce without life.

Upon death the physical body reverts back to the elements from which it originated. Where life returns upon separation from the body is thus far incomprehensible to proponents of the "big bang theory" coupled with the "theory of evolution."

All the elements are composed of microscopic divisions of matter which scientists call atoms. The atoms of each element are composed of protons, neutrons and electrons. The only difference between atoms of different elements is the number of protons within the atom's nucleus. For example, a hydrogen atom contains one proton whereas an atom of uranium contains 92 protons.

Hydrogen is the lightest element and uranium is one of the heaviest elements. The nucleus of an atom is simply protons and neutrons in close proximity to each other. The nucleus of each atom of each element is surrounded by one or more orbiting electrons. Protons are positively charged, electrons are negatively charged, and neutrons are electrically neutral. The term "electrical" with respect to atoms refers to nothing more than the attracting and repelling forces holding atoms together.

Atomic forces binding atoms together are called "the strong nuclear force and the weak nuclear force." Both forces are known to exist but the origin thereof is an unsolved mystery which baffles theoretical physicists striving to understand the relationship between energy, matter, velocity and momentum.

There are three primary sources of energy in the universe referred to as nuclear energy, radiation energy and magnetic energy. Energy in motion is kinetic energy. Kinetic energy at rest is potential energy, and kinetic energy produces both heat and pressure. Within the atom of an individual element, kinetic energy drives the orbiting electrons which appear to vibrate.

A charged atomic particle in motion (such as electrons) generates magnetic energy. Nuclear energy (the strong nuclear force and the weak nuclear force) keeps the nucleus of every atom (except hydrogen) from self-destructing due to the repelling force exerted by positively charged protons within the nucleus (hydrogen atoms contain a single proton).

Radiation energy pulses in waves when an element changes into another element (such as hydrogen into helium) through nuclear fusion within the core of stars. Each star functions as a giant nuclear reactor. There are billions of galaxies and an individual galaxy contains billions of stars.

The process of nuclear fusion within stars emits continuous electromagnetic radiation (light) and nuclear energy resulting from the uncoupling of the strong and weak nuclear forces bonding the nucleus of individual atoms within the fusing elements.

The nuclear energy released in the form of waves of radiation creates massive magnetic energy waves which push against the radiation waves at right angles. This joint energy force is what causes the spin of orbiting masses in space.

The trillions of stars in space are emitting continuous waves of nuclear energy and magnetic energy waves which means that space is not empty between galaxies. The continuous pulsing of energy waves from each galaxy is what causes the expanding universe over a visible radius (through the Hubble telescope) of roughly thirteen billion light years. The velocity of energy waves is reinforced by the continuous energy waves pulsing behind them causing the galaxies to eventually recede from each other faster than the speed of light.

A proton in a hydrogen atom is identical to a proton within an atom of uranium. All neutrons are also the same but atoms of a particular element may contain more or less neutrons than another atom of the same element and are referred to as isotopes of the element.

For example, the isotope of uranium (U-235) is much rarer than the common uranium atom (U-238) but is more susceptible to transmutation through nuclear fission. Hence, U-235 is the fuel originally used in nuclear power plants.

Atoms that are electrically neutral have the same number of electrons orbiting the nucleus as the number of protons within the nucleus. All of the atom outside its nucleus is mostly empty space. Electrons within this space orbit the nucleus completing billions of cycles every millionth of a second. The amazing speed of electron orbit makes the atom appear to be a solid mass.

Each proton has a mass equal to the mass of 1,836 electrons. The mass of an electron has been calculated to be 0.000000000000000000000000009 of one gram which is very close to zero mass. It takes 1,839 electrons to equal one neutron's mass. The protons and neutrons are confined within the tiny nucleus of the atom and are in constant motion. The higher the velocity, the higher the temperature. Every element has a freezing point, melting point and boiling temperature. At extremely high temperatures some elements convert to plasma.

The "strong nuclear force" keeps the nucleus from flying apart by overcoming the mutual repulsion of the positively charged protons.

Atoms can gain, lose or share electrons during chemical reactions with atoms of another element. An atom that loses one or more electrons becomes a positive ion whereas an atom that gains one or more electrons becomes a negative ion.

A negative or positive ion results when the negative charge on the atom's total electrons does not match the positive charge on the atom's total protons.

If an atom easily gives up electrons, its valence is positive, and atoms that tend to gain electrons have a negative valence.

Sodium tends to lose its one electron and thus has a valence of (+1). Chlorine tends to accept one electron from another atom and therefore has a valence of (-1). Negative ions can chemically bond with positive ions.

Thus, a molecule of ordinary table salt consists of one atom of sodium linked to one atom of chlorine. This type of chemical interaction between the atoms of the known elements is how all the matter in the universe, both organic and inorganic, is structured.

The nucleus makes up nearly all the mass of an atom. Protons and neutrons which make up the nucleus are roughly 100,000 times smaller than the atom.

Electrons are not known to be composed of smaller particles of matter whereas protons and neutrons are composed of smaller particles called quarks.

Each proton and each neutron is made up of three quarks. Quarks can be manipulated by researchers within a science laboratory to form other particles of matter besides protons and neutrons but such particles are highly unstable and break down within a tiny fraction of a second. Therefore, these unstable particles are not found outside the laboratory.

Each electron has inherent energy in proportion to its orbiting velocity. The incredible velocity of orbiting electrons resembles vibration rather than orbit. The strong nuclear force binding protons within the atom's nucleus also appears to vibrate and is believed to be the actual source of gravitational attraction between masses.

The positively charged protons within the nucleus exert a force on orbiting negatively charged electrons that keeps them within the atom when the atom is not involved in a chemical reaction, nuclear fission, or nuclear fusion. The inherent energy within an electron generates resistance to the attracting force of the nucleus. The more energy the electron has, the farther from the nucleus it will be. Consequently, electrons are arranged in energy shells at varying distances from the nucleus as determined by the level of their inherent energy. Electrons with the least energy are located in the inner shells and those with higher energy levels are in the outer shells.

Each electron energy shell is identified by a number or letter. The shell closest to the nucleus is shell #1 or shell K. The other shells, in order of increasing distance from the nucleus, are numbered 2 through 7 or labeled L through Q. Each shell can hold a limited number of electrons. Shell 1 can hold no more than 2 electrons. Shell 2 can hold 8 electrons, shell 3 can hold 18, shell 4 can hold 32, shell 5 can hold 50, shell 6 can hold 72, and shell 7 can hold 98. However, the outer shells are never completely filled. The number of filled shells is determined by the number of electrons contained within the atom. An atom that has lost all its electrons will become a positively charged free nucleus.

There can also be free electrons (negative charge), and free neutrons (neutral charge) as the result of radioactive decay, nuclear fission and nuclear fusion. In the atoms of radioactive elements the nucleus will change as the atom gives off radioactive particles.

The change in the nucleus may be rearrangement of its protons and neutrons or the actual loss of one or more. If only the arrangement of the nucleus changes, gamma rays are emitted from the atom. If the number of protons changes, alpha or beta radiation is given off. When an atom loses one or more protons, it changes to an atom of a different element.

If one or more neutrons escape from the nucleus, the atom becomes an isotope of the radiating element. All elements heavier than bismuth are radioactive as well as the isotopes of some of the lighter elements. Isotopes of nearly all the elements can be created by bombarding their atoms with subatomic particles.

The atomic number denotes how many protons the atom of an element contains, and the mass number identifies the sum of the protons and neutrons within the nucleus. Atomic weight is the weight of an atom expressed in "atomic mass units" (amu). One amu or "dalton" equals 1/12 the weight of an atom of carbon 12. There are 602 billion trillion amu in one gram.

All atoms of the same element have the same number of protons. Since every hydrogen atom contains one proton, the atomic number of hydrogen is 1. The atomic numbers range successively up to 94 for plutonium because this element has 94 protons in each atom. Elements with more than 94 protons in each of its atoms can be created by scientists in the laboratory.

There exists more than one isotope for most of the elements. For example, hydrogen has three. The most common has no neutron in the nucleus of each atom. In the other two isotopes, the nucleus contains one to two neutrons. The mass number is used to distinguish the three isotopes; hydrogen 1, hydrogen 2 and hydrogen 3. These isotopes are also called protium, deuterium and tritium respectively.

Most of the lighter elements contain about the same number of protons and neutrons in the nucleus of their atoms. The heavier elements have more neutrons than protons. The heaviest elements have about three neutrons for every two protons. U-238, for example, has 92 protons and 146 neutrons.

Atoms of different elements which have the same mass number but different atomic numbers are called isobars. The isobars argon and calcium have a mass number of 40 but argon's atomic number is 18 (18 protons) and calcium's atomic number is 20 (20 protons).

The way an atom of an element behaves during a chemical reaction is largely determined by the number of electrons in its outermost electron shell. When atoms combine and form molecules, electrons in the outermost shell are either transferred from one atom to another or shared between atoms.

The number of electrons involved in the chemical reaction is referred to as "valence." The atoms of some elements can have more than one valence depending on the number and kind of atoms they can combine with.

Electrons are restricted to a limited set of motions, each of which has a specific energy value. These motions are referred to as quantum states or energy levels. When an electron is in a given quantum state, it does not give off or absorb energy. An atom can lose or gain energy only when one or more electrons change from one quantum state to another.

Electrons seek the lowest state of energy but only one electron at a time can occupy each quantum state. When the lower states are filled, other electrons are forced to occupy higher states. When all electrons are in the lowest available state, the atom is in "ground state" which is the normal condition for atoms at ordinary temperatures.

When matter is heated to a few hundred degrees, sufficient energy is then available to raise one or more electrons to a higher energy level. The atom is then transformed into an "excited state" which lasts for a fraction of a second. An excited electron quickly drops to a lower state and continues dropping until the atom returns to its ground state.

During each succeeding drop, the electron gives off a tiny packet of radiant energy called a photon. The energy of the photon equals the difference between the two energy levels the electron passed through. These photons are detected as visible light and other forms of electromagnetic radiation.

One neutron and one proton can occupy each quantum state in the nucleus of an atom. A light nucleus has about the same number of protons and neutrons but a proton and neutron in the same state do not have the same amount of energy because each proton is electrically repelled by all other protons in the nucleus thereby increasing the energy of each proton.

In a heavy nucleus, the difference in energy levels between protons and neutrons is significant and more low energy states are available for neutrons than for protons. This helps explain why a heavy nucleus contains more neutrons than protons.

Most of the 91 elements found in and on Earth (as

contrasted to the elements created in scientific laboratories and nuclear reactors) are in compound form. They are combined with other elements forming soil, rocks, gas, liquids, minerals, crystals, etc. Oxygen and silicon are the most plentiful elements in Earth's crust and make up 3/4 of the crust's weight. A few elements are found in pure form in small amounts such as gold, copper, carbon and sulfur.

It is easy to confuse energy, force and power. Energy is the word used to describe the ability to make things happen, like raising the temperature of liquids, gases and solids. Energy propels, directs and accelerates all types of matter; produces light; binds subatomic particles within the nucleus of all atoms; and numerous other activities classified as "work." The amount of activities which can be accomplished depends upon the strength of the energy force used and the distance through which it moves. Power measures the rate at which the work is performed.

All matter is held together by the energy which prevents the nucleus of every atom from self-destructing. Therefore, energy existed within the universe before any of the elements came into being. An atom of any of the elements is mostly empty space invaded by energy emitting from the tiny nucleus and the orbiting electrons.

The incredible amount of energy present within the strong nuclear force which offsets the repelling force of the positively charged protons is measured by

Einstein's formula: energy equals mass times the speed of light squared (E = MC squared).

The destructive power of nuclear weapons results from releasing the strong nuclear force from within the atoms of certain radioactive elements.

Since energy preceded the formation of matter and matter is composed of atoms, atoms were perfectly designed so that energy could hold them together. In other words, atoms had to come into existence within the universe in the form of their existing irreducible level of complexity.

Although closely intertwined, energy and matter are not the same. It is obvious from the very structure of matter that it is mostly energy in motion. Yet, the force which holds matter together is not matter; it is energy. Energy and matter were applied to a specific preplanned design and living beings were introduced into a physical environment that had already been carefully crafted to nurture and sustain them.

The questions that physicists, chemists, astronomers, and biologists wrestle with are extremely basic but not simple. How did the universe come into existence? Was the birth of the universe accidental or designed? When did the universe appear? Is the universe progressing from a beginning to an end? Which elements make up the bulk of the matter contained in the universe? How did this combination of elements originate? How were living organisms introduced into the universe? What forces account for the delicate balance between energy, matter, and momentum? Where did viruses and bacteria come from? Where and how did the hierarchy of bacteria, insects, plants, animals and humans originate? How do inorganic compounds acquire life? What exactly is life? Is there life after physical death for humans? For other living organisms? How and when does the human fetus acquire life? Does my life force contain a form of energy? If so, what kind of energy?

What in is the substance of energy? Scientifically speaking, all energy is the gravitational, electromagnetic, and nuclear force fields created by the constant molecular interaction bound up within the atoms of the elements thereby creating potential, kinetic and heat energy.

By definition, I am referring to the elements which combine to form all plasma, gases, liquids and solids.....just like the various elements in my physical body. Does my physical body contain anything whatsoever that is not listed among the primordial elements? No. It does not. I see. And, none of the primordial elements or other elements make up my life force? I never before heard anyone address this question. Is it not an interesting thought? Yes indeed. Since the life force does not result from molecular combining of the elements, life and the physical body must be separate entities. The body is composed of the same elements as dirt, water, and other inorganic compounds that do not contain the life force. That is an absolutely established fact and not disputed even by Darwin's disciples.

But, what then does the life force consist of? With that puzzling issue put aside for the moment, what about the universe itself? Is it not also composed of the elements just like my physical body but in different compounds? Yes. Then, it is certain that the elements had to be in existence before the universe could emerge in either a primordial form or the form we behold today. It would seem so as there is no other explanation being voiced in opposition to the premise that the elements (most certainly hydrogen and helium) had to exist prior to what they indisputably combined to create through nuclear fusion and nuclear fission.

Then does it not also follow that the most primitive form in which the universe ever existed, whether as parallel universes or collapsed universes (or universes that languished for unknown eons of time within outer darkness) must have also been formed by the primordial elements (before light began emitting from billions of galaxies filled with stars including our sun)? Are not the sun and other stars giant circular clouds of hydrogen and lesser amounts of other elements spinning in space and ignited by the heat generated by total inherent mass and internal molecular energy emitting from the fusion of hydrogen into helium? [24]

So then, common logic dictates that some of the elements existed prior to the heavens and Earth and interstellar masses of whatever size, configuration and elemental composition.

Okay. I am convinced that some of the elements preexisted the universe and that the physical human body is distinct from the life force causing moving, feeding and reproducing. Now, if only we can unravel the origin of the elements, and each life force possessed by each diverse living organism, the actual composition of the universe will be definable. Those who spend their short lives studying astrology, astronomy and astrophysics tell us that the sun represents 99.86% of the mass of our **solar system**. The planets, comets, asteroids, and miscellaneous interstellar masses make up the other 0.14%.

The sun's diameter is estimated at 1,392,000 kilometers and its total mass is 330,000 times the mass of Earth. The sun orbits the Milky Way at a distance roughly equal to 25,000 light years with a velocity approaching 370 kilometers per second completing one orbit each 250,000,000 years. The chemical composition of the sun is 75% hydrogen, 23.31% helium and 1.69% oxygen, carbon, neon, and iron plus trace elements heavier than helium. This 1.69% of the sun's mass is 5,628 times the mass of Earth. The sun is just one of the 200 billion or more stars within Milky Way.

The Milky Way is one of an estimated 200 billion galaxies and its velocity is calculated at 550 to 600 kilometers per second. Milky Way's diameter is approximately 120,000 light years (one light year is just under ten trillion kilometers – the distance light travels in one year at a velocity of around 300,000 kilometers per second).

The number of individual stars within the known universe number into the trillions. The sun converts its hydrogen mass through nuclear fusion into helium at the rate of 620 million metric tons per second. The fused helium contains less mass than the converted hydrogen. The excess mass resulting from the fusion of hydrogen into helium radiates out from the sun in the form of pulsating waves of electromagnetic energy which we call sunlight.

With respect to origin of the elements, is it not obvious that if the universe is composed of the elements, then the origin of elements must have occurred outside of all space, distance and measured time relative to the known universe? Yes. That seems elementary. All the Phd folks describe the universe as everything physical that exists within known distance, space and time

Would it not also be just as obvious that since the elements could not arise within our three dimensional universe there must exist another dimension or dimensions not perceivable within our recognized three dimensional habitat? Yes. That is a rational thought.

Doesn't that raise the question as to how many dimensions actually exist? And, if the elements sprang from perhaps seven dimensions, as Einstein believed, would not such dimensions have to be more complex than our perceived three dimensions (by virtue of such dimensions giving birth to the primordial elements)?

Is it not also quite feasible that some life force possessing creative power over the matter, energy and motion within our three dimensions most probably exists somewhere within perhaps seven dimensions?

Okay. I am beginning to see where I am headed. Since only a supreme and creative life force could create the primordial elements from nothingness, what shall we call such a supreme being? Well, "God" works for me. God is a word coined to refer to a creative life force existing outside of that which has been created by Him (I think a masculine pronoun is acceptable when referring to such a supreme life force).

It appears most logical that all matter of whatever description and composition is absolutely the result of the molecular combining of the elements listed on the Periodic Table of the Elements and taught to every high school student electing to study basic chemistry.

A prudent question would be "how does such molecular bonding occur?" Theoretical physics leaps into the murky depths of "might be," "could be," "perhaps," "seems to," "most likely" and figments of sheer imagination in an attempt to describe the force fields that make up the atoms of every element known to science. Such purely theoretical theories are hotly disputed among those with graduate degrees in physics.

Therefore, a dummy like me must for lack of higher education stick with the body of scientific knowledge that is not disputed and which has been tested for compatibility with the law of cause and effect, the laws of the conservation of matter, energy and momentum, plus the first, second and third laws of thermodynamics.

Such alleged scientific facts have been subjected to numerous scientific experiments worldwide which have repeatedly yielded the same results. Many evolutionists (desperately hoping to hang onto random chance evolution of simplicity into complexity thereby voiding the second law of thermodynamics) postulate that entropy only applies to isolated and closed systems. However, our universe is a closed system in that it encompasses all matter, energy and motion existing within time distance and space. It has been consistently demonstrated that all the elements are composed of subatomic force fields that have been named electrons, neutrons and protons. The "weak nuclear force" existing within the universe is the primary force permitting trans-mutation of the elements.

Electrons can be added, subtracted or shared between atoms of different elements to form molecules and molecules can be bonded together to form compounds such as my eyes, teeth, heart, and my other physical body parts. In fact, my physical body contains over 37 trillion individual cells and each cell is composed of the primordial elements in the form of atoms, molecules and compounds.

The molecular mix of chemical compounds making up a physical human body (to the nearest .01%) are 65% oxygen, 18% carbon, 10% hydrogen, 3%

nitrogen, 1.5% calcium, 1.2% phosphorus, .2% potassium, .2% sulfur, .2% Chlorine, .1% sodium, .05% magnesium, <.05% iron, <.05% cobalt, <.05% copper, <.05% zinc, <.05% iodine, <.01% selenium, and <.01% fluorine, plus a few trace elements less than .01% each.

Okay. That sounds very scientific but what accounts for what specific compounds are formed and why? Let's look again at the 37 trillion or so individual living cells that make up my physical body. Charles Darwin, a botanist and inventor of the theory of evolution, knew absolutely nothing about the molecular structure of living cells nor the reality of DNA coding.

Darwin sailed around a remote island and observed metamorphosis peculiar to certain living organisms and minor genetic adaptions within some species of living creatures to accommodate changes in physical habitat. From such limited observations, Charlie concluded that all living creatures evolved over eons of time by random chance genetic mutations from a single celled organism into humans. It never occurred to Charlie that his erroneous conclusion might be chemically, genetically, and mathematically impossible.

Darwin's friend, Charles Lyell, an atheistic lawyer, who, like Darwin, could not imagine a living creature more intelligent than them, decided God is a figment of religious bigots' imaginations, because after all, there is similarity between embryonic stages of living creatures and for sure millions of years elapsed between layers of sediment deposited by erosion and embedded within Earth's crust. Thus, Lyell developed his famous "Geologic Column" as a yardstick to measure how old fossils would be based upon how deep such fossils were buried within Earth's crust.

Well, neither one of the Charlies got around to explaining how whale skeletons and petrified trees were found protruding through several layers of rock sediment laid down millions of years apart from each adjoining layer. Neither did they explain why billions of fossils of living creatures and organisms undergoing evolutionary magic (missing links) are totally absent from Earth's fossil record.

And, neither Charlie explained how odds of one chance in ten to the forty thousands power or one chance in ten to the billionth power could be successfully achieved on a regular basis by simply adding together eons of time. And, of course, neither Darwin nor Lyell nor any other atheist have explained the origin of the life force possessed by every living creature including bacteria.

Then, for Darwin's scientifically confounded disciples there is the sticky problem as to exactly how a chain of minor genetic adaptions occurring separately over eons of time suddenly emerged and functioned in precise coordination with each other at a specific point in measured time to produce a sensory ability such as vision. Even Darwin, himself, believed the evolution of vision to be a physical impossibility (read his book on origin of the species).

Moreover, the impossibility of the evolution of vision pales in comparison to the complexity of the brain of living creatures and the birth of their offspring.

Also, by what evolutionary magic and genetic randomness evolved psychic drives and emotions such as libido, love, hate, jealousy, spite, revenge, imagination, conscience, etc.?

Evolutionists and big bang advocates proclaim that all "true scientists" have accepted the random chance formation of the universe and spontaneous generation of life forms as scientific fact. However, most of the scientists who fathered every existing field of science between the first and twentieth centuries believed in a supreme being and were very vocal about their faith. These scientists include:

Leonardo da Vinci, Johann Kepler, Francis Bacon, Blaise Pascal, Robert Boyle, John Ray, Nicolaus Steno, Thomas Burnet, Athanasius Kircher, John Wilkens, Walter Charleton, Sir William Petty, Isaac Barrow, Increase Mather, Nehemiah Grew, Galileo, Robert Hooke, William Harvey, Christian Huygens, Tycho Brahe, Nicholas Copernicus, Isaac Newton, William Whiston, John Woodward, Carolus Linnaeus, Jonathan Edwards, William Herschel, John Harris, Gottfried Wilhelm Leibnitz, John Flamsteed, William Derham, Cotton Mather, John Hutchinson, Gustavus Brander, Jean Deluc, Richard Kirwan, James Parkinson, Michael Faraday, Humphrey Davy, George Cuvier, Timothy

Dwight, Benjamin Silliman, Charles Bell, William Buckland, Charles Babbage, David Brewster, John Herschel, John Dalton, William Kirby, Jedidiah Morse, Benjamin Barton, Samuel Miller, John Kidd, Peter Mark Roget, Thomas Chalmers, William Prout, Samuel F. B. Morse, Joseph Henry, Matthew Maury, James Simpson, James Joule, Adam Sedgwick, William Whewell, Henry Rogers, Louis Agassiz, James Dana, John William Dawson, George Stokes, Charles Piazzi, Rudolph Virchow, Phillip H. Gosse, Gregor Mendel, Louis Pasteur, Henri Fabre, Lord William Thomas Kelvin, Joseph Lister, Joseph Clerk Maxwell, Bernhard Riemann, John Bell Pettigrew, George Romanes, Richard Owen, Edward Hitchcock, Sir Henry Rawlinson, Sir Joseph Henry Gilbert, Thomas Anderson, Sir William Huggins, Balfour Stewart, P. G. Tait, John Murray, James Glaisher, Edward H. Maunder, William Mitchell Ramsey, Lord John W. S. Rayleigh, Alexander MacAlister, A. H. Sayce, John Ambrose Fleming, Howard A. Kelly, George Washington Carver, Charles Stine, Douglas Dewar, Paul Lemoine, William Ramsey, Wernher von Braun, Sir William Abney, A. Rendal Short, L. Merson Davies, and Sir Cecil P. G. Wakeley.

In the field of theoretical physics (unlimited personal imagination) built upon quantum mechanics (combining proven and unproven theories in the field of physics and theoretical mathematics), there are three additional popular evolutionary explanations as to how the universe came into being: the "string theory;" the "M theory;" and "the theory of everything." However, these concepts are in the hypothetical stages and remain mostly imagination and conjecture aimed at explaining away impossibilities within the big bang and evolutionary explanations of how everything sprang from nothingness without design, order or purpose.

Such purely speculative, unfounded hypotheses ignore every proven and established law of physics and are demonstrated by "a wise old scientist" chalking incomprehensible (even to a venerable physicist) mathematical equations on a blackboard and finally exclaiming: "eureka!!! There is no God!!!"

It is worth remembering that mathematical equations are meaningless when the scales of such equations are balanced with nothing but imagination and unfounded speculation. A valid scientific equation must be based upon proven facts.

Another ruse used to make singularities appear more plausible is to invent new words and phrases which describe imaginary physical forces. Such forces are represented by mathematical equation models jammed with unknowable values pertaining to purely theoretical elementary particles such as the "Higgs boson" and the "gravitron." Such unproven and thus imaginary sub-atomic structures are just two of several theoretical particles of atomic matter believed to be partially responsible for various discernible manifestations of energy bound up within the atoms of the elements.

Every form of organic or inorganic matter, other than pure elements, consists of chemical compounds which under heat and pressure break down into molecules which further break down into atoms of the known elements, and then into subatomic particles comprising the atoms.

This simplistic description of molecular structure is actually the present state of scientific knowledge concerning the composition of the universe and reveals absolutely nothing concerning the origin of energy, matter and momentum.

More than 2,500 scientists, engineers, and researchers have now gone public stating that the big bang is both delusional and intellectually insulting.

Recently, Stephen Hawking admitted that he has been wrong for thirty years about black holes and the loss of information into parallel universes. Intellectually honest theoretical physicists can no longer ignore the fact that Einstein, Planck, Hawking and other theoretical physicists were simply wrong. Their mathematical models were based on equations using faulty mathematical assumptions. They also borrowed formulas from other physicists that are based on hypotheses that have never been subjected to scientific testing yielding identical and repetitive results conforming to the law of cause and effect.

Many of these false hypotheses are being

presented in our public schools as proven facts in spite of the known fact that such hypotheses have never been elevated to a theory which can be scientifically tested and cannot ever become a fact if scientific testing of the theory has not yielded anticipated and consistent results.

Einstein's hypothesis concerning general relativity was accepted as fact based upon one experiment of deflected starlight during a total eclipse of our sun. Thus, big bang, evolution, black holes, parallel universes, and other theoretical hypotheses based only on personal imagination are still merely hypotheses and not theories and certainly not facts.

Einstein's theory of general relativity is based on faulty mathematics (the use of a constant for what is now proven to be a variable on one side of the equation $E = MC$ squared) as recently demonstrated by feedback from orbiting satellites and the Hubbel Space Telescope. The speed of light is not a constant).

The two "basic proofs" quoted by big bang supporters are "the expanding universe" and the "microwave radiation echoes emitting from deep space;" which are both true but do not in any way whatsoever support the imaginary big bang. The microwave radiation echoes are related to electromagnetic radiation emitting from every galaxy. The expanding universe is driven by a combination of galactic emissions and magnetic fields created by the intersecting forces of radiation and magnetic waves pulsing from every galaxy.

It is now observed that the assumed speed of light is not the maximum attainable speed with respect to a real mass with straight line velocity. The Hubble Space Telescope has detected galaxies receding from other galaxies faster than the speed of light.

Newtonian gravitational concepts in terms of description (quantitative) have been proven reliable over three centuries. However, Newton never discovered nor tried to explain the actual source (qualitative) of gravitational forces. It now appears that gravity is a force that results from the continuous vibration of the "strong nuclear force" that binds the nucleus of every atom in the universe thereby binding all matter together with a force in proportion to the mass of the matter and inversely proportional to the distance between masses.

Chapter two

Is Charles Darwin supported or contradicted by DNA coding? What do the established scientific facts reveal?

"Deoxyribonucleic acid or DNA, is a nucleic acid that contains the genetic instructions used in the development and functioning of all known living organisms (with the exception of RNA viruses). The main role of DNA molecules is the long-term storage of information. DNA is often compared to a set of blueprints, like a recipe or a code, since it contains the instructions needed to construct other components of cells, such as proteins and RNA molecules. The DNA segments that carry this genetic information are called genes, but other DNA sequences have structural purposes, or are involved in regulating the use of this genetic information.

DNA consists of two long polymers of simple units called nucleotides, with backbones made of sugars and phosphate groups joined by ester bonds. These two strands run in opposite directions to each other and are therefore anti-parallel. Attached to each sugar is one of four types of molecules called bases. It is the sequence of these four bases along the backbone that encodes information. This information is read using the genetic code, which specifies the sequence of the amino acids within proteins. The code is read by copying stretches of DNA into the related nucleic acid RNA, in a process called transcription.

Within cells, DNA is organized into long structures called chromosomes. These chromosomes are duplicated before cells divide, in a process called DNA replication. Animals, plants, fungi, and Eukaryotic organisms (protists) store most of their DNA inside the cell nucleus and some of their DNA in organelles, such as mitochondria or chloroplasts. In contrast, prokaryotes (bacteria and various archaea) store their DNA only in the cytoplasm. Within the chromosomes, chromatin proteins such as histones compact and organize DNA. These compact structures guide the interactions between DNA and other proteins, helping control which parts of the DNA are transcribed."

The above Wikipedia (internet encyclopedia) excerpt is included here to emphasize the fact that DNA is a genetic blueprint that cannot possibly evolve by random chance. One of the simplest single-celled life forms is the bacteria E. coli which has four million pairs of DNA nucleotides arranged in a specific sequence. The odds against mythical "mother nature" randomly evolving four million pairs of nucleotides in a precise sequence permitting E. coli to replicate itself can be compared to winning one million six-number lottery jackpots without missing a single number with respect to the sequence in which the winning lottery numbers are randomly selected. This is simply mathematically impossible.

Moreover, if single-celled organisms evolved into higher life forms, it would be axiomatic that simplicity must be continually evolving into complexity. This assertion is directly contrary to the established fact that left to random chance and the elements complexity always degenerates into simplicity tending toward chaos (the law of entropy). Evolutionists will chide that chicks randomly evolve from eggs. Does an egg hatch out over eons of time randomly without design, order or purpose in the absence of DNA coding? Or, does an egg hatch out in less than 30 days while demonstrating perfect design, order and purpose in total accord with its cellular DNA?

If a used Chevy is left exposed to the elements for a few million years, it will become a pile of chaotic elements rather than a better engineered car; and the contents of a junkyard are not likely to evolve into the space shuttle. On the other hand, a single living cell is far more complex than the space shuttle. It is very enlightening to consider the following statements by highly esteemed evolutionists, scientists, and professors:

"Natural selection acts only by taking advantage of slight successive variations; she can never take a great and sudden leap, but must advance by short and sure, though slow steps." (On the Origin of Species by

Means of Natural Selection, or the Preservation of Favored Races in the Struggle for Life," 1859, p. 162; public domain). On page 158, Charles Darwin admitted:

"If it could be demonstrated that any complex organ existed, which could not possibly have been formed by numerous successive, slight modifications, my theory would absolutely break down."

Apparently, Darwin had a hard time swallowing his own theory. On page 155, he wrestled with his own conscience:

"To suppose that the eye with all its inimitable contrivances for adjusting the focus to different distances, for admitting different amounts of light, and for the correction of spherical and chromatic aberration, could have been formed by natural selection, seems, I freely confess, absurd in the highest degree."

"When it comes to the origin of life there are only two possibilities: creation or spontaneous generation. There is no third way. Spontaneous generation was disproved more than a hundred years ago, but that leads us to only one other conclusion, that of supernatural creation. We cannot accept that on philosophical grounds; therefore, we choose to believe the impossible: that life arose spontaneously by chance." ("The Origin of Life," Scientific American, 191, P. 48, May, 1954)

"In the years after Darwin, his advocates hoped to find predictable progressions. In general, these have not been found -- yet the optimism has died hard, and some pure fantasy has crept into the textbooks." ("Evolution and the Fossil Record," Science, vol. 213, July, 1981, pg. 289)

"The pathetic thing is that we have scientists who are trying to prove evolution which no scientist can ever prove." (Nobel prize winning physicist Robert A. Millikan)

"The theory of evolution is one of the strangest phenomena of humanity; it is entirely destitute of proof." (World famous geologist from Canada, Sir William Dawson)

"The Darwinian theory of descent has not a single fact to confirm it in the realm of nature. It is not the result of scientific research, but purely the product of imagination. (Professor Fleischmann, University of Erlangen zoologist}

"There is not the slightest evidence that any of the major [animal] groups arose from any other." (Dr. Austin H. Clark, world famous American biologist)

"Darwin's theory of natural selection has never had any proof..." (Dr. Richard Goldschmidt, Professor of zoology, University of California)

"The Darwinian approach has consistently been to find some supporting fossil evidence, claim it as proof for evolution, and then ignore all the difficulties. It is, in fact, a common fantasy..." (Roger Lewin, science journalist).

Earth's fossil record is consistently touted by big bang advocates and evolutionists as proof of the age of Earth and the evolution of bacteria into humans by evolving through marine, amphibian, reptilian, and mammalian life forms over the course of a few billion years. Actually, Earth's fossil record alone is sufficient to completely debunk Darwinian evolutionary concepts.

Human fossils have been found buried along with dinosaur remains. In Texas and the Dakotas, human tools and bones are found in the same fossil layer as dinosaur bones. Human footprints mingle with dinosaur and other mammal footprints in the same fossil layers in Texas and New Mexico.

In Utah and Colorado, cliff and cave drawings depict dinosaur species dating between 400 and 1300 A.D. Decorated burial stones in Inca, Peru show various species of dinosaurs interacting with human figures dating between 500 and 1500 B.C. In Acambaro, Mexico, stone and ceramic figurines dated between 800 B.C. and 200 A.D. depict many species of dinosaurs. Since the first dinosaur fossils were not discovered until the nineteenth century, how would humans know about such monstrous reptiles hundreds of years earlier? According to big bang and Darwinian evolutionary claims, dinosaurs were blasted into extinction 65 million years ago by a little bang pursuant to a mass from space smacking into Earth; and humans did not pop out of monkeys until 200,000 years ago.

Approximately 95% of all Earth's fossil remains found to date are marine invertebrates; 4.74% are plant fossils; 0.25% are land invertebrates including insects; and 0.0125% are vertebrates (mostly fish). Over 90% of all vertebrate fossils discovered and recorded to date have consisted of less than one bone. Intermediate life forms only exist in text books promoting Darwinian evolutionary theory. Considering the abundance of species, both extinct and non-extinct, which all evolved according to the atheists and evolutionists from a single living cell randomly formed through time and chance over billions of years, the fossil record should be literally teaming with billions of intermediate life forms.

An interesting fossil did turn up which evo-lutionists were quick to claim as an intermediate life form. This fossil was named Archaeopteryx and hailed as a transition between reptiles and birds. Why? Well, it has teeth, and claws on its wings (it was later discovered to be a hoax). Great!! Now, where are the fossils of some intermediate life forms prior to and pursuant to Archaeopteryx? After all, there would have to be countless random mutations to transform a reptile into a bird.

"Piltdown man" (Eoanthropus Dawson) was

disturbed from eternal rest in 1912. He was presented by the evolutionists who conveniently discovered him as a missing link between man and ape. More than 500 scientific essays were penned over four decades extolling the striking similarities between ape and man exemplified in the form of Piltdown man. He was a curious fossil. He consisted of two human skulls, an orangutan jaw, an elephant molar, a hippopotamus tooth, and a canine tooth from a chimpanzee. The skulls had been treated with acid, and the other "remains" were stained with an iron sulfate solution. The canine tooth was painted and the molars were filed down.

The orangutan jaw was modified to hide the fact that the jaw did not belong to a human skull. This concoction was strewn around a quarry in Piltdown, England for later discovery as the long awaited missing link. The individuals linked to the "discovery" were world famous evolutionists with impeccable credentials. Hence, no scientist bothered to closely examine Piltdown man for forty one years. When the shameless hoax was uncovered in 1953, Sir Kenneth Oakley found the human skulls to belong to Ona Indians and the other remains were then properly identified as to origin.

"Ramapithecus" was widely acclaimed by evolutionary intellectuals as a "direct ancestor of humans." This fossil has been now identified as an extinct specimen of orangutans.

"Nebraska man" turned out to be a fraud based on a single tooth from a rare pig.

"Java man" consisted of pieces of bone, a skull cap and three teeth scattered over a wide area and dug up over twelve months. Today, we know the bones came from a human burial site; the femur is considered human; and the skull cap is believed to be from an ape.

"Neanderthal man" was promoted as a stooped ape-man. The fossil was eventually discovered to have been formed from a diseased primate.

"Australopithecus afarensis" or "Lucy" promised hope for a "missing link" find. Non-biased examination of Lucy's inner ear, skull and bones determined Lucy to be a pygmy chimpanzee with an upright stance.

"Homo erectus" fossils have been found through-out Earth. The fossils are human in origin and reflect individuals of small stature with proportionally smaller head and brain cavity, but within the range of people today. Middle ear studies show Homo erectus to be human. The fossils have been found in close proximity to other humans.

"Australopithecus africanus" and "Peking man" were hailed for years as true missing links but are now considered simply Homo erectus.

"Homo habilis" is now generally considered to be comprised of fragments from other fossils such as Homo erectus and Australopithecus.

"Toumai" is presented by promoters to be the "earliest member of the human family found thus far." A number of scientists examined the fossil and ident-ified it as coming from an ape (October 2002).

Quibbling over an occasional faked or misidentified fossil is absolutely an exercise in mental nonsense. If evolutionary theory is anything more than a self-inflicted delusion, the fossil record would be vomiting intermediate life forms. The fossil record alone is sufficient to boot Darwinian evolutionary theories from our public schools.

How long have human beings inhabited Earth? Currently, Scientists do not have an answer that does not rely upon erroneous measurement techniques. However, The available evidence pertaining to this question weighs heavily in favor of roughly sixty centuries.

Sixty centuries match up with current world population. Sixty centuries match up with recorded human history. Sixty centuries match up with human and dinosaur remains in the same time period and human footprints alongside dinosaur tracks. Sixty centuries match up with human genealogies given in the Bible covering the period between the expulsion of humans from the Garden of Eden and the birth of Jesus Christ.

According to the Biblical book of Job, dinosaurs were living on Earth during the sixteenth century B.C. Job lived in Mesopotamia in a small area called Uz. God speaks to Job out of a whirlwind around 1520 B.C. Job had been questioning God as to why the righteous suffer. God tells Job to answer questions about how various animals were created. God describes two creatures that we call dinosaurs. The dialogue is recorded in the book of Job, chapters 40 and 41:

    "Then answered the Lord unto Job and said, gird up thy loins now like a man: I will demand of thee, and declare thou unto me. Behold now **behemoth,** which I made with thee; he eats grass as an ox. Lo now, his strength is in his loins, and his force is in the navel of his belly. He moves his tail like a cedar: the sinews of his stones are wrapped together. His bones are as strong pieces of brass; his bones are like bars of iron. Behold, he drinks up a river, and hastens not: he trusts that he can draw up Jordan into his mouth........Can you draw out **leviathan** with a hook?.......shall not one be cast down even at the sight of him? None is so fierce that dare stir him up.......I will not conceal his parts, nor his power, nor his comely proportion......Who can open the doors of his face? His teeth are terrible round about. His scales are his pride, shut up together as with a close seal, one is so near to another that no air can come between them........His heart is firm as a stone; yea, as hard as a piece of the nether millstone. When he raises up himself, the mighty are afraid......he esteems iron as straw, and brass as rotten wood. The arrow cannot make him flee; sling stones are turned with him into stubble; darts are counted as stubble: he laughs at the shaking of a spear......He makes the deep to boil as a pot: he makes the sea like a pot of ointment.....Upon Earth there is none his like, who is made without fear." (Book of Job: portions of chapters 40-41; partial quotation with minor paraphrasing. KJV Holy Bible).

Evolutionists and big bang advocates teaching in our public schools drum into our children that carbon-14 dating and radiometric dating combined with tree ring dating prove that humans appeared on Earth roughly 200,000 years ago. In so doing, these self-worshipers hide a few facts from our boys and girls.

The same pattern of illogical thought that conceived the big bang also invented faulty mathematical models for dating both the universe and the planet, Earth. If we tell an adolescent that a measurement technique is based upon a false assumption, but we use the technique anyway, the child will probably doubt our sanity. But, that is precisely what so-called scientists do with respect to carbon-14 dating.

The evolutionary approach to dating Earth is to find some ongoing process such as radioactive decay within the atoms of radioactive elements; make some very favorable conclusions concerning equilibrium between radioactive and non-radioactive elements; apply mathematical formulas to such equilibrium relationship; and derive the age of Earth therefrom. Two such measurement techniques massaged by disciples of Darwin are carbon-14 dating and radiometric dating.

Carbon dating is a highly controversial and inconsistent dating technique. The method is based on the rate of decay of the radioactive carbon isotope, carbon-14, which is formed in the upper atmosphere through the effect of cosmic ray neutron bombardment of nitrogen-14.

The carbon-14 is rapidly oxidized and enters Earth's organic life through photosynthesis (plants) and the food chain (animals). Carbon-14 also enters the earth's oceans in an atmospheric exchange and dissolved carbonate. Plants and animals, which utilize carbon in organic functions absorb carbon-14 during their lifetimes.

The totally false assumption is that the earthbound carbon exists in equilibrium with the carbon-14 in the atmosphere; which means that the number of carbon-14 atoms and non-radioactive carbon atoms stays approximately the same over time. As soon as a plant or animal dies, it ceases its carbon intake. Thereafter, there is no replenishment of radioactive carbon-14, only decay. The carbon-14 dating mathematical model is scientifically invalid because the atmospheric equilibrium between carbon-14 and non-radioactive carbon does not exist; and there is no evidence whatsoever that such equilibrium ever existed.

Carbon dating advocates have resorted to Dendrochronology (tree ring dating) to create a smoke screen to draw attention away from the "equilibrium dilemma." They claim that Dendrochronology allows them to determine past concentration levels of Carbon-14 in the atmosphere by measuring the Carbon-14 to Carbon-12 ratios in tree rings.

The unavoidable errors inherent in this red herring cross reference is that no trees have been shown to exceed 4,500 years in age. The Methuselah Tree in southern California has been designated as the oldest living tree, and it has been dated at roughly 4,500 years.

Carbon-14 advocates use tree rings from dead trees thought to perhaps overlap the Methuselah Tree to mathematically determine ages exceeding 4,500 years. They determine whether a dead tree's age exceeds the ancient Methuselah Tree's age by ring patterns, and then they assume that the dead trees are older through a comparison of ring patterns, carbon ratios, etc.

It has repeatedly been demonstrated that dead tree ring patterns are typically inconsistent; and living trees can show dissimilar patterns caused by differing soil nutrients, direction of prevailing sunlight, fire history, distance to water sources, etc.

Radiometric Dating is another yardstick employed by evolutionists to determine the age of Earth. Radiometric dating techniques are predicated upon the natural decay of radioisotopes. An isotope is one or more atoms which have the same number of protons in their nuclei, but a different number of neutrons.

Radioisotopes are unstable isotopes. They spontaneously decay emitting radiation in the process thereby making them radioactive. They continue to decay going through various transitional states until they finally reach stability.

For example, Uranium-238 (U238) is a radioisotope. It will spontaneously decay until it transitions into lead-206 (Pb206). The numbers 238 and 206 represent the atomic mass for U238 and Pb206. The Uranium-238 radioisotope goes through 13 transitional stages before stabilizing into Lead-206: (U238> Th234> Pa234> U234> Th230> Ra226> Po218> Pb214> Bi214> Po214> Pb210> Bi210> Po210> Pb206).

In this instance, Uranium-238 is called the "parent" and Lead-206 is called the "daughter." By measuring how long it takes for an unstable element to decay into a stable element, and by measuring how much daughter element has been produced by the parent element within a specific rock sample, devout evolutionists believe they are able to determine the age of the rock.

This belief is based upon totally unreasonable assumptions: (1) no daughter element was originally present in the rock from which the sample was extracted; (2) the rate of radioactive decay is an unwavering constant; and (3) no contamination of any kind has occurred within the rock strata (leeching).

The diffusion rate of helium gas from within zircon crystals buried deep within Earth's basement granite demonstrates the gross errors buried within the radiometric dating model.

The amount of helium gas remaining within the zircon crystals (as verified by controlled laboratory testing) date the zircons at approximately six thousand years as opposed to the billion and a half years established by radiometric dating.

Evolutionists argue that the tremendous depth of the basement granite creates sufficient "earth crust pressure" and heat upon the granite rock to retard the diffusion rate of helium from zircon. Gee Whiz! From 6,000 years to 1,500,000,000????? Moreover, the basement granite was still intact and molecularly sound. Otherwise all the helium would have diffused back when reptiles were evolving into birds.

Since 1829, there has been a seven percent deterioration in Earth's magnetic field. When the curve of fixed rate deterioration is graphed over time, it becomes quite apparent that roughly 22,000 years ago Earth's magnetic field would have been as strong as the sun's magnetic field; and that around 10,000 A.D., Earth's magnetic field will be too weak to keep cosmic radiation from destroying all life on the planet. Life on Earth would have been impossible prior to around 20,000 B.C. and cease to exist by 10,000 A.D. or sooner.

Earth's axial speed is deteriorating (slowing down) and scientists measure this slowdown in "leap seconds." Every eighteen months an additional second is required for Earth to complete one axial rotation.

If Earth's spin is slowing, logic dictates that at some time in the past, Earth was spinning faster than it is today. Earth's rate of spin is a significant factor with respect to life on the planet because axial velocity directly contributes to the "Coriolis Effect" which in turn affects the circulation of Earth's atmosphere and weather patterns.

Today's scientists acknowledge that the moon is gradually drifting away from Earth. Here again, at some past date the moon was much closer to Earth than it is today. Based on the current rate of moon-drift, 1.2 billion years ago, the moon would have been touching Earth. In accordance with the "Inverse Square Law" pertaining to the attraction between Earth and its moon, if the moon was one third closer to Earth than it is today the gravitational effect on our tides would be nine times greater causing massive flooding in each hemisphere each tidal cycle. Since the oceans cover about 75% of Earth's surface, such frequent and unrestrained flooding each tidal cycle would prevent air breathing organisms from evolving into humans.

Earth's oceans contain measurable quantities of Aluminum, Antimony, Barium, Bicarbonate, Bismuth, Calcium, Carbonates, Chlorine, Chromium, Cobalt, Copper, Gold, Iron, Lead, Lithium, Manganese, Magnesium, Mercury, Molybdenum, Nickel, Potassium, Rubidium, Silicon, Silver, Sodium, Strontium, Sulfate, Thorium, Tin, Titanium, Tungsten, Uranium and Zinc.

Rivers and other waters draining into the oceans dump chemical solids at a measurable rate. Comparison between amounts already in the oceans with the rates at which more are being dumped indicates a fairly young Earth. The level of current sediments would have been deposited within a few thousand years.

Comets lose rather than gain matter so that over time comets deteriorate to extinction. Short period comets with known, predictable orbits around Earth (the orbital period) should have completely deteriorated within 10,000 to 12,000 years. Yet, the short period comets (like Haley's comet) are still orbiting Earth thereby indicating a young planet.

Jupiter is five times farther from the sun than Earth and is losing heat twice as fast as it gains heat from the sun. Jupiter's surface is still hot indicating a young solar system. In addition, Jupiter's moon, Ganymede, has a strong magnetic field which indicates it is still hot. Saturn's rings are drifting away from the planet and should have cleared Saturn if the planet is billions of years old.

The actual age of the universe and the stars, planets, asteroids, meteorites, comets, and interstellar debris provides not a single clue as to the question of origin. Regardless of whether the Earth is several billion years old or several thousand years of age, longevity provides zero information as to origin.

On the other hand, the actual age of the universe and Planet Earth is critical to every evolutionist because evolution of bacteria into humans requires eons of time according to the basic theory of evolution.

The Biblical record of the creation of "the heavens and the earth" does not indicate the elapsed time between the origin of the heavens and the earth and the time at which the earth was "without form and void, covered by water and existing in complete darkness." Consequently, the actual age of both the universe and Planet Earth is not critical to Biblical veracity.

It is nothing less than intellectual dishonesty to attempt to verify a faulty measurement technique with two more similarly erroneous techniques. But, this is precisely what phoney scientists are doing. "Junk science" is practiced by phoney scientists who champion scientific methods known to be unreliable. [10]

Two to the 100th power expressed in the United States numbering system is: One nonillion, 267 octillion, 650 septillion, 600 sextillion, 228 quintillion, 229 quadrillion, 401 trillion, 496 billion, 703 million, 205 thousand, three hundred and seventy-six. This is obviously an extremely large number.

The current world population "doubling time cycle" is 61 years. In the 1960's it was 35 years. The increase from 35 years to 61 years has been primarily due to abortion of the unborn. At the current doubling rate of 61 years, world population would be approximately 13 billion in 2075. Although the death rate is the highest among the poorest nations, so is the doubling time cycle the lowest because within the poorest nations, the main activity is making babies.

If we consider the effects on world population due to primordial technology; natural deaths; accidental deaths; individuals killed by war, pestilence, murder, and starvation; plus deaths inflicted by non-human living creatures from the time that the first male and female apes made the transition to humans **(roughly 200,000 years ago according to the planet's most brilliant professors of evolution)** until the present time to result in a doubling time cycle averaging out at 2,000 years instead of the current 61 years; then 200,000 years divided by 2,000 years would result in 100 population doubling time cycles (the number two to the 100th power). Considering that two multiplied by two 100 times produces a number 31 digits to the left of the decimal point, a mentally challenged human would suspect that big bang advocates and evolutionists are intellectually dishonest.

On the other hand, beginning with one man and one woman 6,000 years ago and an average doubling time cycle over those 6,000 years of 180 years, the current world population would be produced in 33 doubling time cycles (6,000 divided by 180 equals 33.3). The number 2 to the 33rd power equals 8.6 billion (rounded off) whereas the current world population is calculated at approximately seven billion.

Sir Fred Hoyle, a world famous British evolutionist, assisted by world famous professors of mathematical probabilities, calculated the chances of amino acids arranging themselves by random chance into the building blocks of a single-celled living organism to be one chance in ten to the forty thousandth power. Hoyle further calculated the chances of this amino acid miracle becoming a living organism through spontaneous generation to be one chance in ten to the billionth power. The premise that a living single-celled organism accidentally evolved by random chance through any biological process and then further evolved into every life form that exists today or ever existed on Earth is quite obviously mathematically suspect (even when such spontaneous generation is allowed 14 billion years to occur).

An electron (a tiny particle of matter with a negative electrical charge) is so miniscule that it takes nineteen million years to count a line of electrons one inch long if four electrons per second are counted night and day around the clock. The number of electrons contained within the entire known universe is calculated to be approximately the base number 10 to the 80th power. Compare this tidbit of trivia to mathematical probabilities of one in ten to the $40,000^{th}$ power and to one in ten to the $1,000,000,000^{th}$ power.

What these examples shout at the human race is that the big bang and Darwinian evolutionary pomposity insults the intelligence of those who bother to check the relevant mathematical probabilities.

Chapter three

What about black holes and the singularity giving birth to the big bang? What do we really know about black holes and what exactly is a singularity? Other than variation in star orbital speed near the center of a galaxy, the supporting facts are totally missing. Do black holes and/or a singularity make rational sense?

Theoretical physicists who do not believe in a supreme being and creator of the universe have imagined the concept of a "singularity." What precisely is a singularity? Well, say those who worship themselves: "A singularity is a one-time event such as the big bang. This one-time explosion did not conform to the established laws of physics but rather such laws accidentally govern cause and effect relationships within space, distance, time and motion pursuant to the big bang." [14]

Disciples of Charles Darwin, Carl Sagan, Sir Fred Hoyle, Stephen Hawking, Stephen Jay Gould, Niles Eldridge, and a covey of other die-hard evolutionists with PhD behind their names proclaim very loudly that the universe of matter, energy and motion created itself from the bottom of a black hole.

How did this occur and when? Well, say these intellectual giants, it happened far away and long ago. Matter of fact, it happened so long ago that random chance engineered the entire process which we have dubbed "the big bang." Eons of time before the big bang, there existed prior universes that collapsed upon themselves sort of like a giant star burning up all its hydrogen fuel and shrinking to the size of an atom shrouded by an interstellar black hole with a gravitational suction so strong that the black hole sucked in stars, planets, and other interstellar matter.

Everything, including light, that passed within the black hole's "event horizon" got sucked into the hole; and as the density of the matter and energy increased, the sucked in matter and energy got heavier and heavier, just like dead stars can become a black hole. Now, exactly where these prior universes came from is still under investigation. It may be that they just popped out of nothingness (the absence of any matter, energy or motion) by random chance urged on by Mother Nature.

The matter, energy and motion in the black hole got really, really hot and compacted smaller than a marble. This extremely dense and hot matter, energy and motion finally went "bang" and spewed out our present universe. It was one heck of a bang because the marble-sized compacted matter, energy and motion spewed out clouds of plasma and gases which spawned liquids and solids captured by gravity creating billions of galaxies containing trillions of stars. How much plasma, gas and interstellar debris spewed forth from the "big bang black hole?"

Wow!!! It was a whole bunch because just our sun

alone contains a lot of hydrogen and other elements. For example, to get the sun's cubic miles of hydrogen and other elements we multiply four thirds times pi times 432,500 miles cubed which equals one hundred and twenty-three quadrillion, one hundred and twelve trillion, five hundred and eighty-three billion, five hundred million cubic miles of gas and debris.

Now, multiply this number by at least another trillion (to account for the other stars) and don't bother with all the interstellar debris (probably another hundred billion cubic miles) which all spewed from a marble-sized mass of matter, energy and motion captured within a truly magic black hole. WOW! That would be a whole bunch of forty foot tank trailers filled with hydrogen gas not to mention the other gaseous elements; and all from this tiny black hole core.

Now, isn't that statement an excellent example of gross pride, arrogance and utter stupidity? "Hey, y'all. To explain the unexplainable by random chance, we have elected to ignore the law of cause and effect; the law of the conservation of matter; the law of the conservation of energy; the law of the conservation of momentum; the first law of thermodynamics; the second law of thermodynamics; the third law of thermodynamics; the atomic and molecular structure of plasma, gases, liquids and solids; the fusion of hydrogen into helium under extreme heat and pressure; the transmutation of the primordial elements through the uncoupling of the strong nuclear force within every atom of every element under extreme heat and pressure; the universal proportionality factor between equivalent amounts of energy and mass (matter); plus a myriad of related laws of physics.

Yes, indeed! We are going to stuff billions of trillions of cubic miles of hydrogen into a thimble sized ball of super hot matter and energy along with a few trillion cubic miles of the other primordial elements in gaseous form in order to create everything out of nothing and we are going to use matter, energy and motion that is already in existence to create stars that are already in existence because we need a big black hole to house the magic ball of hot energy and matter (our singularity) before the ball explodes into the unmeasured universe. [18]

So, don't you see? We are going to school you by saying the magic ball exploded into all energy, matter and motion when the magic ball is actually composed of existing energy, matter, and motion by hiding the magic ball in a black hole formed by a burned out star and/or prior universe that burned up its supply of hydrogen such that the heavier primordial elements formed by the fusion of hydrogen into helium became the extremely heavy core left over from the burned out star or collapsed universe; and this super duper, very dense core sucked into it's gravitational field all energy, matter and motion that crossed its "event horizon" thereby creating the little magic ball that became so hot and so heavy that matter and energy flowed into each other and finally exploded (the big bang) into our present universe of matter, energy, and motion.

How are going to convince you? Well, we're going to invent a whole new space concept and use baffle gab to describe how it came about from prior collapsed universes that exist somehow parallel to our universe between which universes matter, energy and motion are routinely exchanged. Just don't ask us where the first universe came from.

Now, we really do not believe this crock of nonsense, but the only other possibility is a supreme being with awesome creative power sufficient to exercise control over all matter, energy and motion and we just cannot believe that such a power exists because such a being would be smarter than us and that is simply out of the question. Now, let us restate the big bang and evolution of bacteria into humans so you can understand what we teach your children in the public schools:

"At the exact moment of the big bang, the tiny speck of matter and energy was flowing between energy and matter such that billions of trillions of cubic miles of hydrogen and primordial debris were flung across a vacuum of nothingness. This spewed out mass cooled over 385,000 years thereby allowing the random formation of an initial quantity of all the other elements without any design, purpose or order.

The "other elements" were created accidentally out of the hydrogen and primordial interstellar debris created by the big bang (or the big eternally expanding energy bubble) plus the fusion of hydrogen into helium within every star formed by the big bang interstellar debris including the stars that preexisted the big bang.

This big bang accidentally produced plasma, solids, liquids and gases along with antimatter (the opposite of matter); dark energy (invisible energy); and dark matter (invisible matter).

And, of course, the big bang spewed forth a tiny fraction more matter than antimatter. For every billion particles of antimatter there were a billion and one particles of matter. Antimatter canceled out an equal amount of matter through nuclear collisions.

The tiny speck of energy and matter blew up or simply expelled energy and matter with so much force that the excess matter not canceled by antimatter became everything in the universe that we see today (galaxies, stars, planets, suns, moons, meteorites, asteroids, comets, bacteria, viruses, insects, plants, animals, humans, etc.).

This big bang happened in a "planck" moment of time (rough estimation = one thousand billion trillionth of one clock second).

The tiny speck of matter and energy which blew up or simply expanded was trillions of degrees hot and moving extremely fast (faster than the speed of light) so that in a few planck units of time the universe expanded several billion light years in diameter (one light year equals 5.88 trillion miles).

Then, after 200 million more years of slow

cooling, more of the other non-gaseous elements randomly formed within billions of stars which randomly formed from vast clouds of hydrogen.

These stars were and are basically billions of gigantic balls of hydrogen gas created by the big bang and held together by the force of gravity being exerted throughout the entire primordial universe by dark matter and dark energy.

Dark matter and dark energy randomly appeared from nothingness in just the right randomly formed proportions (by the big bang) to accidentally impose order out of random and chaotic events transpiring faster than a couple planck units of time.

Such randomly directed primordial energy forced the universe to continue expanding in an orderly and totally balanced fashion. This randomly created but precise order and balance permitted a medium-sized galaxy named "Milky Way" (a grouping of billions of individual stars, moons, planets, comets, asteroids, and other interstellar debris) to accidentally manipulate itself into the precise orbit and exact distribution of inherent gravitational forces to keep Planet Earth safely in perpetual orbit around the star nearest Earth (our sun).

The big bang randomly fixed Earth's orbit at just the right distance, the right speed, orbital tilt, and surface temperature to permit the eventual evolution of various life forms.

The galaxies are receding from each other at a high velocity indicating that the universe is expanding rapidly and there are cosmic background microwave radiation echoes emitting from deep space (as detected from Earth). [15] [20]

The continuously expanding universe and the microwave echoes are sufficient to prove the big bang theory to be fact because the big bang obviously triggered the expanding universe and the microwave echoes are due to the heat left over from the big bang (heat which originated over fourteen billion years ago). Billions of galaxies and trillions of stars (one of which is Earth's sun) are not generating sufficient deep space heat to generate the microwave echoes. The electro-magnetic energy waves known to be pulsating from every star probably contribute somehow to the expanding nature of the entire universe.

The average temperature of the universe is calculated to be about 450 degrees below zero, Fahrenheit (less than three degrees above absolute zero, Kevin). (Golly! Bet it's real hot around the galaxies).

The universe just keeps getting bigger and bigger but retains all the matter and energy not canceled by antimatter during the big bang such that today the universe is probably about 150 billion light years across (150 billion times 5.88 trillion miles).

Dark energy is now pulling the universe apart so that about 100 billion years into the future the universe will collapse in on itself like letting the air out of a balloon. There will probably be another big bang creating a whole new universe."

For all those readers who believe the foregoing explanation for an "accidental universe without design or purpose," I have a bridge in Brooklyn that you might also want to consider.

So, then, why do we allow such utter junk science to be taught as established fact to our children in our public schools? I think mainly for two primary reasons: First, most parents do not really understand the basic scientific foundation for either Darwinism or the big bang and are too occupied with their own lives to pay much attention to the public school text books. Second, there exists today so diverse a selection of world religions and concepts of a supreme being or beings that most parents do not try to educate their children with respect to matters of faith nor science but rather expect tradition, government, churches, Hollywood, National Geographics and the educational institutions to do so.

Then, another factor is that public school teachers generally speaking are atheists, abortionists, homosexuals, and various other vocal minorities because teaching in the public schools provides a forum to promote their personal agendas and parents don't care.

Could the concentration of self-worshipers in our public schools contribute heavily to school shootings, school bullying, eroding educational standards, sex between juveniles (free condoms from the schools), hard core drug addiction and the general atmosphere of violence in our educational facilities? After all, we are teaching the children that they evolved from lower life forms without design, logic, reason or purpose and that natural selection weeds out the weak from among the "most fit and the most aggressive." The only reasonable surprise is that there is not more sex, rape and murder where we send Johnnie and Sally to learn their reading, writing and arithmetic. Neither should it be a surprise that we are graduating high school students who cannot read a bus schedule.

Another factor in the deceiving of our children is the intense burning desire of evolutionists and atheists, who have dedicated their lives to brainwashing our children, to find some kind of fossil evidence, no matter how suspect, to support their denial of a supreme being. Evolutionists compete for the personal recognition and media fame associated with "new discoveries" in the face of astronomical odds against the existence of evidence supporting Darwinian theories. By refusing to acknowledge a supreme being, atheists and evolutionists steadfastly insist on lighting a candle in order to see the sun.

The popular press continues to cast special creation as religion and evolution as science. Advocates of special creation are portrayed as dimwitted religious fanatics who need to be educated in the real world of science. Evolutionists, on the other hand, are revered as true scientists who, with great dignity and saintly patience, persevere along the path of truth regardless of where the path leads. Such an image in the liberal media dates back to the "Scopes Trial," also remembered as the "Monkey Trial," wherein creationists were pictured as bumbling, narrow-minded, bigots; and evolutionists were viewed as persecuted scientists under a state law prohibiting the teaching in public classrooms of monkeys evolving into men.

Hollywood jumped on this image and produced "Inherit the Wind," a true motion picture expose featuring Spencer Tracy as the virtuous defender of truth, freedom and the American way. Cast in the role of Clarence Darrow, he labored in the courtroom to save brave, honest scientists from persecution by defending evolutionary theory. After all, why would any rational person object to the harmless teaching of a theory, even if the theory claims there is no God? There are a couple of reasons that come to mind. Children, especially during their formative years, tend to believe what parents allow the public schools to teach them. If they evolved from beasts, there is no morality other than the law of the jungle. Schoolboys, like instinct driven beasts, can without inhibition copulate with schoolgirls; and, just to make sure they understand that this is to be expected and permissible, schools can furnish condoms.

If some adolescent girls do become pregnant, there is free abortion available and the children can opt for this convenience without parental consent. Then, of course, there is the puzzling matter of drugs, suicide, rebellion and murder in our schools. In the aftermath of teaching our impressionable youth "survival of the fittest," the "purer than driven snow" media ponders why our children are behaving like animals.

Another reason is that children with no morals become adults without morals or respect for human life. What was once just a false theory has become the truth. Life is just a random chance, purposeless existence where the strongest prosper by hoarding life's necessities. Inferior members of the species should be eliminated for the benefit of the superior species. That's just natural selection doing its job and we're helping out.

A good example of the harmless teaching of evolution in our public schools is typified by some students of evolution with familiar names. Let's hear how evolutionary theory affected their outlook on life:

"Nature doesn't desire the mating of weaker with stronger individuals, even less does she desire the blending of a higher with a lower race, since if she did, her whole work of higher breeding, over perhaps hundreds of thousands of years, might be ruined with one blow." (Adolph Hitler, "Mein Kampf," 1924, p. 286)

"......should I not also have the right to eliminate millions of an inferior race that multiplies like vermin?" (Adolph Hitler, quoted in Joachim Fest's, "Hitler," 1974, pgs. 679-680)

Another good student of evolution, Joseph Stalin, made Hitler's murder of six million or so look saintly. Stalin is credited with slaughtering more than sixty million "inferiors." Then, there are other students of evolution like Pol Pot, who patterned his genocide after Hitler and Stalin. These faithful evolutionists are excellent role models for "survival of the fittest." Were these mass murderers deluded and simply misunderstood their evolutionary teachers? Not according to Sir Arthur Keith (1866-1945), world famous British evolutionist, knighted in 1921:

"Hitler is an uncompromising evolutionist, and we must seek for an evolutionary explanation if we are to understand his actions" (Sir Arthur Keith, "Evolution and Ethics," 1947, p. 14). At page 230,   Keith gives us comforting reassurance: "The German Fuhrer, as I have consistently maintained, is an evolutionist; he has consciously sought to make the practice of Germany conform to the theory of evolution."

One would think from his defense of Hitler that Sir Knight, Keith would have aided Hitler in his zeal to practice evolution, given the opportunity. So, in view of historical events, is it insane to teach our children Lucifer's lie of evolution wherein humans are no more than an aberration resulting from random cosmic accidents? If we could put this question to the hundred million or so murdered by evolutionists during the twentieth century alone, perhaps they could shed a little light on the subject. Does what parents allow God-haters to teach our children in our public schools affect their moral perspective and ultimately their behavior? History speaks for itself.

In our textbooks, in the popular media, in judicial

hearings, and sundry public forums, reference is frequently made to "the mountains of evidence" demonstrating evolution is a proven fact. Where is all this voluminous evidence? Apparently, it exists only in the imagination of those making such pompous statements. Scientists who challenge evolution in every field of study cannot find a single shred of evidence supporting evolutionary claims. Evolution is not "pure science," it is pure religion as it must be accepted based on nothing more than simple faith which denies the existence of creative design and, consequently, a creator. As such, the religion of Evolution is no different than any other religion (like Christianity.....which the nine morons in Washington have decided cannot be referred to in America's public schools because it is not "science but faith").

The history of humanity indicates that, in the absence of undisputed scientific facts, biased statements by those believed to be experts in the relevant scientific discipline are generally accepted as facts. The more imaginative the alleged cause and effect relationship the more likely it is to be believed by the public at large. When self-delusion is mingled with a grain of truth a delusional theory of cause and effect may survive long after the law of cause and effect demonstrates the theory to be impossible. Such is the case with the most outrageous lie (the big bang) to ever be foisted upon mankind by Lucifer (Satan), the father of false information. His most zealous supporters sit on the U.S.

Supreme Court.

A postulate is a self-evident fact that does not need to be proven such as "equals divided by equals are equal." A law of physics is derived from an opinion elevated to a hypothesis and further refined into a written theory which has been subjected to numerous scientific tests and experiments yielding in every instance identical results. Consequently, it is totally accurate to refer to established laws of physics as facts.

The other side of the laws of physics coin is simple logic. When considering the big bang and Darwinism, the logical "law of cause and effect" shatters such unrestrained imagination spouting forth an unsupported myth. The law of cause and effect states: "Any factor in whose absence the effect occurs cannot be the cause; and any factor in whose presence the effect fails to occur cannot be the cause." The law of cause and effect is the ultimate test for any hypothesis or theory giving rise to an alleged law of physics.

Can the big bang possibly be the factor giving birth to the universe? The answer is an absolute unshakable "no." The universe existed prior to the fictitious big bang because the big bang involved the preexistence of matter, energy and motion which is the very essence of the universe.

Could a series of prior primordial universes which collapsed in on themselves have provided the matter, energy and motion which produced a series of big bangs? No, because **"THE VERY FIRST"** primordial universe would be irrefutable evidence that a universe existed in the absence of a big bang as tested by the law of cause and effect. Because the ultimate scientific definition of the universe is all matter, energy and motion that exists within space, distance and time, how could a chronological progression of universes possibly have been formed by a few trillion random chance events within space, distance and time (a closed and isolated system of energy, matter and motion)? Matter, energy and motion must be present in order for any random chance event to occur because any "event" or "happening" involves the manipulation of preexisting matter, energy and motion.

Can the continuous pulsing of shock waves of electromagnetic energy emitting from every star as the star's hydrogen fuel is converted into helium account for the galaxies receding from each other creating an expanding universe? Yes. The shock waves are present and the universe is expanding in unison with the fusion of hydrogen into helium.

Can the extreme heat generated by a trillion or so stars be detected from deep space by microwave echoes produced by such heat? Yes. Astrophysicists estimate the number of stars in the universe at approximately one trillion. That quantity of stars will most certainly generate heat waves in the form of electromagnetic energy flowing from deep space.

Can a single-celled life form replicate without an internal DNA code? Absolutely not. DNA coding is necessary for even the simplest bacterium to replicate. A virus is not a life form but rather is an encapsulated protein with "messenger RNA" and cannot replicate without being embedded within a living host cell and using the host cell's DNA to reproduce itself (the virus).

Can simplicity evolve by random chance over billions of years into complexity? No. Simplicity and complexity coexist in the universe and there has never been a proven instance where simplicity evolved by random chance into complexity over eons of time. Conversely, left to time and random chance, complexity has always degenerated into more simplistic molecular structures. Whenever any simple molecular structure becomes more complex in terms of compounding through bonding of elements, there is a discernible cause and effect relationship that is beneficial to order and balance within the universe.

Among numerous laws of physics there are four laws referred to as "Laws of Thermodynamics" which dictate that order within the universe is directly proportional to thermalization (thermal equilibrium) within the entire universe. Thermal equilibrium within the universe means that the temperature throughout the universe will eventually equalize. As the entire universe cools, the amount of entropy (level of randomness and inherent disorder) increases. When the uniform temperature of the universe reaches absolute zero, the level of entropy will also be zero and all molecular motion will cease.

Taken together, the four laws of Thermodynamics prove that the universe is not eternal and is progressing from a beginning to an end because the universe cannot exist in the absence of molecular motion. What this also means, of course, is that the universe could not possibly have evolved because complexity left to time and chance always degenerates into more simplistic molecular structure tending toward chaos (law of entropy).

The hypothesis of single-celled organisms evolving into all life forms in the universe is pure imagination because the entire hypothesis violates both the law of cause and effect and genetic molecular structure (DNA code) as well as the one-way evolution of simplicity into chaos.

Does Earth's fossil record support the evolution of single-celled organisms into all the life forms within the universe? No. It does not. The small number of fossils argued by theoretical reasoning to be proof of any such evolutionary hypothesis cannot account by any stretch of an evolutionist's imagination for the absence in the fossil record of the trillions of intermediate life forms that such evolution would produce over eons of time.

Moreover, there is not in the fossil record intermediate life forms that would relate to the billions of living creatures pertaining to all species that were fossilized during the same geological time window.

Is it logically, biologically, chemically, mathematically and genetically impossible as well as totally incompatible with all known molecular structures for any combination of plasma, gases, liquids and solids to spontaneously generate by pure random chance into a single-celled living organism? Yes, it is absolutely impossible.

Regardless of what type of living cell we look at, whether specialized for a particular function or existing as a one-celled organism, every living cell must carry out certain activities in order to remain alive.

Every living cell must be equipped: (1) to take in nutrients and to get rid of waste; (2) to reproduce itself to avoid extinction; (3) to convert nutrients to energy and capture that energy to fuel activities within the cell; and (4) to carry out predetermined genetic code instructions through its internal DNA.

In other words, a single living cell must be specifically designed and then created to carry out these "minimum functions" before it can, in fact, carry out such specialized, internal, life sustaining activities. Here is an obvious irreducible level of complexity. Looking back at the "primordial soup being electrically charged" theory wherein a single living cell was randomly formed from natural elements bathed in liquids; it is quite easy to comprehend why the chances of producing the irreducible level of complexity detailed above by random chance is one in ten to the billionth power. It just didn't happen and no amount of chest pounding by supporters of Darwinism or modern evolutionary theory will change the cold, hard fact that the first living cell was no cosmic accident. It was first designed and then created by a supreme being regardless of what name or words we may choose to describe this creator.

With unaided eyes we can behold portions of the universe around us. We can handle the leaves of trees, walk upon grass, swim in the ocean, walk along the seashore, eat barbeque, drink beer, caress loved ones, and weep at the graves of departed family members, plus virtually unlimited sensory experiences perceived through sight, hearing, smelling, touching and tasting.

When petting a cat, it would be imbecilic to ponder whether felines exist. While downing a glass of ice water on a hot afternoon, we generally do not doubt that water is a part of our habitat. Gazing upon stars in the night sky, we probably would not deny that stars do indeed exist although understanding stars as giant nuclear reactors would not necessarily brand us as stupid.

We see the sun, we feel the heat, we bask in sunlight, and observe that sunlight has an effect on the growth rate of grass and flowers. We may not know that sun-light results from the conversion of hydrogen into helium within the mass of the sun, but we would be perceived as total morons if we proclaim that the sun does not exist.

Why would we feel justified in laying aside our common sense, simple logic and past sensory experiences when considering questions such as the origin of the universe, the origin of living organisms, or evolution of more complex life forms from single-celled bacteria? While we may not understand astronomy, astrology, DNA coding, chemistry, physics, quantum mechanics, mathematical probabilities, nuclear forces, biology, molecular structure, etc., we would exhibit gross stupidity to state that human intelligence does not exceed that of earthworms.

Individual humans lacking exposure to "higher education" are generally much impressed with "scientific explanations" that are incomprehensible to 85% of the world's population due to the language peculiar to each scientific field of study. A lumberjack in Oregon whose exposure to higher education ended with graduation from high school watching nifty graphics and a "wise old owl professor" explaining the "big bang" theory on the National Geographics TV channel might be duly persuaded that the big bang spewed the universe from the bottom of a black hole in space.

Surely National Geographics would not broadcast an utter impossibility and the professor narrating the "scientific" episode should know what he is talking about. Thus, the Oregon lumberjack might easily be convinced that the "big bang theory" is established scientific fact.

Due to a common human trait best described as mental laziness, the relaxing lumberjack is not consciously evaluating what he is hearing. It is not necessary to be Albert Einstein or Isaac Newton to be mentally insulted by such an obvious and totally impossible explanation for the origin of the universe.

Conversely, the big bang theory being mouthed by such an intellectual and so beautifully detailed in mind blowing graphics on a TV channel known for true devotion to "pure and undefiled science" lends credibility to intellectual dishonesty.

Most National Geographics fans do not bother to check out the funding and management of National Geographics thereby discovering that their NG TV Channel is funded and managed by proponents of Darwinian evolution and the big bang theory.

What if the Holy Bible is truly the written word of the supreme being having creative power over all matter, energy and motion and dictated to the spirits of forty different writers spanning a time period of sixteen centuries. But, you don't believe it because you never really bothered to read the Scriptures with an open mind so as to understand what the Bible actually states. What if you are actually alive forever having an immortal spirit but a mortal body? What if, when you lay aside your mortal body and you still possess your eternal soul and spirit, you find yourself among billions that appear before the judgment seat of the creator (God) of the universe and your only thought about Jesus Christ when you used his name for a curse expression? You did not care that the Scriptures proclaim Jesus Christ to be the sacrificial lamb provided by Almighty God to redeem you from your sins and human abominations. What will you say to the judge of the universe? I never accepted the sacrifice provided because I truly believed the big bang explanation made sense and that my ancestors were bacteria that magically appeared through spontaneous generation? God's answer to you is already recorded and may be read in the Bible in the Book of Romans chapter 1:18-32.

"For the wrath of God is revealed from heaven against all ungodliness and unrighteousness of men who hold the truth in unrighteousness: because that which may be known of God is manifest in them; for God has shown it unto them. For the invisible things of Him from the creation of the world are clearly seen, being understood by the things that are made, even His eternal power and Godhead; so that they are without excuse: because that, when they knew God, they glorified Him not as God, neither were thankful; but became vain in their imaginations, and their foolish heart was darkened.

Professing themselves to be wise, they became fools, and changed the glory of the uncorruptible God into an image made like to corruptible man, and to birds, and four-footed beasts, and creeping things. Wherefore God also gave them up to uncleanness through the lusts of their own hearts, to dishonor their own bodies between themselves: who changed the truth of God into a lie, and worshiped and served the creature more than the Creator, who is blessed forever. Amen.

For this cause God gave them up into vile affections: for even their women did change the natural use into that which is against nature: and likewise also the men, leaving the natural use of the woman, burned in their lust one toward another; men with men working that which is unseemly, and receiving in themselves that recompense of their error which was meet.

And even as they did not like to retain God in their knowledge, God gave them over to a reprobate mind, to do those things which are not convenient. Being filled with all unrighteousness, fornication, wickedness, covetousness, maliciousness; full of envy, murder, debate, deceit, malignity, whisperers, back-biters, haters of God, despiteful, proud, boasters, inventors of evil things, disobedient to parents, without understanding, covenant-breakers, without natural affection, implacable, unmerciful: who knowing the judgment of God, that they which commit such things are worthy of death, not only do the same, but have pleasure in them that do them." (Romans 1:18-32)

The judgment of death is not physical death of the body (which is already past) but rather the symbolic death of your soul and spirit by banishment from God's presence forever to the habitat prepared for Lucifer (Satan) which is a lake burning with fire and brimstone where the smoke of your torment ascends up forever and you have no rest day nor night (Revelation 20:10-15 and Revelation 14:9-11 KJV Holy Bible). Will your banished soul and spirit have a body? Yes, according to the Holy Bible; and it will not be subject to extinction as pertains to a physical, mortal body. Jesus Christ made this clear as recorded in St. Luke 16:19-24 KJV Holy Bible:

"There was a certain rich man, which was clothed in purple and fine linen, and fared sumptuously every day: and there was a certain beggar named Lazarus, which was laid at his gate, full of sores, and desiring to be fed with the crumbs that fell from the rich man's table: moreover the dogs came and licked his sores. And it came to pass that the beggar died, and was carried by the angels into Abraham's bosom (Paradise): the rich man also died and was buried; and in hell he lift up his eyes, being in torment, and saw Abraham afar off, and Lazarus in his bosom. And he cried and said, Father Abraham, have mercy on me, and send Lazarus, that he may dip the tip of his finger in water, and cool my tongue, for I am tormented in this flame. But Abraham said, Son, remember that you in your lifetime received good things, and likewise Lazarus evil things: but now he is comforted, and you are tormented. And beside all this, between us and you there is a great gulf fixed: so that they which would pass from hence to you cannot; neither can they pass to us that would come from thence." (minor paraphrasing)

Does this Scripture depict a three-dimensional and physical environment? No. It reflects a multifaceted spiritual habitat and the rich man possesses an eternal soul and spirit but is banished from the Kingdom of God for all eternity. What kind of body does his soul and spirit inhabit? Well, he has eyes; he hears; he speaks; he remembers; he feels pain; he cries; he has a tongue; he has emotions; he can distinguish mercy from being ignored; he has corrupted his free will and found himself in hell with his free will exhausted.

How can these things be? They certainly do not occur in our three-dimensional universe? Like parting the Red Sea? Raising the dead? Turning water into wine or into blood? Walking on water? Feeding thousands with a few fish and handful of bread? Healing lepers? Restoring withered limbs? Opening blind eyes? Controlling the wind and waves? Forgiving your murderers while being murdered? Rising from the dead? Mocking the idols of a pagan nation with plagues of frogs, lice, flies, hail, locusts, body sores, darkness, only blood to drink, and killing the first born in every household except those smeared with sacrificial blood?

What do you believe accounts for the universe and all its life forms? Big bang and spontaneous generation of single-celled organisms plus Darwinian evolution? Or do you believe in a supreme being existing outside of our universe who created, controls and manipulates all energy, matter and motion? Those are the only two choices. Every other belief system is simply a bastardization of evolution or special creation. Consider the true essence of world religions other than Christianity having enough followers to be included within a summary of established religions:

Islam is the second largest religion on Earth (after Christianity) and was founded more than 500 years after the resurrection of Christ by an Arab named Muhammad who regarded himself as Allah's (Arabic for God's) guardian of the true faith of Abraham. Muhammad proclaimed that Jews and Christians distorted the revelations God gave to Abraham, Moses, Jesus and other prophets by text altering and misinterpretation. The sacred writings of Islam are referred to as the Qur'an (God's revelations to Muhammad) and the Sunnah (words and deed of Muhammad, God's final prophet to Earth). Followers of Islam are known as Muslims who deny that God had a son. They believe that Jesus was a mere prophet, that he escaped into Paradise and did not sacrifice himself for the sins of all humans. Everyone must save themselves from hell by accumulating more good works than evil works, and true believers may have to spend some time in hell to atone for insufficient good works compared to evil works. Upon birth, an individual's record is opened in Paradise and the individual becomes chargeable upon reaching the age of accountability (puberty). It is permissible to lie, steal, kill, rob, rape and pillage in the service of Allah (converting infidels from the error of their ways).

Paradise is a place of feasting, drinking, and sexual gratification surrounded by a swarm of virgins. Muslims who die or commit suicide in service to Allah are ushered directly into Paradise. Muslims condemn homosexuality, adultery, eating pork and gambling. Since Muslims have blatantly bastardized Christianity and do not accept Jesus Christ as the divine sacrifice for their personal sins, the other details of Muslim religious beliefs, laws and customs are unimportant for the purpose of this book. Islam is the most intolerant and most violent "save yourself" belief system in existence.

Zoroastrianism is a religion with approximately 200,000 followers which preaches "save yourself" through good thoughts, good words, and good deeds. Zoroastrianism is also referred to as Mazdaism and first appears in recorded history during the seventh century BC. Zoroaster is the main prophet for the belief system and invented the term "Ahura Mazda" to name the one universal and transcendental god. Mazdaism embraces the concepts of good and evil. There exists an immortal adversary of Ahura Mazda dedicated to evil (Druj). Humanity is drawn into the conflict wherein Ahura Mazda is ultimately victorious and time ends with the renovation of the universe. Thereafter, all creation is reunited in Ahura Mazda. The collection of sacred texts are called "Avesta." Good thoughts, words and deeds are required to ensure happiness and ward off chaos. Today, followers of Zoroastrianism are located primarily in Iran, India and Pakistan.

Unitarian Universalists promote world unity and the inherent goodness of humans. All religions are embraced and are considered to be of equal merit. The ultimate achievement is religious unity and a single world government. Peace through good thoughts, good deeds and unbiased tolerance is the main tenet. Otherwise, all followers are encouraged to worship as they choose. Consequently, Unitarian Universalists are everything to everybody and humans will eventually live together happily as quickly as unity becomes reality. Abortion, homosexuality, and same sex marriage are smiled upon.

A fiction writer, L. Ron Hubbard, gave birth in 1960 to what has become known as Scientology and described as the study and handling of the human spirit in relationship to itself, others, and all life. The sacred texts are various books written by Hubbard. Man (a gender neutral term to encompass all humans) is basically good but life experiences lead him into evil. Man errs by trying to solve his problems from his own point of view rather than achieving greater spiritual awareness through learning, auditing and training. Man is a spiritual being whose existence spans more than one lifetime. Man is endowed with abilities well beyond those he normally considers he possesses. What is true for man is what he has observed to be true. During each reincarnation, man applies the knowledge and increased spiritual awareness he acquired during the previous life. Man can improve his quality of life to the degree he continues to preserve his spiritual integrity and remains honest and decent thus achieving certainty of spiritual existence and a relationship with whatever supreme being he believes exists outside of himself. Scientology organizations provide ongoing auditing and counseling. Because man alone controls his earthly and eternal existence, Scientology is a somewhat unusual "save yourself" belief system with Hubbard's home spun psychiatry and hypnosis imbedded within the pseudo-scientific orientation.

The Bahai followers believe in one god who created everything; but the Bahai god is transcendent and unknowable who has and will continue to send great prophets to humanity through which the unknown deity has revealed a series of messages. Bahai prophets thus far have been Adam, Abraham, Moses, Krishna, Zoroaster, Buddha, Jesus Christ, Mohammed, The Bab, and Bahaullah. Another prophet is not expected for many centuries into the future. Bahai teaches the essential unity of the great world religions as arising from the same spiritual source but splintered by conditions at the time of founding and by accretions following the death of the founder.

The Bahai faithful believe that all individuals possess an immortal soul not subject to decomposition. At death, the soul is freed to travel throughout the spiritual universe which is a timeless and placeless extension of the known universe. The sacred texts are a collection of the writings of Abdul-Baha, The Bab, and Bahaullah plus miscellaneous Bahai scriptures which were first circulated during the nineteenth century AD.

Bahai further teaches that the happiness of mankind as well as world peace and security are unattainable until global unity is firmly established. Bahai promotes gender and race equality, world government, freedom of expression and assembly, world peace, religious tolerance, and religious cooperation. Bahai rejects homosexuality while calling for equal dignity and respect for all peoples, the elimination of poverty and excessive wealth, universal education and economic justice. Mankind must control the present and future through unity and global cooperation.

The sacred texts of Hinduism are collectively referred to as "the Vedas" and the written forms date between 600 to 300 BC. Hinduism views the entire universe as one divine entity who is at one with the universe but transcends it as well. Brahma is the creator who is always creating new realities. Dharma is the eternal order, religion, law and duty. Vishnu preserves the creations of Brahma and travels between heaven and earth in one of ten incarnations. Shiva is the destroyer of eternal order but can be compassionate and erotic. Hinduism is splintered into various groupings which worship local gods and goddesses. The two major divisions of Hinduism are Vaishnavaism (Vishnu is the ultimate deity) and Shivaism (Shiva is the ultimate deity). The main tenet of Hinduism is the transmigration of the soul -- a continuous cycle of birth, life, death, and rebirth through many lifetimes (referred to as "samsara"). Hindu priests serve at rituals and worship ceremonies but are considered unnecessary in rural areas where priestly duties are carried out by local non-Brahmins.

The four aims of Hinduism or "the doctrine of the fourfold end of life" are Dharma (religious righteousness), Artha (economic success and wealth), Kama (gratification of the senses such as sex, pleasure, and mental enjoyment), and Moska (liberation from samsara). The three goals of the "pravritti" (those who are in the world) are Dharma, Artha, and Kama. The main goal for the "nivritta" (those who renounce the world) is Moska.   Liberation from samsara, thus becoming one with the universe, is the supreme goal of mankind.

Kama also refers to the accumulation of an individual's good and bad deeds. An overload of bad Kama might result in rebirth as an animal or insect. The unequal distribution of wealth, prestige, and suffering is believed to be the result of one's previous acts during the current life and previous lives. Meditation is practiced with Yoga being the most observed. Other Hindu activities include rituals, daily prayers, and ceremonial dinners for various deities.

Hinduism is a "save yourself" belief system where good thoughts, good intentions, and good deeds will ultimately be rewarded with cessation of reincarnation.

Buddhism was founded during the second half of the sixth century BC by Siddhartha Gautama, son of King Gautama who ruled over a small district in the Himalayas between India and Nepal. As a young man, Siddhartha wandered outside the palace and observed a leper, a corpse, and an ascetic whereupon he concluded that happiness is an illusion. After he fathered a son to ensure the royal bloodline, Siddhartha began a pilgrimage of inquiry and asceticism wherein he was influenced by two Brahmin hermits and later by five monks.

After years of seeking communion with the supreme cosmic spirit, Siddhartha claimed to have discovered the four noble truths (Pativedhanana) and pronounced himself the Buddha. He labored some forty years spreading the Buddha doctrines and died a questionable death at age 80 (it is reported that he was poisoned by a blacksmith). The teachings of Buddha are referred to as Dharma. Following Siddhartha's death, his followers convened to create tenets they could all accept within the caste system which required a series of rebirths to move up through the system. The Buddha rejected the concepts of a supreme being and eternal souls. Whatever gods inhabit the cosmos are impermanent and are reincarnated like humans. The cessation of rebirths is named "nirvana" wherein the individual being becomes one with the Universal Soul. Nirvana is the ultimate achievement.

Karma (tally of good and bad deeds) determines

the kind of rebirth and quality of life after rebirth. The path to nirvana is to follow the four noble truths -- the universality of suffering; the origin of suffering; overcoming of suffering; and the suppression of suffering. Lustful desires cause suffering which is experienced during rebirth, aging, death and rebirth. Suffering can be overcome by suppression of the desires causing one to suffer. The way leading to suppression of suffering is a noble path with eight branches -- right aspirations, right speech, right conduct, right livelihood, right effort, right concentration, right views of understanding, and right mindfulness. The eight branches are different dimensions of a total way of life.

Several lives are required to achieve nirvana. The journey is long and difficult with inner peace and harmony as one approaches nirvana; then nothingness. The sacred texts of Buddhism were compiled around 80 BC and are referred to as the Pali Canon (also called the Tripitaka). In summary, Buddhism rejects the concept of a supreme being and teaches that human works are disciplined by cycles of reincarnation.

Jainism, a heretical movement within Hinduism, was founded by a man named Mahavira. The sacred texts of Jainism are the twelve "angas" plus lesser writings which appeared in written form around 1600 AD. At age 30, it is believed by followers of Jainism that Mahavira decided to live a life of self-denial and wandered naked through India for twelve years before achieving "enlightenment." In his thirteenth year of naked wandering, in a squatting position exposed to the sun with his knees high and his head low, in deep meditation, Mahavira reached nirvana whereupon he stopped living by himself and attracted disciples. He preached his revelations until his death at which time he allegedly boasted of 14,000 monks within his brother-hood.

Although Mahavira was steadfastly opposed to the concept of God or gods, his followers elevated him to deity claiming that he descended from heaven without sin and having all knowledge. Jainism preaches self denial as the path to nirvana. The Five Great Vows renounce killing any living thing; lying, greed, sexual pleasure, and worldly attachments. Monks were taught to avoid women entirely because Mahavira believed they were the cause of all types of evil.

Taoism traces its roots to Lao-Tzu around 600 BC. The sacred text is Tao-te-Ching (also known as Daodejing). Taoism was originally a hodgepodge of psychology and philosophy that became a religion in 440 AD and benefited from state support until the fall of the Ching Dynasty in 1911 AD. Today, Taoism has roughly twenty million followers centered mainly in Taiwan off the mainland of China.

Taoism rejects the concept of a personalized deity. Tao is the life force which flows through the universe and all life. The ultimate achievement is to harmonize with Tao. Taoists believe in letting nature take its course unimpeded by mankind. Time is cyclical and not linear. Kindness is always reciprocated. Left to themselves, people will be compassionate without expecting a reward. Tao regulates and balances natural processes and embodies the harmony of opposites -- no love without hate; no light without dark; no male without female, etc. There is no God to hear prayers or to act on them. Taoists seek answers to life's questions through inner meditation and outer observation.

Evolution is the religion of atheists who deny that any supreme being exits; and that all life forms evolved from a single living cell which created itself through a chain of unrelated and purely random events. From this original living cell evolved every life form that exists today or has ever existed in the past eons of time. The elements within the universe emerged from nothingness by random chance for no reason and without purpose. There is no life of any kind following physical death. Humanity is simply an accidental life form produced by natural selection and survival of the fittest.

Judaism is a belief system traced back to a man called Abraham who lived in Ur of the Chaldees within the fertile crescent around 1900 BC. Although his family worshiped idols, Abraham believed there is an unseen supreme being who created the universe and all life forms. According to Judaism, Abraham meditated upon and prayed to the invisible God until God called him out from among the idol worshipers and instructed him to travel to a land which God would give to him and to his seed. The "promised land" would be shown to him as he traveled. Abraham obeyed God and went out not knowing where he was going. God led him to the land of Canaan where Abraham lived as a shepherd and fathered Ishmael and Isaac. Ishmael was the firstborn, but his mother was a bond-servant. Isaac's mother was Sarah, Abraham's wife. Ishmael and his seed fathered the Arabs; and Isaac's descendants became known as Jews. Isaac's wife birthed two sons named Jacob and Esau. Jacob's name was changed to Israel and his twelve sons begat twelve tribes who collectively are referred to as "the children of Israel." Esau's descendants are called Edomites. Esau, being the firstborn, sold his birthright to Jacob for a bowl of stew.

The sacred texts of Judaism are the thirty-nine narratives which make up the total writings within the Old Testament of the Holy Bible. Followers of Judaism believe in one true God, sin and righteousness, resurrection from the dead, heaven and hell, Satan and the angels, eternal life, and eternal punishment. They further believe in sacrificial offerings (animal sacrifices) to obtain forgiveness for breaking God's law. Moses, the greatest of God's prophets, received God's law while seeking God on Mount Sinai around 1491 BC. The Law of Moses covers criminal, civil and religious law. Religious law involves a priesthood, rituals, sacrifices, holy days, annual feasts, an annual Day of Atonement, a Sabbath day (every 7th day), the Sabbath year (every 7th year), and the year of Jubilee (every 50th year wherein all bond servants are freed and all real estate reverts to the original tribal family).

The ten main points of the Law of Moses are referred to as God's Ten Commandments -- worship God only; do not set up nor worship any graven image; do not speak of God in an irreverent manner; remember and keep the Sabbath day; do not commit adultery; do not steal; do not murder; do not bear false witness; do not covet; and honor both father and mother. The thirty-nine Old Testament narratives were written and compiled between 1491 and 397 BC by a total of thirty-one different authors. The first five narratives are ascribed to Moses and are referred to as the "Pentateuch" (Genesis, Exodus, Leviticus, Numbers and Deuteronomy).

Followers of Judaism who rejected the teachings of Jesus Christ are still waiting for their prophesied Messiah who the Hebrew prophets said would restore Israel to the glory the nation enjoyed under King David and would make Jerusalem the center of world government.

Jews (children of Israel) have been the most hated and persecuted of all nationalities (anti-Semitism) since 825 BC and continuing to the present time. Following approximately 2,000 years of dispersion among Gentile nations, the Jews began returning to their homeland pursuant to a United Nations mandate issued in 1948 AD. During the same year, the tiny nation of Israel declared its independence. The nation of Israel has remained independent and has become one of the worlds most lethal military powers.

With reference to all world religions other than Judaism and Christianity, there is not a single fact to support the various belief systems. Reincarnation was plucked from the imagination of humans. There has never been a documented case of reincarnation. The basic goodness of mankind has been repeatedly proven to be an illusion along with global unity. Good thoughts, good words and good deeds may be exhibited from time to time due to will worship and voluntary self-denial, but do not represent routine human behavior. Mankind generally exhibits greed, selfishness, envy, cruelty, and hatred for the socially outcast. Past and present wars are very obvious examples of true human nature.

The Law of Cause and Effect eliminates reincarnation as being factual. The basic goodness of humanity has never been demonstrated within relationships between the races, nor between general populations, nor between nations; and very seldom between individuals. Bastardized versions of Christianity, such as Islam, seek to justify greed, lust. and violence.

Although Judaism is Christianity concealed; and Christianity is Judaism revealed, followers of Judaism still look to personal works and animal sacrifices as the ticket to eternal life with God. Only Christians believe and teach that redemption from personal sins and eternal life in Heaven flow solely from faith in and acceptance of a divine sacrifice provided by God; and that the very best of human works fall short of the standards reflected in God's law. Prior to the law of Moses, sin was not charged to individuals because in the absence of law there can be no sin. God gave the law to demonstrate to every human the need for a divine sacrifice. Jesus said he is that sacrifice; and that the souls of the dead prior to his offering of himself before God were confined to either Paradise or Hell awaiting his coming; and that he, himself, would descend into Hell and provide all therein the opportunity to accept him as "the Lamb of God."

The ten commandments on the surface appear easy to keep yet the Bible declares that no man except Jesus ever kept God's laws. The reason that humans cannot keep God's law is because sin originates in our thoughts and does not depend upon execution of our mental rebellion and lust. We conceive sin in our mind and when we act upon sinful thoughts we incur the consequences of our acts. However, because sin originates in our thoughts, humans are not capable of living a sinless life. Therefore, we can only be redeemed back to God by a divine sacrificial lamb (Jesus Christ).

The roots of Christianity within Judaism and the teachings of Jesus Christ are found within the pages of the Holy Bible. Those who reject Jesus as the Son of

God have labored for twenty centuries to disprove Biblical Scriptures. To date, the enemies of Jesus have failed to come up with a single proven example of Biblical error. On the other hand, the Holy Scriptures repeatedly demonstrate the unerring accuracy found therein. There are Biblical statements which cannot be proven to be true, but neither can they be proven to be false. That is why the Scriptures declare that the redemption of human souls results from grace through faith in Jesus Christ and not through that which is yet to be revealed.

Because no religion nor belief system, other than Christianity, predicates eternal life with God in Heaven as God's "free gift to humanity," it is more than prudent to consider what the Holy Bible reveals to mankind concerning life, death, time and eternity. For the reader's convenience, each of the thirty-nine books within the Old Testament and each of the twenty-seven books making up the New Testament are summarized herein using common English vernacular for clarity and brevity. The essential truths contained within each of the sixty-six books have been paraphrased by the author.

Jesus Christ, through the works he performed, has already demonstrated to any logical and rational person that God exists. If, then, an individual accepts God's existence, the acts attributed to God as described within the Holy Bible are insignificant displays of his unlimited power. Just one glimpse at the atomic structure of atoms or the awesome design obvious within DNA indicates the unfathomable intelligence and preexistence of our creator. The question is not whether the described events occurred. The question is -- does God exist? It is most advisable to avoid the "killing Lazarus" mindset when reading God's revelation to humanity. During Jesus' earthly ministry He raised a man named Lazarus from the dead before numerous eyewitnesses. Lazarus had been dead for four days and was already decomposing. The enemies of Jesus decided the only way to deal with such a miracle was to kill Lazarus thereby destroying the evidence of his resurrection.

Chapter four

When considering the question of how the universe came into being, it is very easy to become confused by the astronomical numbers we immediately encounter which makes it difficult to mentally separate the macro universe from the micro composition.

Could the life force possessed by every living organism spring from nothingness? Such a spontaneous generation of life violates the law of cause and effect. Plasmas, gases, liquids and solids have coexisted with the known universe. Yet, there has never been such a spontaneous generation of life in any molecular form even with the concentrated supportive efforts of expert physicists and geneticists.

Any molecular structure having the physical capacity to move, feed and reproduce has life by scientific definition. The human reproductive cycle begins with the merging of the female egg with the male sperm. Neither the egg nor the sperm is a living organism because neither has the ability to feed and reproduce although the sperm moves with a whip-like tail and the egg by pressure variation travels within the fallopian tube.

The fertilization of the egg by the sperm produces a zygote or human embryo which moves and reproduces by means of cellular mitosis while extracting nutrients from the mother's bloodstream. Thus, the embryo consists of cellular tissue and a life force. The cellular tissue is the product of conception but where did the life force come from? The egg did not feed nor reproduce and neither did the sperm. The embryo consists of the inorganic elements but what does the life force consist of?

Since the life force does not consist of matter, energy, and motion and therefore is definitely not composed of the elements, the life force is a separate entity from the cellular tissue and exists separate from the matter, energy and motion comprising the embryo. The most common words used to designate the life force is "spirit" or "soul."

The logical deduction from the separate existence of the physical body and the spirit is that there is a physical, three-dimensional universe visible to humans and there is also a spiritual, multidimensional universe which is invisible to humans while the spirit is confined within the physical body. When the physical body loses the ability to accommodate the spirit by moving, feeding and reproducing on the cellular level, the spirit departs from the physical body into the spiritual universe.

It is worth restating that the most intelligent, most imaginative and most educated of humans as well as the most illiterate, most simple and most aboriginal among humans have conceived only two explanations for the universe and its various life forms: (1) the universe and its life forms created themselves through random chance events over eons of time such that human life is without meaning, purpose or immortality; or (2) the universe and its life forms were created by a supreme being or beings existing outside of that which was created; and humans possess a soul or spirit which is both separate from the physical body and immortal.

The basic belief of all atheists, evolutionists and agnostics is that the accidental, random chance universe gave birth to life forms by means of spontaneous generation since there is no "creator" nor life after physical death of the body because the physical body and life perish simultaneously.

Conversely, the rest of humanity believes in some form of God or Gods responsible for creation of the universe and its life forms plus granting or withholding of fellowship with such supreme being or beings within a created paradise in accordance with faith and or good works during physical life on Earth. Such belief tenets may rely upon faith alone, or good works alone, or a combination of both faith and good works.

Lack of faith and/or good works result in spiritual eternal life within a very unpleasant environment whereas faith and/or good works guarantee eternal spiritual life in some sort of paradise.

Christianity is the world's largest religion followed by Islam. Both belief systems are fractured by doctrinal divisions as to whether faith, or faith plus good works, determine one's eternal destiny. The other major world religions embrace some variation of reincarnation based upon good works versus bad works with the ultimate reward being cessation of reincarnation and "oneness with the universe." Several minor world religions espouse the basic goodness of mankind leading to world peace and a spiritual life through reincarnation or in a paradise peculiar to each religion.

Religions referred to as "pagan" or "heathen" generally involve idol worship and cults along with various tenets pertaining to a spiritual immortality.

Okay. So, what do we know for certain? Well, we know the universe exits as demonstrated by the undisputed fact that we are alive and living on Planet Earth. We see the sun and moon. We admire the stars. We experience the cycle of the seasons. We experience heat and cold, light and darkness, and the force of gravity. We watch the earth and seas produce our food. We strive to satisfy our libido, hunger and thirst while breathing in oxygen and exhaling carbon dioxide. We feel the aging of our physical bodies and try not to think too much about how soon we must lay our flesh aside.

Thus, we know for an absolute fact that the universe exists and that we are an integral entity within it. It is also a very safe bet that the universe did not pop out of nothingness and that everywhere we turn within Earth we observe total design, order and mind-boggling complexity. It is even a safer bet that humans did not evolve from lower life forms because such evolution is both illogical and physically impossible as detailed herein.

We therefore are left with an inescapable conclusion. There is a supreme being or beings who created the universe and all its life forms. That being so, it is without doubt most prudent to endeavor to understand the divine nature of such a supreme being or beings and how humanity relates past, present and future to our creator or creators.. That challenge I will address carefully within the remaining chapters.

An individual's faith, tradition and/or religion is very private and it is the author's intention to simply encourage every reader to carefully apply logic and common sense to his/her personal faith, religion, tradition or lack thereof. Perhaps by applying only established scientific facts, cold logic and common sense to the questions pertaining to life, death, time and eternity, each reader of this book will feel that the author has made a significant contribution to his/her comfort level.

Because the supernatural war involving our spirit, soul and body is waged by God against evil powers who are the rulers of the spiritual darkness of this world (Satan, fallen angels, and demonic spirits), Christians are persecuted unto physical death by Satan's spiritual children among atheists, evolutionists, agnostics, and religions spawned by Satan opposing Christianity. Such deadly persecution rages today in Islamic controlled nations and nations ruled by Satanic dictators. In nations where Christians are not being killed, such as the United

States, laws are being passed to prohibit Christians from practicing their faith in all public forums. It is a short step from such laws to actually executing Christians. In the United States, every religion except Christianity is freely tolerated and free to worship in any and all public forums.

Christian martyrs who know that the death of their physical body is a small price to pay for openly practicing their faith accept death with such peace and fortitude that both executioners and spectators are often converted to Christianity. Satan's children have tried very hard to make execution of a Christian extremely degrading and exceedingly tortuous. A few examples from Foxe's Book of Martyrs (public domain book) are certainly enlightening:

Stephen, a deacon in the church, preached to a crowd of Jews declaring that Jesus fulfilled the Old Testament prophecies. He was mobbed, actually chewed by the teeth of his assailants, then stoned to death. Among those consenting to his death was Saul of Tarsus who became known as Paul, the apostle to the Gentiles (after his conversion on the road to Damascus).

James, the apostle, son of Zebedee, and brother of the apostle, John, was beheaded under the rule of Herod's son to please the Jews. The apostle, Philip, was thrown into prison and afterward crucified. The apostle, Matthew was beheaded with a blunt instrument in the city of Nadabah. The apostle, James the Less, was elected to the oversight of the church at Jerusalem, and authored the Epistle of James (Holy Bible). At the age of ninety-four, he was beaten and stoned by Jews before his brains were splattered with a fuller's club. Matthias (selected by lot to replace Judas Iscariot) was stoned at Jerusalem and then beheaded. Andrew, the apostle and brother of Simon Peter, preached in Asia. At Edessa, he was attacked and crucified on a cross, the two ends of which were fixed transversely in the ground (hence the derivation of the term, "St. Andrew's Cross").

Mark, author of the Gospel bearing his name, was dragged to pieces by a mob in Alexandria, during a pagan festival. The apostle, Peter, was crucified in Rome, upside down at his own request (because he felt he was unworthy to be put to death in the same position as Jesus). Paul, apostle to the Gentiles, was beheaded at Rome during the reign of Nero. Jude, also called Thaddeus, was crucified at Edessa. The apostle, Bartholomew, preached in several countries. He also translated the Gospel of Matthew into the language of India. He was crucified by the pagans he sought to convert. Thomas, called Didymus, the apostle, preached in Parthia and India. Enraged pagan priests thrust him through with a spear. Luke, the beloved physician and author of the Gospel bearing his name, traveled often with Paul, the apostle to the Gentiles. He was hanged by pagan Greeks. The apostle, Simon Zelotes, preached in Africa and what is now Britain. He was crucified by an angry mob.

The apostle, John, author of the Gospel of John,

three epistles, and the Revelation (Holy Bible), was cast into a cauldron of boiling oil. The boiling oil had no effect upon John whereupon he was banished to the Isle of Patmos where he wrote the Book of Revelation. John was the only apostle to escape martyrdom.

The first of ten primitive persecutions occurred during the reign of the Roman Emperor, Nero. Nero, himself, set fire to Rome and blamed the ensuring inferno upon the Christians living in Rome. Nero amused himself dreaming up the most novel means whereby to torture and execute Christians. They were sewn up in the skins of wild beasts and chewed upon by dogs; smeared with pitch and used as human torches to light his gardens; crucified upon flaming crosses; and fed to lions and other meat eaters that had been starved to enhance their appetites for blood.

The second persecution was headed by the Roman Emperor, Domitian, and commenced around 81 A.D. A law was passed that no Christian, once brought before the tribunal, should be exempt from punishment without renouncing his religion. Church leaders were favorite targets for torture and public execution. During this period, many hideous tortures were invented to encourage Christians to renounce Jesus Christ.

The third persecution under Roman emperors began during the reign of Trajan, 108 A.D. and continued throughout the reign of Adrian. Executing Christians in large numbers in the arena before heckling spectators gained in popularity. Eustachius, a high ranking Roman commander, was ordered to join in an idolatrous sacrifice to celebrate some of his victories. Being a Christian, Eustachius declined the invitation whereupon the emperor ordered his execution along with his entire family.

At the martyrdom of Faustines and Jovita, brothers and citizens of Brescia, their torments were so many and their patience so great, that Calocerius, a pagan, was struck with such admiration that he exclaimed in a kind of ecstasy, "Great is the God of the Christians!" for which he was arrested and given a similar execution. Adrian died about 138 A.D. and was succeeded by Antoninus Pius who held no animosity toward Christians.

Emperor Marcus Aurelius Antoninus initiated the fourth persecution in 162 A.D. The cruelties used during this period were such that many of the spectators shuddered in horror at the sight, and were astonished at the intrepidity of the victims. Some of the martyrs were forced to pass with wounded feet over thorns, nails, broken shells, etc. Others were scourged until their sinews and veins lay bare, then subjected to excruciating tortures before being executed in the most horrible manner. Germanicus, a young man, being delivered to wild beasts because of his faith, behaved with such courage that several pagans became converts to the faith which inspired such fortitude.

Polycarp, the bishop of Smyrna, hearing that he was being hunted, escaped, but was discovered by a child and burned alive tied to a stake. Metrodorus, a bold minister, and Pionius, a church leader were also burned alive. An illustrious Roman lady and mother to seven sons converted to Christianity. Her eldest son was scourged and pressed to death with weights. Two more sons had their brains dashed out with clubs. The fourth son was thrown from a precipice. The remaining three sons were beheaded. The mother was then beheaded with the same sword. A deacon of Vienna, Sanctus, was tortured with red hot plates of brass placed upon the most tender parts of his body. Blandina, a Christian woman, having a weak constitution, was suspended on a piece of wood fixed in the ground and offered as food to wild beasts. None of the meat eaters touched her and she was remanded to her cell. She was brought out again and still was not attacked. When she was dragged out the third and final time, a teenager was forced out with her. Blandina encouraged the youth such that the constancy of their faith enraged the crowd. They were then subjected to multiple tortures and finally executed with a sword.

In spite of the ferocity of cyclical waves of persecution, Christianity continued to spread throughout the Roman empire. By the time of the fifth cycle of persecution during the reign of Severus, 192 A.D., many Roman soldiers as well as Roman citizens had converted from idol worship to Christianity. The steadfast refusal of Christians to renounce Christ in the face of barbaric, hideous, and prolonged torture did not go unnoticed among the jeering, bloodthirsty spectators. Between the sixth and tenth cycles of primitive Roman persecution (235 A.D. -- 313 A.D.), Christians continued to worship in secret within private homes and in the catacombs beneath the city of Rome.

Traveling evangelists, at the risk of torture and death, introduced the teachings of Christ throughout the civilized world. It was not a time for lip service and lukewarm stewardship (as is the case within Christianity today). Devoted converts shrank not from martyrdom to preach Christ in every city, town, and village. It was the realization of the challenge of stewardship spoken by Jesus, Himself:

"Whosoever therefore shall confess Me before men, him will I confess also before My Father which is in heaven. But whosoever shall deny Me before men, him will I also deny before My Father which is in heaven. Think not that I am come to send peace on earth: I come not to send peace, but a sword. For I am come to set a man at variance against his father, and the daughter against her mother, and the daughter in law against her mother in law. And a man's foes shall be they of his own household. He that loveth father or mother more than Me is not worthy of Me: and he that loveth son or daughter more than Me is not worthy of Me. And he that taketh not his cross, and followeth after Me, is not worthy of Me. He that findeth his life shall lose it: and he that loseth his life for My sake shall find it. He that receiveth you receiveth Me, and he that receiveth Me, receiveth Him that sent Me." (Matthew, chapter 10, verses 32-40)

"And He said unto them, Go ye into all the world, and preach the gospel to every creature. He that believeth and is baptized shall be saved: but he that believeth not shall be damned." (Mark, chapter 16, verses 15-16)

"But take heed to yourselves: for they shall deliver you up to councils; and in the synagogues ye shall be beaten: and ye shall be brought before rulers and kings for My sake, for a testimony against them. And the gospel must first be published among all nations. But when they shall lead you, and deliver you up, take no thought before hand what ye shall speak, neither do ye premeditate: but whatsoever shall be given you in that hour, that speak ye: for it is not ye that speak, but the Holy Ghost. Now the brother shall betray the brother to death, and the father the son; and children shall rise up against their parents, and shall cause them to be put to death. And ye shall be hated of all men for My name's sake: but he that shall endure unto the end, the same shall be saved." (Mark, chapter 13, verses 9-13)

In view of such warnings from Jesus, the severity of the cyclical persecutions was no surprise to early Christians who went joyfully to their deaths, to be ushered into the kingdom of God. Such persecutions drew the attention of humanity to the gospel of Jesus Christ and resulted in countless conversions to

Christianity. The death of the martyrs also served as an accusation before God against those taking pleasure in their torture and execution:

"Wherefore ye be witnesses unto yourselves, that ye are the children of them which killed the prophets. Fill ye up then the measure of your fathers. Ye serpents, ye generation of vipers, how can ye escape the damnation of hell? Wherefore, behold, I send unto you prophets, and wise men, and scribes: and some of them ye shall kill and crucify; and some of them shall ye scourge in your synagogues, and persecute them from city to city: That upon you may come all the righteous blood shed upon the earth, from the blood of righteous Abel unto the blood of Zacharias son of Barachias, whom ye slew between the temple and the altar. Verily I say unto you, All these things shall come upon this generation." (Matthew, chapter 23, verses 31-36)

"And I say unto you my friends, Be not afraid of them that kill the body, and after that have no more that they can do. But I will forewarn you whom ye shall fear: Fear Him, which after He hath killed hath power to cast into hell; yea, I say unto you, Fear Him." (Luke, chapter 12, verses 4-5)

The martyrdom of a Christian, regardless of the measure of cruelty involved, occurs over a brief period, and the suffering is mitigated by the joy for which it is endured. But, the suffering of those inflicting torture and death is eternal and of far greater intensity. Consider for a moment, the reality of eternity (timelessness): If an immortal ant should carry, one single grain at a time, all the sand from every desert and from every beach on Earth and drop each grain into a continually expanding abyss, and repeat the entire process a hundred billion trillion times, eternity would still be in its initial beginning.

After the first twenty centuries within the bowels of hell, Nero is probably more or less getting the message that God is loving and merciful, but also just. It is prudent to keep God, the righteous judge, in mind while contemplating additional examples of Christian martyrs.

Perpetua, a young married lady, and Felicitas, a married lady big with child, were stripped naked before the spectators and presented to a mad bull. The animal initially charged Perpetua, stunning her, then ran upon Felicitas goring her through her stomach. Both women were afterward finished off with a sword. A mere lad was placed naked into a scalding bath, left there to broil, then beheaded. Hippolitus, a Christian of exemplary reputation, was tied behind a wild horse and dragged to shreds. Julian, a native of Cilicia, was seized for his confession of Christ, stuffed into a leather bag filled with snakes and tossed into the sea. Peter, a young convert, refused to sacrifice to Venus whereupon he was stretched upon a torture wheel until all his bones were broken, afterward his head was struck off with a sword.

Alexander and Epimachus, of Alexandria were apprehended for being Christians, and after confessing the accusation were beaten with staves, their bodies were ripped with hooks, and then they were both burned alive. Trypho and Respicius, two eminent men, were seized as Christians and imprisoned. Their feet were pierced with nails; they were dragged through the streets; scourged with iron hooks; scorched with lighted torches; and finally beheaded. Agatha, a Sicilian lady, was scourged, burned with red-hot irons, and torn with sharpened hooks. She was afterward laid naked upon live coals intermingled with broken glass, then carried back to her cell where she died.

Julianus, an old man, lame with gout, and Cronion, another Christian, were bound upon the backs of camels, severely beaten, then thrown into a fire and consumed. At Utica, three hundred Christians were placed around a burning lime kiln. They were commanded to either sacrifice to Jupiter or be thrown into the pit. Unanimously refusing, they jumped into the flames. Maxima, Donaltilla, and Secunda, three virgins of Tuburga, were forced to drink gall and vinegar; mercilessly beaten; tormented at length upon a gibbet; scorched with a gridiron; worried by wild beasts; and eventually beheaded. In 286 A.D., over six thousand Roman soldiers were executed for refusing to renounce Christ. Zoe, the wife of a jailer who had custody of some Christians, was converted to the faith. She was hung upon a tree with a fire of straw lighted under her. Her body was taken down, a large stone was tied to her corpse, and the remains heaved into a river.

Quintin, a native of Rome, was arrested for preaching the gospel of Christ. He was stretched with pulleys until all his joints were dislocated. His body was torn with wire scourges; boiling oil and pitch were poured upon his naked flesh; and lighted torches were then applied to his sides and armpits. He was dragged back to his cell where he expired.

Victor, a Christian who spent his personal fortune relieving the poor was seized by imperial order. He was bound and dragged through the streets before being subjected to numerous cruelties and indignities. Remaining steadfast, his courage was deemed obstinacy. Being stretched upon the rack, he prayed to God to endue him with patience, after which he underwent additional tortures with great fortitude. After his tormentors tired of brutalizing him, he was remanded to prison where he converted his jailers. The emperor ordered the execution of the jailers and they were beheaded. Victor was again tortured upon the rack, unmercifully beaten and thrown back into his cell. Being a third time examined concerning his faith, a small altar was set before him, and he was commanded to immediately offer incense upon it. Fired with indignation at the command, he boldly stepped forward, and with his foot overturned both altar and the incense. The emperor, Maximilian, who was present, ordered the foot with which Victor had kicked the altar to be immediately cut off. Victor was then thrown into a hole and crushed to pieces with stones.

Romanus, a native of Palestine, was a Christian spokesman. He was scourged; put to the rack; his body torn with hooks; his flesh ripped with knives; his face lacerated; his teeth beaten from their sockets; and his hair plucked out from his scalp; thereafter he was strangled to death. Peter, a eunuch belonging to the emperor, was a Christian of singular modesty and integrity. He was stretched upon a gridiron and broiled over a slow fire. Eulalia, a Spanish lady of a Christian family, was remarkable for her sweetness of temper and gentleness to others. Being apprehended as a Christian, the magistrate attempted to convert her back to paganism, but she ridiculed the pagan deities with such contempt that the magistrate, incensed at her faith, ordered that she be tortured to death. She was stripped and her sides were torn with hooks. Then her breasts were burned until she expired. Eustratius, secretary to the governor of Armina, was thrown into a heated furnace for exhorting some Christians who had been arrested to persevere in their faith.

Nicander and Marcian, two eminent Roman military officers, were arrested for being Christians. As both men possessed revered abilities, great effort was expended to induce them to renounce Christianity; but these efforts were ineffectual. They were beheaded. In the kingdom of Naples, a dozen Christians were ordered to be devoured by wild beasts. The savage animals would not touch them whereupon all twelve were summarily beheaded. In Arethusa, the bellies of apprehended Christians were opened up and corn stuffed inside. Swine were brought to feed on the corn, and in the process the entrails of the condemned were also devoured.

Hundreds of thousands of Christians were butchered during the ten cycles of persecution permitted by Roman emperors. The foregoing examples demonstrate the mindset against the teachings of Christianity and the existence of God as preached by Christians. This mindset, by and large, remains the same today. In the east, especially within Muslim controlled lands, Christians are still being displaced, tortured, and murdered with the consent of the governing powers. Islam, despite its peaceful claims, is nothing more than a religion of terrorists.

Leaders of political movements and resulting governing bodies have, in the name of Christianity, committed acts of persecution that rival the brutality of the Roman emperors and the pagan powers that ruled the civilized world until the time of Constantine, who, in 313 A.D., proclaimed himself a Christian. As emperor of the Roman empire, he granted freedom to all Christians and official status to Christianity alongside paganism. Because Christianity became a recognized religion within the empire, the emperor became the defacto head of the Christian church. Constantine was primarily interested in unifying the empire by establishing peace between rival ideologies.

Thus, he became the first ecumenist and introduced that fatal error into church doctrine. He convened the Council of Nicea in 325 A.D. and presided over its proceedings. He also continued to head the pagan priesthood. He officiated over pagan celebrations and endowed pagan temples. To the pagans, Constantine was "Pontifex Maximus," and to the Christian church he became "Bishop of Bishops," and "Vicar of Christ." Consequently, under Constantine, there was a Satanic mixing of paganism and Christianity. Lucifer, the angel of light sought to conquer Christianity from within. A position of leadership within the Christian church became the fastest route to power and wealth. This acted as a magnet to attract the most base and greedy individuals within the empire to Christian leadership.

The concept of a priesthood with all its trappings and rituals was introduced along with a hierarchy of bishops, cardinals and a papacy. The Roman Catholic Church became a formidable political force as well as a pagan religion masquerading under the name of Christianity. The Catholic Church claimed the power to excommunicate (doom souls to hell), to forgive sins in exchange for payment therefor (sale of indulgences), and other such nonsense. Heads of state had to cater to the church fathers in order to be accepted by the general population.

By the Middle Ages, the bishops of Rome claimed to be the sole representative of Christ upon earth and absolute ruler over kingdoms, people, and property. They took to themselves the titles of Vicar of Christ,

Bishop of Bishops, and Pontifex Maximus; and forbade any other bishops to be called "pope" (papa). With support from the simple among Christianity, the Papal claims were realized and great corruption engulfed the Roman Catholic Church. In time, the universal church (Catholic) would torture and murder millions of Christians who refused to accept corruption of their faith. In addition, the Roman Catholic Church would torture and murder millions of non-Christians in an effort to force conversion of "nonbelievers." The church "fathers" in Rome claimed dominion of all Christians around the world.

After the death of Constantine, there were renewed cycles of persecution by Roman emperors as well as nonstop persecution within lands not governed by Rome. But, the Roman Catholic Church would become the greatest enemy of uncorrupted Christianity. The marriage between the state recognized church and the state itself was maintained by the sword and by perpetuating the ignorance of the people concerning the actual content of the Holy Scriptures. The church hierarchy carefully collected and enshrined the Scriptures, and it was only the clergy that was permitted to explain the Word of God to the masses.

The church was pagan in both origin and practice. The decision of the pope was final in all matters of Scriptural interpretation, and all dissenters were ruthlessly tortured to death. It is imperative to keep in mind that the Roman Catholic Church represented

Christianity in name only whereas true followers of Jesus Christ rejected the papal doctrines and defied the pope at the risk of their lives. Popery shrouded the teachings of Christ with darkness and superstition in order to achieve tremendous power and wealth. The sons of Satan who often filled the papal chair claimed the absolute right to reign over the nations as well as the church.

Peter Waldo, a native of Lyons, a man of great learning and integrity became a major opponent of popery, and his converts became known as Waldenses or Waldoys. Pope Alexander III ordered the bishop of Lyons to exterminate the Waldenses, giving rise to the formation of the "inquisition." Pope Innocent III found the persecution of the Waldenses to be ineffective whereupon he sent monks to convert them back to popery. Dominic, one of the monks, was especially zealous and instituted a new order of monks which became the "Dominican friars." Members of this order have been the principal inquisitors in the inquisitions ordered by the Roman Catholic Church.

The inquisitors were given unlimited powers and they proceeded against whom they pleased without regard to status, wealth or gender. The validity of the accusations which triggered an inquisition might be wholly suspect and the charges of little significance, but the inquisitors were more interested in personal enrichment than protecting popery. Wealthy citizens were often accused of giving aid to heretics in order to extract large sums of money or land from them. The bones of alleged heretics and those charged with providing aid to them were dug up and put on trial as an excuse to confiscate their estates and defraud the heirs. Such practices continued for several centuries under the protection of the Catholic Church hierarchy.

The Albigenses, like the Waldenses, rejected Catholic doctrine and were subjected to papal persecution. The pope raised an army by promising paradise to those who would bear arms against the heretics for forty days. About the same time, heavy persecutions ran rampant throughout Lithuania and Poland. In 1524, at Melden, France, a dissenter named John Clark fixed a bill on the church door which denounced the pope. He was repeatedly whipped and branded in his forehead. He later traveled to Mentz, in Lorraine, and demolished some graven images. His right hand and nose were cut off and his breast ripped with pincers. He endured these attacks with such fortitude that he sang the 115th Psalm which expressly condemns idolatry, whereupon he was burned to death.

Other dissenters were racked, beaten and burned at Paris, Malda, and Limosin. A native of Malda was roasted by a slow fire for proclaiming the Mass to be a denial of the teachings of Christ. Soon thereafter, a bloody campaign was executed throughout France. The streets were strewn with bodies as men, women, and children were methodically slaughtered. Some priests, holding a crucifix in one hand and a dagger in the other, exhorted the attackers to spare neither relatives nor friends. At Anjou, many women were raped before being murdered. The president of Turin, after giving a large sum for his life, was mercilessly beaten, stripped and hung. His belly was slit open, his entrails plucked out, and his heart carried about the city upon a spear. The Roman Catholic Church proved itself, by means of prolonged tortures and the cruelest methods of execution, to be more barbarian than the emperor, Nero. Dissenters became known as "Protestants," and entire populations were indiscriminately slaughtered.

Courts of inquisition were established in several countries, but the Spanish Inquisition became the most powerful and most dreaded. The most ruthless of the popish monks were the Dominicans and the Franciscans and they were given the exclusive right to preside over the courts of inquisition. Even the kings of Spain were taught to dread the power of the inquisition, and multitudes who rejected popery were careful to conceal their sentiments. The pope granted the inquisitors power to represent the papal presence; to excommunicate; to sentence to death upon mere suspicion of heresy; to publish crusades against all whom they deemed to be heretics; and to enter into alliances with sovereigns to join forces to carry out crusades.

The officers of the inquisition were three inquisitors (or judges), a fiscal proctor, two secretaries, a magistrate, a messenger, a receiver, a jailer, an agent of confiscated possessions, several assessors, counselors, executioners, physicians, surgeons (to treat the victim so more torture could be inflicted during a state of consciousness), door-keepers, families, and visitors, who were sworn to secrecy. The principle accusation against those brought before the inquisition was heresy, which encompassed all that was written, or spoken, against any of the articles of the creed, or traditions of the Roman Catholic Church. The inquisition also took authority over those accused of reading the Bible in the common language, and those accused of being magicians or witches.

A defense before the inquisition had little value since suspicion alone was sufficient for condemnation, and the wealthier the accused, the more probable his condemnation. The accused was never allowed to see the face of his accusers or the witnesses against him. Torture and threats were used to encourage the accused to condemn himself and thus corroborate the evidence. High birth, distinguished rank, great dignity and eminent employment were no protection from the severity of the inquisition, and its lowest officers could make the highest characters tremble.

The immense wealth of the Catholic Church has remained in stark contrast to the poverty of the masses under its influence. The Protestant reformation which began under the leadership of Martin Luther combined with the collapse of the Eastern Roman Empire has significantly undermined the power of the papacy. The papal hierarchy today still claims all the powers of its predecessors.

Today, Christianity is embraced by more humans than any other religion. In the United States, recent polls show that over eighty percent of Americans consider themselves to be Christians. Sadly, however, the professions of Christianity are mostly lip service only. Religious freedom still exists within the United States, but is now being seriously threatened because of the apathy of collective Christianity. Homosexuality, abortion, greed and vanity are being accepted as permissible behavior on the part of professing Christians.

By and large, American Christians are doing very little to address the creeping influence of Satan's disciples within our churches, schools, courts, and popular media. This is especially tragic because Christians have the necessary votes and purchasing power to correct every social evil within American society. Yet, a small, loudmouthed, obnoxious minority are trampling upon the moral values that have made America the greatest nation on Earth. In the seventh century before Christ, Isaiah foresaw the apostasy of today's Christians:

"His watchmen are blind: they are all ignorant, they are all dumb dogs, they cannot bark; sleeping, lying down, loving to slumber. Yea, they are greedy dogs which can never have enough, and they are shepherds that cannot understand: they all look to their own way, every one for his gain, from his quarter. Come ye, say they, I will fetch wine, and we will fill ourselves with strong drink; and tomorrow shall be as this day, and much more abundant." (Isaiah, chapter 56. verses 10-12; 698 B.C.)

Jesus also, in 96 A.D., spoke to the apostle, John, concerning the apostasy of the church just prior to the end of the dispensation of grace and mercy: "I know thy works, that thou art neither cold nor hot: I would thou wert cold or hot. So then because thou art lukewarm, and neither cold nor hot, I will spew thee out of My mouth. Because thou sayest, I am rich, and increased with goods, and have need of nothing; and knowest not that thou art wretched, and miserable, and poor, and blind, and naked. I counsel thee to buy of Me gold tried in the fire, that thou mayest be rich; and white raiment, that thou mayest be clothed, and that the shame of thy nakedness do not appear; and anoint thine eyes with eye salve, that thou mayest see. As many as I love, I rebuke and chasten: be zealous therefore, and repent." (Revelation, chapter 3, verses 15-19; Patmos vision; 96 A.D.)

Chapter five

Does a record exist of "the beginning?" Beginning of what? Of the primordial elements? Of the universe? Of Planet Earth? Of original life forms? Of bacteria? Of mammals? Of humans? To answer such a question, we must identify the subject matter relating to the question. In order to be coherent it might help to answer in accord with chronological time as measured by humans.

Is there a record of the beginning or origin of the primordial elements? No. There is not. There is not even a theory that addresses the origin of the most abundant, the lightest, and simplest in molecular structure among the primordial elements. 21st century scientific literature reports that physicists believe the universe consists of roughly 73% hydrogen, 25% helium and that only around 2% of the universe consists of all the remaining primordial elements totaling 82 (there are 84 elements which do not involve any laboratory synthesis and are therefore referred to as "primordial").

Hydrogen subjected to intense heat and pressure fuses into helium and such atomic fusion occurring within stars provides Earth with sunlight and sunlight is reflected from other masses within our solar system such as our moon. [24] [25]

Physicists today speculate that the 2% of the

universe composed of primordial elements other than hydrogen and helium originates as the by-product of the fusion of hydrogen into helium within all the galaxies. Whether or not such speculation is factual the question remains as to the origin of hydrogen. The only rational and logical explanation is that hydrogen was created by a spiritual power existing outside of that which was created.

This "supreme being" and all powerful creator is also the only answer that makes sense to the other questions of "beginning or origin" of all matter, energy and motion including the life force within all living organisms. Because we cannot otherwise explain the origin of hydrogen (from which all the other elements are believed to derive) we must accept the same explanation we accept for hydrogen for all matter, energy and motion associated with the molecular structure of the elements and the bonding of the atoms of the elements into the physical bodily composition of all life forms within the universe.

Once we truly accept the premise that a supreme being and all powerful creator exists, it is a minor decision to accept the premise that the same supreme being created the life force existing within all living organisms.

When was the universe created? Many scientists believe that the universe including our solar system has existed for billions of Earth years. The validity of this belief is of little importance other than the issue of a supreme being versus random chance evolution without design, order or purpose. However, bearing heavily on this dispute is the question of when humans first appeared on Earth. Regardless of how long Planet Earth has existed within the universe, humans first appeared on the planet roughly six thousand years ago. This hard conclusion is supported by every field of 21st century science, logic and mathematical probabilities as well as common sense expounded upon in previous chapters.

Does a realistic, credible, and detailed account of human history upon Planet Earth exist which has been investigated for veracity and stood the test of time in spite of continuous hostile scrutiny by many thousands of individuals with very impressive credentials including atheistic self worshipers? Yes, Indeed. Such a written history does exist and is the most widely printed, circulated and read document ever produced by mankind.

What is this written history? It is the Holy Bible and the Scriptures therein were penned down by forty different authors over a period spanning sixteen centuries and yet the Scriptures read in total accord with each other with zero contradictions between the forty different authors. Such continuity and total agreement of thought, message and prophecy among forty writers over sixteen hundred years has confounded, awed and frustrated Biblical critics and all other seeking to discredit the Holy Scriptures. Moreover, the Bible contains hundreds of detailed prophecies spanning the entire recorded history of humanity that have been fulfilled precisely as written down over periods of several years to several centuries prior to fulfillment.

How do we know that Julius Caesar, or Alexander the Great, or Pharaoh Ramses, or Moses, or Nero, or Jesus Christ, or George Washington, or anyone who lived centuries ago actually lived and acted as history records rather than such personages simply being the figment of some historian's imagination? Well, in addition to existing remains of associated buildings, monuments, and archaeological artifacts, the primary evidence supporting historical records is the written testimony of eye witnesses that actually lived during the time period in question and whose written testimony has survived in the original written form or in authenticated copies of the original. This describes precisely how the Holy Scriptures were compiled in the original Hebrew and Greek and then translated into virtually every language spoken and read today.

Recorded history verified by numerous eye witness testimonies written down and preserved to the present time prove that Jesus Christ lived, ministered to the Jewish nation, was crucified by the Romans and then was buried in another man's virgin tomb during the first century A.D.

The recorded eye witness testimonies state that Jesus Christ healed lepers, restored withered limbs, gave sight to those born blind, healed all manner of sickness and disease, raised the dead, walked on water, stilled the wind and waves by his command, and fed with a handful of bread and fish thousands of people gathered to hear him. While being crucified he forgave those killing him and rose from the dead three days after his execution.

Following his resurrection, for forty days he walked, talked, ate with and instructed his twelve apostles concerning their eternal relationship with him and God, his father. He explained Biblical prophecies to them and gave them total authority to continue his ministry to humanity. He was the living word of God incarnate and revealed to humanity the divine nature of God and God's plan for redeeming mankind back to himself. During the forty days he ministered to his apostles, Jesus Christ in his resurrected body was seen in person by more than five hundred individuals at the same point in time. He told his apostles that seeing him they had in fact seen God because he and God were one and the same. He taught them that God is triune in H is being and that the Godhead consists of God, the Father, God, the Son (Himself, Jesus Christ) and God, the Holy Ghost.

While walking along a roadway to a village with two of his followers Jesus reviewed with them the many Biblical prophecies concerning himself which were written centuries before his virgin birth. The odds of all such prophecies coming true in minute detail by sheer happenstance have been calculated by several expert mathematicians to be less than one chance in ten to the

100th power whereas ten to the 80th power would account for all the electrons in the known universe. All of the following prophecies concerning Jesus Christ were written down at least 400 centuries before his birth:

"Therefore the Lord Himself shall give you a sign; Behold, a virgin shall conceive and bear a son, and shall call His name Immanuel." (Isaiah 7:14 KJV); Isaiah lived and prophesied in the early part of the 700th century before Jesus Christ was born.

"For unto us a Child is born, unto us a Son is given: and the government shall be upon His shoulder: and His name shall be called Wonderful, Counselor, The Mighty God, The Everlasting Father, The Prince of Peace." (Isaiah 9:6-7)

"Behold, My servant shall deal prudently, He shall be exalted and extolled, and be very high. As many were astonished at Thee; His visage was so marred more than any man, and His form more than the sons of men." (Isaiah 50:13-14)

"I gave My back to the smiters, and My cheeks to them that plucked off the hair: I hid not my face from shame and spitting." (Isaiah 50:6)

"Who hath believed our report? And to whom is the arm of the Lord revealed? For He shall grow up before Him as a tender plant, and as a root out of dry ground: He hath no form nor comeliness; and when we see Him, there is no beauty that we should desire Him. He is despised and rejected of men; a man of sorrows, and acquainted with grief: and we hid as it were our faces from Him; He was despised, and we esteemed Him not. Surely He hath borne our griefs, and carried our sorrows: yet we did esteem Him stricken, smitten of God, and afflicted. But He was wounded for our transgressions, He was bruised for our iniquities: the chastisement of our peace was upon Him; and with His stripes we are healed. All we like sheep have gone astray; we have turned every one to his own way; and the Lord has laid upon Him the iniquity of us all. He was oppressed, and He was afflicted, yet He opened not His mouth: He is brought as a lamb to the slaughter, and a sheep before her shearers is dumb, so He openeth not His mouth. He was taken from prison and from judgment: and who shall declare His generation? For He was cut off out of the land of the living: for the transgression of my people was He stricken. And He made His grave with the wicked, and with the rich in His death; because He had done no violence, neither was there any deceit in His mouth. Yet it pleased the Lord to bruise Him; He hath put him to grief: when Thou shall shalt make His soul an offering for sin, He shall see His seed, He shall prolong His days, and the pleasure of the Lord shall prosper in His hand. He shall see of the travail of His soul, and shall be satisfied: by His knowledge shall My righteous servant justify many; for He shall bear their iniquities. Therefore will I divide Him a portion with the great, and He shall divide the spoil with the strong: because He hath poured out His soul unto death: and He was numbered with the transgressors; and He bare the sin of many, and made intercession for the transgressors." (Isaiah 53:1-12)

In Isaiah, Chapter 61:1-3 we are given a preview of the earthly ministry of Jesus as He sets His face as flint toward His cross:

"The Spirit of the Lord God is upon Me; because the Lord hath anointed Me to preach good tidings to the meek; He hath sent Me to bind up the brokenhearted, to proclaim liberty to the captives, and the opening of the prison to them that are bound; to proclaim the acceptable year of the Lord, and the day of vengeance of our God; to comfort all that mourn; to appoint to them that mourn in Zion, to give unto them beauty for ashes, the oil of joy for mourning, the garment of praise for the spirit of heaviness; that they might be called trees of righteousness, the planting of the Lord, that He might be glorified."

The prophet Zechariah predicted the precise price of the betrayal of Jesus by Judas: "And I said unto them, if ye think good, give me my price; and if not, forbear. So they weighed for My price thirty pieces of silver. And the Lord said unto me, Cast it unto the potter: a goodly price that I was prised at of them. And I took the thirty pieces of silver, and cast them to the potter in the house of the Lord." (Zechariah, 11:12-13; 487 B.C.); 520 years later, the remorse of Judas is recorded:

"Then Judas, which had betrayed Him, when he saw that He was condemned, repented himself, and brought again the thirty pieces of silver to the chief priests and elders, saying, I have sinned in that I have betrayed innocent blood. And they said, What is that to us? See thou to that. And he cast down the pieces of silver in the temple, and departed, and went and hanged himself. And the chief priests took the silver pieces, and said, it is not lawful for to put them into the treasury, because it is the price of blood. And they took counsel, and bought with them the potter's field, to bury strangers in." (Matthew, Chapter 12:3-7. 33 A.D.)

The Hebrew prophet Micah foretold the precise hamlet where Jesus would be born:

"But thou, Bethlehem Ephratah, though thou be little among the thousands of Judah, yet out of thee shall He come forth unto Me that is to be ruler in Israel; whose goings forth have been from old, from everlasting." (Micah, Chapter 5:2, 710 B.C.)

More than 1,000 years before the birth of Jesus, the Spirit of God Almighty stirred King David's soul and he penned down in Psalms 22:

"My God, My God, why hast thou forsaken Me? Why art Thou so far from helping Me, and from the words of My roaring? ....But I am a worm, and no man; a reproach of men, and despised of the people. All that see Me laugh Me to scorn: they shoot out the lip, they shake their head, saying, He trusted on the Lord that He would deliver Him: let Him deliver Him, seeing He delighted in Him.........They gaped upon Me with their mouths, as a ravening and a roaring lion. I am poured out like water, and all My bones are out of joint: My heart is like wax; it is melted in the midst of My bowels. My strength is dried up like a potsherd; and My tongue cleaveth to My jaws; and Thou hadst brought Me unto the dust of death. For dogs have compassed Me: the assembly of the wicked have enclosed Me: they pierced My hands and My feet. I may tell all My bones: they look and stare upon Me. They part My garments among them, and cast lots upon My vesture." (Portions of Psalms 22, ten centuries B.C.)

In Psalms 69, David again writes down what God lays upon his heart concerning the suffering of Jesus as despised and rejected:

"They that hate Me without a cause are more than the hairs of Mine head: they that would destroy Me, being Mine enemies wrongfully, are mighty; Then I restored that which I took not away......Reproach hath broken My heart; and I am full of heaviness: and I looked for some to take pity, but there were none; and for comforters, but I found none. They gave Me also gall for My meat; and in My thirst they gave Me vinegar to drink." These verses in Psalms 69 paint an exact portrait of Jesus upon His cross reuniting humanity with God while being ridiculed, mocked, jeered at and given vinegar mixed with gall to drink.

Although the total body of inspired Scriptures within the Holy Bible contains numerous specific and detailed prophecies concerning the birth, life, ministry, sacrificial death, resurrection and return of Jesus to God, the Father, which all came to pass precisely as spoken and written, the writings of Isaiah concerning Jesus are the most incredible and comprehensive within the Old Testament and have been carefully preserved down through the centuries as demonstrated by the discovery of the Dead Sea Scrolls which contain a complete scroll of Isaiah which exactly parallels the text within the King James version of the Holy Bible.

In addition to the many Biblical prophecies concerning Jesus Christ, there are hundreds of companion prophecies pertaining to world events that were fulfilled precisely as prophesied long before fulfillment. A fair sampling of such prophecies would be:

Around 975 B.C., Jereboam, king of Northern Israel (ten of the twelve tribes), set up golden calves in the cities of Dan and Beth-el. Jereboam arrogantly proclaimed: "......behold thy gods, O Israel, which brought thee up out of the land of Egypt." (I Kings, chapter 12, verse 28) This brazen act of idolatry on the part of Jereboam was followed by a visit from a prophet during the same time window (around 975 B.C.):

"And, behold, there came a man of God out of Judah (Southern kingdom of Israel – two tribes) by the word of the Lord unto Beth-el: and Jereboam stood by the altar to burn incense. And he cried against the altar in the word of the Lord, and said, O altar, altar, thus saith the Lord; Behold, a child shall be born unto the house of David, Josiah by name; and upon thee shall he offer the priests of the high places that burn incense upon thee, and men's bones shall be burnt upon thee." (I Kings, chapter 12, verses 1-2)   Note that the prophet actually names the king, Josiah, who approximately 350 years later will offer upon the altar the priests who are then practicing idolatry. A Hebrew prophet named Ahijah also tells Jereboam:

"Thus saith the Lord God of Israel, Forasmuch as I exalted thee from among the people, and made thee prince over My people Israel, and rent the kingdom away from the house of David, and gave it thee: and yet thou hast not been as My servant David who kept My commandments, and who followed Me with all his heart, to do that only which was right in Mine eyes; But hast done evil above all that were before thee: for thou hast gone and made unto thee other gods, and molten images, to provoke Me to anger, and hast cast Me behind thy back: Therefore, I will bring evil upon the house of Jereboam, and will cut off from Jereboam him that pisseth against the wall, and him that is shut up and left in Israel, and will take away the remnant of the house of Jereboam, as a man taketh away dung, till it be all gone. Him that dieth of Jereboam in the city shall the dogs eat; and him that dieth in the field shall the fowls of the air eat: for the Lord hath spoken it."   (I Kings, chapter 14, verses 7-11, prophecy spoken around 956 B.C.)

Jereboam died suddenly within a few years after this prophecy by Ahijah. The latter prophecy came to pass in 624 B.C.:

"And the high places that were before Jerusalem, which were on the right hand of the mount of corruption, which Solomon the king of Israel had builded for Ashtoreth the abomination of the Zidonians, and for Chemosh the abomination of the Moabites, and for Milcom the abomination of the children of Ammon, did the king defile. And he brake in pieces the images, and cut down the groves, and filled their places with the bones of men. Moreover the altar that was at Beth-el, and the high place which Jereboam the son of Nebat, who made Israel to sin, had made, both that altar and the high place he brake down, and burned the high place, and stamped it small to powder, and burned the grove.

And as Josiah turned himself, he spied the sepulchers that were there in the mount, and sent, and took the bones out of the sepulchers, and burned them upon the altar, and polluted it, according to the word of the Lord which the man of God proclaimed, who proclaimed these words. ....And he slew all the priests of the high places that were there upon the altars, and burned men's bones upon them, and returned to Jerusalem." (II Kings, chapter 23, verses 13-20)

Moses prophesied to Israel that, if they forsook the commandments and statutes of God, their enemies would besiege them in all their cities and they would eat their own children:

"And thou shalt eat the fruit of thine own body, the flesh of thy sons and of thy daughters, which the Lord thy God hath given thee, in the siege, and in the straitness, wherewith thine enemies shall distress thee....." (Deuteronomy, chapter 28, verse 53, prophecy spoken 1451 B.C.) This prophecy was precisely ful- filled in 892 B.C. during the Syrian siege of Samaria (capitol of Israel's northern kingdom after the civil rebellion under Solomon's son, Rehoboam):

"And it came to pass after this, that Ben-hadad king of Syria gathered all his host, and went up, and besieged Samaria. And there was a great famine in Samaria: and, behold, they besieged it, until an ass's head was sold for four score pieces of silver, and the fourth part of a cab of dove's dung for five pieces of silver. And as the king of Israel was passing by upon the wall, there cried a woman unto him, saying, Help, my lord, O king. And he said, If the Lord do not help thee, whence shall I help thee? out of the barn floor, or out of the wine press? And the king said unto her, What aileth thee? And she answered, This woman said unto me, Give thy son, that we may eat him today, and we will eat my son tomorrow. So we boiled my son, and did eat him: and I said unto her on the next day, Give thy son that we may eat him: and she hath hid her son. And it came to pass, when the king heard the words of the woman, that he rent his clothes; and he passed by upon the wall, and the people looked, and, behold, he had sackcloth within upon his flesh." (II Kings, chapter 6, verses 24-30, siege of Samaria, 892 B.C.)

In 899 B.C., Ahab, the king of Israel, coveted his

neighbor's vineyard which grew nearby the palace. Jezebel, Ahab's wife, arranged to have the neighbor murdered so Ahab could possess the vineyard. Ahab was taking possession when the prophet, Elijah, was sent to give him a message from God:

"And the word of the Lord came to Elijah the Tishbite, saying, Arise, go down to meet Ahab king of Israel, which is in Samaria: behold he is in the vineyard of Naboth, whither he has gone down to possess it. And thou shall speak unto him, saying, Hast thou killed, and also taken possession? And thou shalt speak unto him, saying, Thus saith the Lord, in the place where dogs licked the blood of Naboth shall the dogs lick thy blood, even thine......And of Jezebel also spake the Lord, saying, The dogs shall eat Jezebel by the wall of Jezreel." (I Kings, chapter 21, verses 17-19; verse 23, prophecy 899 B.C.)   Three years later, the prophecy concerning Ahab was fulfilled; and twelve years after Ahab's death, the prophecy pertaining to Jezebel came to pass:

"And a certain man drew a bow at a venture, and smote the king of Israel between the joints of the harness: wherefore he said unto the driver of his chariot, Turn thine hand, and carry me out of the host; for I am wounded. And the battle increased that day: and the king was stayed up in his chariot against the Syrians, and died at even: and the blood ran out of the wound into the midst of the chariot. And there went a proclamation throughout the host about the going down of the sun, saying, Every man to his own city, and every man to his own country. So the king died, and was brought to Samaria; and they buried the king in Samaria. And one washed the chariot in the pool of Samaria; and the dogs licked up his blood; and they washed his armour; according unto the word of the Lord which he spake." (I Kings, chapter 22, verses 34-38, Syrian battle 896 B. C.)

"And when Jehu was come to Jezreel, Jezebel heard of it; and she painted her face, and tired her head, and looked out at a window. And as Jehu entered in at the gate, she said, Had Zimri peace, who slew his master? And he lifted up his face to the window, and said, Who is on my side? Who? And there looked out to him two or three eunuchs. And he said, Throw her down. So they threw her down; and some of her blood was sprinkled on the wall, and on the horses: and he trode her under foot. And when he was come in, he did eat and drink, and said, Go, see now this cursed woman, and bury her: for she is a king's daughter. And they went to bury her: but they found no more of her than the skull, and the feet, and the palms of her hands. Wherefore they came again and told him. And he said, This is the word of the Lord, which he spake by his servant Elijah the Tishbite, saying, In the portion of Jezreel shall dogs eat the flesh of Jezebel:....." (II Kings, chapter 9, verses 30-36, Jehu proclaimed king, 884 B.C.)

In 713 B.C., the prophet Isaiah predicted the

Medes would destroy Babylon: "Behold, I will stir up the Medes against them, which shall not regard silver; and as for gold, they shall not delight in it. Their bows also shall dash the young men to pieces; and they shall have no pity on the fruit of the womb: their eye shall not spare children. And Babylon, the glory of kingdoms, the beauty of the Chaldees' excellency, shall be as when God overthrew Sodom and Gomorrah." (Isaiah, chapter 13, verses 17-19)

This prophecy was fulfilled one hundred and seventy-four years later. Belshazzar, son of Nebuchadnezzar, was throwing a party for a thousand of his lords. In an arrogant display of contempt for the God of Israel, Belshazzar had the golden and silver vessels brought forth which had been taken by his father from the temple in Jerusalem. He and his lords, and his wives, and his concubines drank wine from the sacred vessels and praised their idols.

The fingers of a man's hand appeared and wrote on the wall next to the candlestick: "MENE, MENE, TEKEL, UPHARSIN." None of the Chaldeans could interpret the writing, and the king was petrified with fear. Among the princes brought to Babylon from Judah was Daniel, who was known for his wisdom. Daniel was summoned and he interpreted the writing:

"And this is the writing that was written, MENE, MENE, TEKEL, UPHARSIN. This is the interpretation of the thing: MENE; God hath numbered thy kingdom and finished it. TEKEL; Thou art weighed in the

143

balances, and art found wanting. PERES (upharsin); Thy kingdom is divided and given to the Medes and Persians. ....In that night was Belshazzar the king of the Chaldeans slain. And Darius the Median took the kingdom, being about three score and two years old." (Daniel, chapter 5, verses 25-28; 30-31, event 538 B.C.)

More than a century before Cyrus, king of Persia was born, the prophet Isaiah called him by name and said Cyrus would open the two leaved gates of Babylon and allow a remnant of Judah to return to Jerusalem:

"That saith of Cyrus, He is My shepherd, and shall perform all My pleasure: even saying to Jerusalem, Thou shalt be built; and to the temple, Thy foundation shall be laid. Thus saith the Lord to his anointed, to Cyrus, whose right hand I have holden, to subdue nations before him; and I will loose the loins of kings, to open before him the two leaved gates; and the gates shall not be shut." (Isaiah, chapter 44, verse 28; chapter 45, verse 1)

When this prophecy was spoken by Isaiah in 712 B.C., the Medes and Persians were not a threat to Babylon. The southern kingdom of Israel (Judah) had not been taken into captivity yet by the king of Babylon. Cryus, king of Persia, the subject of the prophecy was not yet born. The prophecy was fulfilled one hundred and seventy-six years later:

"Thus saith Cyrus king of Persia, The Lord God of heaven hath given me all the kingdoms of the earth; and He hath charged me to build Him an house at

Jerusalem, which is in Judah. Who is there among you of all His people? his God be with him, and let him go up to Jerusalem, which is in Judah, and build the house of the Lord God of Israel (He is the God), which is in Jerusalem." (Ezra, chapter 1, verses 2-3; proclamation 536 B.C.)

Jeremiah, the prophet, in 607 B.C., foretold the destruction of Jerusalem by the king of Babylon in 588 B.C., and the deportation of Judah into Babylon. Jeremiah also foretold the exact duration of the Babylonian captivity (seventy years):

"Therefore thus saith the Lord of hosts: Because ye have not heard My words, Behold, I will send and take all the families of the north, saith the Lord, and Nebuchadrezzar the king of Babylon, My servant, and will bring them against this land, and against the inhabitants thereof, and against all these nations round about, and will utterly destroy them, and make them an astonishment, and a hissing, and perpetual desola- tions........And this whole land shall be a desolation, and an astonishment; and these nations shall serve the king of Babylon seventy years. And it shall come to pass, when seventy years are accomplished, that I will punish the king of Babylon, and that nation, saith the Lord, for their iniquity, and the land of the Chaldeans, and will make it perpetual desolations." (Jeremiah, chapter 25, verses 8-9; 11-12; 607 B.C.)

This prophecy, with respect to Judah, was fulfilled as predicted in 588 B.C. Seventy years later, the remnant of Judah was allowed to return to Jerusalem by the Persians who overthrew the Babylonians:

"And in the fifth month, on the seventh day of the month, which is the nineteenth year of king Nebuchadnezzar, king of Babylon, came Nebuzaradan, captain of the guard, a servant of the king of Babylon, unto Jerusalem: And he burnt the house of the Lord, and the king's house, and all the houses of Jerusalem, and every great man's house burnt he with fire. And all the army of the Chaldees, that were with the captain of the guard, brake down the walls of Jerusalem round about. Now the rest of the people that were left in the city, and the fugitives that fell away to the king of Babylon, with the remnant of the multitude, did Nebuzaradan the captain of the guard carry away." (II Kings, chapter 25, verses 8-11; event 588 B.C.)

Under King Cyrus of Persia, an advance pilgrimage was allowed for Jews to return to Jerusalem and begin to rebuild the city walls and lay the foundation for the temple. In 518 B.C., the Persian king, Artaxerxes, allowed all Jews to return to Jerusalem:

"Artaxerxes, king of kings, unto Ezra the priest, a scribe of the law of the God of heaven, perfect peace, and at such a time, I make a decree, that all they of the people of Israel, and of His priests and Levites, in my realm, which are minded of their own free will to go up to Jerusalem, go with thee. (Ezra, chapter 7 verses 12-13, event 518 B.C.)

The prophet, Daniel, during the reign of

Belshazzar, king of Babylon, foretold the overthrow of the Persian empire by Alexander the Great. At the time of the prophecy, the Babylonian empire had not yet fallen to the Persians; and Alexander was yet to be born:

"In the third year of the reign of king Belshazzar a vision appeared unto me, even unto me Daniel, after that which appeared unto me at the first. And I saw in a vision; and it came to pass, when I saw, that I was at Shushan in the palace, which is in the province of Elam; and I saw in a vision, and I was by the river of Ulai. Then I lifted up mine eyes, and saw, and, behold, there stood before the river a ram which had two horns; and the two horns were high; but one was higher than the other, and the higher came up last. I saw the ram pushing westward, and northward, and southward; so that no beasts might stand before him, neither was there any that could deliver out of his hand; but he did according to his will and became great.

And as I was considering, behold, an he goat came from the west on the face of the whole earth, and touched not the ground: and the goat had a notable horn between his eyes. And he came to the ram that had two horns, which I had seen standing before the river, and ran into him in the fury of his power. And I saw him come close unto the ram, and he was moved with choler against him, and smote the ram, and brake his two horns; and there was no power in the ram to stand before him, but he cast him down to the ground, and stomped upon him: and there was none that could deliver the ram out of his hand. Therefore the he goat waxed very great: and when he was strong, the great horn was broken; and for it came up four notable ones toward the four winds of heaven ......And it came to pass, when I, even I Daniel, had seen the vision, and sought for the meaning, then, behold, there stood before me as the appearance of a man.

And I heard a man's voice between the banks of Ulai, which called, and said, Gabriel, make this man to understand the vision. So he came near where I stood: and when he came, I was afraid, and fell upon my face: but he said unto me, Understand O son of man: for at the time of the end shall be the vision. Now as he was speaking with me, I was in a deep sleep on my face toward the ground: but he touched me, and set me upright. And he said, Behold, I will make thee know what shall be in the last end of the indignation: for at the time appointed the end shall be. The ram which thou sawest having two horns are the kings of Media and Persia. And the rough he goat is the king of Grecia: and the great horn that is between his eyes is the first king. Now that being broken, whereas four stood up for it, four kingdoms shall stand up out of the nation, but not in his power." (Daniel,chapter 8, verses 1-8; 15-22; vision 553 B.C.)

We know from documented history that Alexander the Great conquered Persia in 331 B.C., and that he died prematurely whereupon his kingdom was divided between four of his generals.

Before the Babylonians destroyed Jerusalem, Jeremiah, the prophet, pronounced God's judgment upon the city of Babylon: "Because of the wrath of the Lord, it shall not be inhabited, but it shall be wholly desolate...... ......Therefore the wild beasts of the desert with the wild beasts of the islands shall dwell there, and the owls shall dwell therein: and it shall be no more inhabited forever; neither shall it be dwelt in from generation to generation." (Jeremiah, chapter 50, verses 13, 39; 600 B.C.)

At the time Jeremiah wrote this prophecy, Babylon was the most powerful and most impregnable city in the world, and the Babylonian empire was at the very zenith of its power. The site where the city of Babylon once sprawled is a trackless wasteland where the owl, scorpion, viper and the jackal prowl. The city was destroyed over two thousand years ago and the site has never been rebuilt although it lies within the fertile crescent. For about sixty days within each year, the ruins of Babylon are flooded by the annual overflowing of the Euphrates. The rest of the year, the ruins are parched and dry. Concerning the great city of Tyre, once the trading center of the ancient world, the prophet Ezekiel wrote in 590 B.C.:

"And they shall destroy the walls of Tyrus, and break down her towers: I will also scrape her dust from her, and make her like the top of a rock. It shall be a place for the spreading of nets in the midst of the sea:

for I have spoken it, saith the Lord God: and it shall become a spoil to the nations." (Ezekiel, chapter 26, verses 4-5; prophecy 590 B.C.)

Two hundred and fifty years after the city of Tyre was initially destroyed by the Babylonians, the ruins of the city remained whereas the prophecy stated the city site would be like the top of a rock and fishing nets would be spread thereon. Then, came Alexander the great with his army and used the ruins of Tyre to build a causeway one half mile into the Mediterranean Sea in order to attack the island of new Tyre. The ruins of the former city were scraped clean, like the top of a rock, and later, fishermen spread their nets over the ruins of the once mighty city.

For roughly nineteen centuries the Jews were dispersed among the nations following the destruction of Jerusalem by the Romans in 70 A.D. In 1948 A.D., the Jews began returning to the land of Israel as foreseen by Ezekiel, the prophet: "And I will bring them out from the people, and gather them from the countries, and will bring them to their own land, and feed them upon the mountains of Israel by the rivers, and in all the inhabited places of the country." (Ezekiel, chapter 34, verse 13, prophecy 587 B.C.)

When Israel was established again in 1948 A.D. as a sovereign nation, every Biblical prophecy from the beginning of human existence upon Earth to the "rapture of all believers having accepted Jesus Christ as their redeemer was fulfilled in exquisite detail. Critics and skeptics will say that such fulfillment came about by sheer random chance just like the protein building blocks for the physical makeup of a living cell evolved by random chance in spite of the odds being one chance in ten to the 40,000th power. It is a waste of breath trying to logically reason with a self-worshiper. Jesus referred to such wasted effort as "casting pearls before swine." The elite religious hypocrites and self-worshipers in 31 A.D. watched Jesus heal lepers, give sight to the blind, feed thousands with a handful of bread and fish, restore withered limbs, and raise the dead. How did the human swine respond to the miracles performed by Jesus? "Then the Pharisees went out, and held a council against him, how they might destroy him." (Matthew 12:14 KJV)

Chapter six

How long does the Bible state that Planet Earth existed within the universe before humans first appeared on the planet? The short answer is that the Bible does not address this question.

When was the beginning and when will the end be? The Bible does not contain a date for either the beginning or the end, and it gives more information concerning the end than it does about the beginning. The Bible does state: "In the beginning God created the heaven and the earth." (Genesis, chapter 1, verse 1; writer, Moses, 15th century B.C.). It is important to note that in this statement, it is proclaimed that "in the beginning" God created Earth and its atmosphere (the heaven containing the clouds of water vapor). But, in the very next verse, the atmosphere is missing: "And the earth was without form, and void; and darkness was upon the face of the deep. And the Spirit of God moved upon the face of the waters" (Genesis, chapter 1, verse 2).

How much time elapsed between the creation of Earth stated in verse 1 and the condition of Earth pictured in verse 2? It could have been a very long period of time, or a brief period. Within the vastness of the universe, time as measured by humans doesn't appear to be a significant consideration.

Today's scientists tell us that it takes billions of years for the light coming from distant stars to reach Earth. Time is only important to those who know their life is brief. To an eternal being, the passing of time doesn't count for much. It is clear from the two statements that Earth suffered a devastating catastrophe and languished in a chaotic state for an undisclosed period of time. There are Scriptures which indicate that Earth had undergone a cataclysmic change as the result of divine judgment:

"I beheld the earth, and, lo, it was without form, and void: and the heavens, and they had no light." (Jeremiah, chapter 4, verse 23, vision 612 B.C.)

"Behold, the Lord maketh the earth empty, and maketh it waste, and turneth it upside down, and scattereth abroad the inhabitants thereof." (Isaiah, chapter 24, verse 1, vision 715 B.C.)

"For thus saith the Lord that created the heavens; God himself that formed the earth and made it; he hath established it, he created it not in vain, he formed it to be inhabited: I am the Lord; and there is none else." (Isaiah, chapter 45, verse 18, 712 B.C.)

"How art thou fallen from heaven, O Lucifer, son of the morning!.....For thou hadst said in thine heart, I will ascend into heaven, I will exalt my throne above the stars of God: I will sit also upon the mount of the congregation, in the sides of the north; I will ascend above the heights of the clouds; I will be like the Most High. (Isaiah, chapter 14, verses 12 -14, vision 712

B.C.)

"........Thus saith the Lord God; Thou sealest up the sum, full of wisdom, and perfect in beauty. Thou hadst been in Eden the garden of God; every precious stone was thy covering, the sardius, topaz, and diamond, the beryl, the onyx, and the jasper, the sapphire, the emerald, and the carbuncle, and gold: the workmanship of thy tabrets and of thy pipes was prepared in thee in the day that thou wast created. Thou art the anointed cherub that covereth; and I have set thee so; thou wast upon the holy mountain of God; thou hast walked up and down in the midst of the stones of fire. Thou wast perfect in thy ways from the day that thou wast created, till iniquity was found in thee." (Ezekiel, chapter 28, verses 12-15, vision 588 B.C.)

"And there was war in heaven: Michael and his angels fought against the dragon; and the dragon fought and his angels, and prevailed not; neither was their place found any more in heaven. And the great dragon was cast out, that old serpent called the Devil, and Satan, which deceiveth the whole world: he was cast out into the earth, and his angels were cast out with him." (Revelation, chapter 12, verses 7-9, Patmos vision A.D. 96)

The composite of these passages implicates Earth in the "fall of Lucifer," (also called "Satan", "Devil", and "Dragon"). There was an absence of energy lighting the planet, and there was no division of liquids and gases on Earth's surface. Whatever living creatures inhabited Earth at that time perished as well as plant life. However, plant seed remained dormant within Earth. The physical shape of Earth reflected chaos such that it appeared "without form and void," and completely covered with water.

Genesis, chapter 1, verse 2 begins the account as to how God brought order out of chaos, created humans and gave them dominion over the planet. The intense, eternal hatred Lucifer (Satan, Devil, Dragon) exhibits toward mankind is also understandable in the light of these composite Scriptures. As the first step in bringing order out of chaos, Genesis, chapter 1, verse 3 records:

"And God said, Let there be light: and there was light" (made to appear, made visible; the sun and moon were created "in the beginning" but some mass had invaded the solar system and blocked out the light radiating from the sun and reflecting from the moon).

A close examination of the actual recorded text contained within Genesis, chapters 1 and 2 reveals that the past tense (in the beginning) and the time period spanning the end of chaos and restoration of order upon Earth (preparing Earth for dominion by humans) are intertwined in order to maintain the continuity of the narrative in summary form.

The Hebrew word for "made" translates into English as both "made" and "had made." Keeping that fact in mind, the narrative in Genesis, chapters 1 and 2 makes perfect sense in its summary form. Chapter 1 presents a complete summary of "in the beginning" and "bringing order out of chaos." Chapter 2 adds specific details concerning the creation of humans within Earth prepared for dominion by mankind. Genesis, chapter 2, verses 7-9 explicitly state that mankind was created:

"And the Lord God formed man of the dust of the ground, and breathed into his nostrils the breath of life; and man became a living soul. And the Lord God planted a garden eastward in Eden; and there he put the man whom he had formed. And out of the ground made the Lord God to grow every tree that is pleasant to the sight, and good for food; the tree of life also in the midst of the garden, and the tree of knowledge of good and evil."

Although the Scriptures do not reveal the elapsed time spanning "in the beginning," nor how long Earth languished in a state of chaos, we can trace how long humans have inhabited the planet by the sum of the life spans of Adam and his descendants prior to the "days of Noah" (recorded in Genesis, chapter 5), plus the passing of time since Noah's death (grand total equal to roughly sixty centuries). There is no conflict between the veri-fiable scientific body of knowledge existing today and the Biblical account of how humans came into being. The Scriptures do, however, answer many questions for which scientists have no other explanation whatsoever.

The fossilized remains of ancient, extinct life forms have been found, but there are absolutely no fossilized remains of humans more than sixty centuries old. When fossilized remains of life forms, other than humans, do appear in the fossil record, they are either extremely ancient or essentially the same as non-human life forms that inhabit Earth today, or have become extinct; and they all appear in the same time period.

It is patently obvious chemically, physically, biologically, mathematically, atomically, and just using common sense that the universe and all matter therein could only have been designed and then created by God (an awesome creative power existing outside time and space). The perfect order, balance, orbital precision, and gravitational interaction within our solar system could not possibly have originated as the result of chaotic mingling of energy, matter and motion. Our solar system and the entire universe display the unmistakable evidence of intelligent thought, design and predetermined order.

The chronological Biblical narrative is primarily the written account of the creation of the heavens and the earth; the creation, disobedience, fall, and redemption of humanity through the sacrificial death and subsequent resurrection of Jesus Christ; and the composite makeup of the "Kingdom of God" time without end.

Seven dispensations and eight covenants can be easily traced through Biblical Scriptures beginning forty centuries before the birth of Jesus Christ and ending with the "second coming" of Jesus and his reign over Planet Earth for 1,000 years prior to the "new heavens and the new Earth."

The seven dispensations can be identified as the

dispensation of innocence; of conscience; of human government; of promise; of law; of grace; and of "the kingdom." During a specific dispensation one phrase of God's overall plan to redeem humanity from a fallen state back to himself is initiated and completed.

The eight covenants are also chronological in time and are traced as the Edenic; the Adamic; the Noahic; the Mosaic; the Abrahamic; the Palestinian; the Davidic; and the new covenant. A covenant is a binding agreement between the parties to the covenant and may be either conditional or unconditional. With respect to the eight Biblical covenants recorded, only the Mosaic covenant was conditional and pertained to the keeping or the breaking of the law given to Moses by God. Keeping the law resulted in God's blessings and breaking the law triggered cursing, the opposite of blessings.

The Bible teaches that a human being is a spirit possessing a soul and living in a physical body. Through his spirit man has God consciousness. The soul is the seat of libido, other psychic drives, emotions, and free will through which emotions are expressed and the appetites and lusts of the physical body are either satisfied or denied. The exercise of free will also determines levels of love, hate, pride, arrogance, spite, anger, and jealousy, plus desire for status, admiration, vengeance, etc. The physical body is the tabernacle housing the spirit and soul. The soul and spirit are forever joined in existence whereas the body will suffer physical death at which time the soul and spirit will be translated to the spiritual dimension where the spirit originated (from the breath of God).

Thus, through his spirit man has God consciousness. Through his soul man has self-consciousness, and through his body man has world consciousness. The soul is what makes every human being different from every other human. The Bible declares that God is intimately familiar with every individual soul and even knows the number of hairs on the individual's head prior to death of the individual's physical body.

It seems both reasonable and logical to ask why God went ahead and created humans knowing that they would disobey him and lose their physical body immortality whereas their freed immortal spirits would require a spiritual new birth and their souls would require a total transformation in order to rejoin his eternal kingdom.

Although the Bible does not directly address this question, it is crystal clear from the plan for human redemption revealed in considerable detail within the Scriptures that God desired a large population of living creatures having a free will and created in his own image and after his likeness who would fellowship with the Godhead (Father, Son and Holy Ghost) willingly without any form of divine coercion. Such a population of living creatures were deemed by the Godhead to be of infinite value even though the price of redemption would be enormous. The full cost of redemption was discussed within the Godhead and the Son was willing to pay the price. The cross of Jesus Christ was the planned redemptive price allowing God to dispense justice and mercy simultaneously as the righteous judge of the universe.

"Forasmuch as ye know that ye were not redeemed with corruptible things, as silver and gold, from your vain conversation received by tradition from your fathers; but with the precious blood of Christ, as of a lamb without blemish and without spot; who verily was foreordained before the foundation of the world, but was manifest in these last times for you." (I Peter 1:18-20)

The cross of Jesus Christ is the center of all the Holy Scriptures. Every redeemed human is saved by the blood of Christ freely offered up to God to atone for the individual's sins. Humans living, making their decisions whether to love and honor God, and dying before Christ, were redeemed by looking forward to the cross. Thereafter, humans were and are redeemed by looking back at the cross. God, who ever foresaw the cross, accepted the innocent blood of sacrificial animals as a foreshadow of the sacrifice to be offered up by Jesus Christ "in the fullness of time." The blood of bulls and goats can never take away sins but they did provide a covering for sins until Jesus actually appeared in person on Earth and offered up his body and blood.

"For it is not possible that the blood of bulls and

of goats should take away sins. Wherefore when he cometh into the world, he saith, sacrifice and offerings thou wouldest not, but a body thou hast prepared me: In burnt offerings and sacrifices for sin thou hast had no pleasure. Then said I, Lo I come (in the volume of the book it is written of me,) to do thy will, O God." (Hebrews 10:4-7)

Redemption from sins is by grace (unmerited favor) through faith (in what God has said) and not of works but simply believing and accepting what God says as being absolute truth.

"For by grace are ye saved through faith; and that not of yourselves; it is the gift of God. Not of works, lest any man should boast." (Ephesians 2:8-9)

What then? Are believers in Christ today no longer subject to the laws given to Moses? No, they are not. The Biblical book of Galatians directly addresses this question:

"Knowing that a man is not justified by the works of the law, but by the faith of Jesus Christ, even we have believed in Jesus Christ, that we might be justified by the faith of Christ, and not by the works of the law: for by the works of the law shall no flesh be justified." (Galatians 2:15-16)

"I do not frustrate the grace of God: for if righteousness comes by the law, then Christ died in vain." (Galatians 2:21)

What purpose is then served by the law? The Bible also squarely answers this question:

"Wherefore the law was our schoolmaster to bring us unto Christ, that we might be justified by faith." (Galatians 3:24)

In other words, the law given to Moses was given by God to expose to humanity the "nature of inherited sinfulness" bequeathed to mankind by the first man and woman created by God. The law forced humanity to confess that keeping a perfectly righteous law was a total impossibility for mortal humans poisoned by the disobedience of immortal ancestors who became mortal.

"Wherefore, as by one man sin entered into the world, and death by sin; and so death passed upon all men, for that all have sinned; (For until the law sin was in the world: but sin is not imputed where there is no law. Nevertheless death reigned from Adam to Moses, even over them that had not sinned after the similitude of Adam's transgression, who is the figure of him that was to come. But not as the offence, so also is the free gift. For if through the offence of one many be dead, much more the grace of God, and the gift by grace, which is by one man, Jesus Christ, hath abounded unto many. And not as it was by one that sinned, so is the gift: for the judgment was by one to condemnation, but the free gift is of many offences unto justification. For if by one man's offence, death reigned by one; much more they which receive abundance of grace and of the gift of righteousness shall reign in life by one, Jesus Christ.). Therefore, as by the offence of one judgment came upon all men to condemnation; even so by the righteousness of one the free gift came upon all men unto justification of life. For as by one man's disobedience many were made sinners, so by the obedience of one shall many be made righteous." (Romans 12-19; epistle of Paul; 60 A.D.)

So, then, the direct Biblical answer to the question "why was the law of Moses given and what purpose does it serve?.....is this: The law was given to bring all humanity to the end of self-righteousness seeking and will worship and to make mankind aware that redemption back to God from a fallen state depended solely upon a divine sacrifice acceptable to God thus allowing a righteous God and judge of the universe to dispense total justice and abounding grace simultaneously.

Hot dog! You mean I can just believe in Jesus as my divine sacrificial lamb and live like Satan is my spiritual father? No. Of course not. Believing in and accepting Jesus Christ as your personal sacrificial lamb to redeem you back to God triggers a spiritual rebirth which is the sovereign act of God whereby you become a new creation upon whom God bestows his own righteousness so that you forever after will love and reverence God and seek to please him in everything that you think, say and do.

Are you then saying that I will become a perfect person and be faultless before God? No. You will become perfect in your desire to love, honor, worship and please God. However, until you lay aside your body of sinful and corruptible flesh and pass into the presence of God for eternity, you will be subject to becoming overwhelmed by the desires and lusts of your mortal body. The spirit of God (the Holy Ghost) dwelling in your physical body will convict you of your wrong doing and lead you into immediate sorrow and repentance such that in the eyes of God you remain sinless because you are not under law but rather under grace (God's unmerited favor).

Again, the Bible directly addresses this logical and two-pronged question:

"........Verily, verily, I say unto thee, Except a man be born again, he cannot see the kingdom of God. Nicodemus saith unto him, How can a man be born again when he is old? Can he enter the second time into his mother's womb and be born? Jesus answered, verily, verily, I say unto thee, Except a man be born of water *(natural birth)* and of the Spirit, *(Holy Spirit)* he cannot enter into the kingdom of God. That which is born of the flesh is flesh; and that which is born of the Spirit is spirit. Marvel not that I said unto thee, Ye must be born again. The wind bloweth where it listeth, and thou hearest the sound thereof; but canst not tell whence it cometh, and whither it goeth: so is everyone that is born of the Spirit. (Gospel of John 3:3-8)

"For that which I do I allow not; but what I hate I do. If then I do that which I would not, I consent unto the law that it is good. Now then it is no more I that do it, but sin that dwelleth in me. For I know that in me (that is, in my flesh) dwelleth no good thing: for to will is present with me; but how to perform that which is good I find not. For the good that I would I do not: but the evil which I would not, that I do. Now if I do that I would not, it is no more I that do it, but sin that dwelleth in me. I find than a law, that, when I would do good, evil is present with me. For I delight in the law of God after the inward man: But I see another law in my members, warring against the law of my mind, and bringing me into captivity to the law of sin which is in my members. O Wretched man that I am! Who shall deliver me from the body of this death? I thank God through Jesus Christ, our Lord. So then with the mind I myself serve the law of God; but with the flesh the law of sin. There is therefore now no condemnation to them which are in Christ Jesus, who walk not after the flesh, but after the Spirit. (Romans 7:15-25; 8:1)

Okay. How should a believer in Jesus Christ view the law of Moses? A believer should view the law given to Moses by God as having fulfilled the purpose for which it was given..... to make individuals aware of the need of every human for a sacrificial lamb for redemption back to God and forgiveness of personal sins past, present and future. Where there is no law, there is no sin. A believer is brought out from under the law and redeemed by grace through faith in Jesus Christ. The law simply does not apply to believers for the purpose of judgment but rather as a guide as to how a believer can satisfy the desire to please God complete with the full knowledge that no human being in a mortal, physical body can keep the perfect law of God otherwise Jesus Christ died in vain. Nevertheless, right believing (in Jesus Christ) will lead to the undeniable desire to love, honor, worship and please God

Consequently, it is no longer the "sin question" but rather the "Son question:" "What think ye of Christ?" Did you believe in him and accept him as your personal sacrificial lamb? If not, you are forever banned from God's presence and God's kingdom. Well, if my eternal spirit is banned from God and God's kingdom, what eternal spiritual dimension will I inhabit? You will inhabit the same spiritual habitat as your spiritual father, Satan, and that habitat is referred to as "the lake of fire)." You will be there forever and it is not a desirable place to dwell.

"And the devil that deceived them was cast into the lake of fire and brimstone, where the beast and false prophet are, and shall be tormented day and night forever and ever." (Revelation 20:10)

"And the sea gave up the dead which were in it; and death and hell delivered up the dead which were in them: and they were judged every man according to their works. And death and hell were cast into the lake of fire. This is the second death. And whosoever was not found written in the book of life was cast into the lake of fire." (Revelation 20:13-15)

It is surely true that every individual must at some point weigh the difference between imagination and reality. It is also true that the future of man's physical mortal existence has already been determined. The author watched his father (as his caretaker) slip through that thin veil between the dimensions of mortality and immortality and wrote down the remembrance:

"He had been without frontal vision for years but had learned to cope with limited peripheral sight. During the last three years, his quality of life had diminished to commuting slowly from his bed to the kitchen table. The cartilage in both knees had thinned allowing bone to grind against bone. He gasped for breath when hobbling to the bathroom and his bowels became more irregular. He suffered cramps in his hands, legs and feet and his skin had turned a bluish black. He depended on nine prescription drugs and three inhalers to maintain his fragile pulmonary and cardiac functions. His hearing aids and dentures became more and more useless. Early one morning, he fell in the kitchen and could not get up again. His caretaker could not lift him. An ambulance came and took him to his deathbed. He was a mere child in years having seen only ninety-five winters. He had been born with an immortal soul but with a mortal body. His death had been appointed for sixty centuries and now the sentence was being carried out. William V. Alexander was returning to the dust from which his ancestors had been created approximately forty centuries before the birth of Jesus Christ.

The hospital room was stark, quiet and smelled of death. William's breathing was barely perceptible as his lungs struggled against pneumatic fluid. His kidneys failed and his eyes turned upward showing only slits of white. He came into the world with nothing and he was leaving with nothing.

He struggled to hold on to his flesh with every last beat of his heart; and then he was gone. His body would soon be laid to rest with the powerful of the earth, the wise, the good, aborted fetuses, drunks, mutilated children, harlots, whore mongers, murderers homosexuals, atheists, fools, self-appointed wise men, those who believed in Jesus Christ and those who did not. His life was like a vapor that appeared for a little while and then vanished. He had a body, a spirit and a soul. His body was like every other body in that it required daily nurturing and began to die from birth. His spirit consisted of the breath of God which He breathed into Adam's nostrils causing Adam to become a living soul. His spirit maintained God consciousness thereby distinguishing between good and evil. His soul had developed into his innermost seat of emotions and desires, having been shaped by personal   decisions which now followed him into eternity. William V. Alexander believed in Jesus Christ and was heading into everlasting life where mortal regains immortality -- that which was lost in the Garden of Eden.....the redemption for which God sacrificed even Himself."

Chapter seven

How should a believer in Jesus Christ approach a careful study of the Holy Scriptures in order to obtain an unbiased understanding of what the Holy Bible actually reveals concerning humanity's relationship to God and each other? It is indispensable to a cohesive grasp of the Biblical record to know up front what each of the forty different Biblical authors is writing about and who is being addressed by the writer. To that end, the following synopsis of each writer's contribution may prove to be helpful. The Bible not only contains the "word of God" but also includes the words of devils, scoffers, angels, scorners, evil principalities, and powers ruling the darkness of this world. It is thus of extreme importance to know who is saying what is recorded.

Biblical Synopsis
Chapters 7 through 13

Genesis describes the creation of the universe by God (the God revealed in the Holy Bible) as well as all plant and animal life. The time stated is "in the beginning." Heaven and Earth were created, but Earth lapsed into a condition of chaos for an undetermined time period.......perhaps due to divine judgment involving the inhabitants of Earth prior to the planet becoming dark, without form and void, and flooded with water. During God's creative acts turning chaos into perfect order, darkness became light; excess water turned to vapor and formed a new atmosphere; the dry land appeared as the surface water formed oceans, seas, rivers and lakes; Earth's vegetation reappeared. God ordained lights to divide day from night and to provide signs for days, seasons, and years. The sun, moon and stars appeared in the firmament. God filled the oceans, seas, rivers and lakes with marine life; and filled the air and dry land with living creatures of every variety.

After five days filled with bringing order out of chaos, God created man from the dust of the ground and breathed His own breath into man's nostrils causing man to become an immortal living soul. God named man "Adam" and gave him complete dominion over Earth and all its life forms. Adam named all the living creatures God brought before him. God caused Adam to sleep while He formed a woman from one of Adam's ribs. God placed Adam and the woman in a garden paradise which He planted for them and told them to be fruitful and to replenish Earth. On the seventh day God rested from his creative activities.

God gave the man the power to disobey Him. He instructed Adam not to eat of a designated tree (in order to test man's obedience). God warned Adam that if he ate of the "tree of the knowledge of good and evil" he would die. The woman, tempted by an evil spirit (Satan in the form of a serpent), ate of the forbidden tree and gave some to Adam whereupon they were immediately banished from God's presence and from their garden paradise. God cursed Earth because of Adam's disobedience. Man was appointed to physical death and to wrestle food from a hostile Earth. Adam and Eve died spiritually and began to age physically the day Adam disobeyed God, but God was already executing His plan to redeem human souls back to himself.

Adam called his wife "Eve" and settled down to till the ground for food. Adam begat sons and daughters who began life with an immortal soul, but with a mortal body. Adam's firstborn son (Cain) murdered his younger brother (Abel) following a misunderstanding concerning sacrificial offerings to God. Cain took a sister with him, fled from Adam and Eve, and initiated his own bloodline. Seth, Adam's third son, was born when Adam was one hundred and thirty years old.

The descendents of Cain and Seth began to intermarry and to drift deeper into evil and violence until only one man (Noah) retained any God-consciousness. In accordance with His plan for redeeming mankind, God decided to repopulate Earth with Noah's seed. God flooded the planet while preserving Noah and his immediate family inside an ark built by Noah according to God's instructions. God caused a male and female representing every air breathing creature to come to Noah for preservation inside the ark. Noah's descendents repopulated Earth and pooled their efforts to build a city and a tower to escape future flood waters.

God confounded their communications and scattered them over the continents. Because mankind became more and more wicked, God shortened the human lifespan to a maximum of one hundred and twenty years. Between the death of Adam and the death of Joseph, Abraham's great grandson, life expectancy diminished more than eighty-five percent (Joseph lived to age 110).

Approximately 1975 BC, God selected a man named Abraham for special blessing because Abraham believed God existed and wanted to please Him. God promised Abraham that he would father many nations and instructed him to leave his homeland and travel to a country which God would give to him and to his seed forever. Abraham gathered his household and journeyed from Ur of the Chaldees to Canaan where he became a shepherd and waited for the fulfillment of God's promises. Because Sarah, his wife, was barren, Abraham took her advice and fathered a son (Ishmael) by her handmaid. God rejected Ishmael as Abraham's heir and told Abraham that Sarah would bear him a son with whom God would honor his promises to Abraham. Abraham begat Isaac when he was a hundred years old and when Sarah was far beyond the age of childbearing.

Abraham and his nephew, Lot, departed from each other because their herds became too large for them to share common land. Abraham gave Lot first choice of which direction to travel and Lot chose to settle in the lush plains outside the twin cities called Sodom and Gomorrah. Abraham remained in Canaan. God selected circumcision as the sign of the covenant He made with Abraham and his seed after him.

Because the populations of Sodom and Gomorrah practiced open homosexuality mixed with extreme violence and wickedness, God sent angels to destroy the cities. Abraham interceded with God on Lot's behalf and God promised He would spare Sodom and Gomorrah plus the smaller cities round about if ten righteous persons could be found therein. Only Lot and his two daughters were spared and the angels had to force them to flee to Zoar, a small city above the plain of Jordan. In a drunken stupor, Lot fathered two sons (Moab and Benammi) by his two daughters. Moab's descendants are known as Moabites and Benammi's descendants are called the children of Ammon. Ishmael, Abraham's son by Sarah's handmaid begat the patriarchs of the Arab nations.

God told Abraham to offer his son, Isaac, as a sacrificial offering and then provided a substitute ram when Abraham actually raised his knife over Isaac as Isaac lay bound upon the altar (a preview of the sacrifice of God, the Son). After the death of Sarah, Isaac took his cousin, Rebecca, as his wife and she bare twin sons named Esau and Jacob. Esau exited the womb first but sold his firstborn birthright to Jacob for a bowl of pottage to assuage his temporary hunger. Jacob thus inherited the covenant promises God made to Abraham and Esau's descendants are the Edomites.

God changed Jacob's name to Israel and he begat twelve sons who are the twelve patriarchs of the "twelve tribes of Israel" (the tribes of Reuben, Judah, Gad, Asher, Simeon, Levi, Dan, Naphtali, Issachar, Zebulun, Joseph, and Benjamin).

Pursuant to the birth of Benjamin, during a fit of jealousy, Joseph's brothers sold him into slavery and told Jacob that a wild beast had apparently devoured Joseph. In Egypt, Joseph became a slave in the household of Potiphar, an officer serving Pharaoh. God blessed Joseph in Egypt and he became Potiphar's chief steward. Joseph spurned efforts by Potiphar's wife to seduce him whereupon she claimed Joseph tried to rape her, and Potiphar had him cast into prison.

During his time in prison, God continued to bless Joseph and he was put in charge of the prisoners (which eventually included Pharaoh's chief butler and chief baker). Joseph interpreted the dreams of the chief butler and chief baker and told them that in three days Pharaoh would restore the chief butler to his duties and hang the chief baker. Joseph's interpretation proved true -- the butler was freed and the baker was hanged within three days.

Pharaoh dreamed he saw seven lean cattle devour seven fat cattle followed by a dream wherein he saw seven withered ears of corn devour seven healthy ears. Pharaoh called his wise men and magicians but they could not interpret his dreams. The chief butler remembered that Joseph could interpret dreams and Pharaoh summoned him from prison. Joseph told Pharaoh that his two dreams were God's warning to Pharaoh that seven bountiful years were going to be followed by seven years of severe famine; that the two dreams were the same warning indicating that God had revealed the future to Pharaoh.

Joseph advised Pharaoh to appoint someone honest and wise to store twenty percent of the food produced during the bountiful years to provide relief during the seven years of famine. Pharaoh appointed Joseph head of his royal house and all of Egypt to carry out his advice.

Jacob and his family were suffering in Canaan during the seven years of famine and Jacob sent ten of his sons to buy grain in Egypt. Joseph's brothers did not recognize him but he knew them and forgave their treatment of him. Joseph sent for Jacob and Benjamin and the rest of Jacob's descendents and servants. The children of Israel abandoned the land promised to Abraham and settled down to the easy, good life in Egypt. Joseph fathered two sons in Egypt (Manasseh and Ephraim).

The children of Israel (also called Hebrews) settled in the land of Goshen, Egypt where they prospered and multiplied. Joseph's generation died in Goshen, and Joseph was embalmed and placed in a coffin. Thus, Genesis begins in the paradise of God and ends with a mummy in Egypt.

The book of Exodus begins with the Hebrew slavery in Egypt. A Pharaoh came to power in Egypt who was unfamiliar with Joseph's deeds on Egypt's behalf. The Hebrews had become exceedingly numerous and Pharaoh viewed them as a threat to Egypt's security. Pharaoh ordered the Hebrews reduced to slavery and decreed that all their male infants be thrown into the Nile River. The mother of Moses placed him into a basket lined with leaves and pitch and placed the basket among the flags alongside the river. Miriam, Moses' sister, watched the basket to see what would happen to it. Pharaoh's daughter came to bathe in the river and heard the child crying. She took pity on Moses and Miriam asked her if she would like a Hebrew nurse. Pharaoh's daughter told Miriam to fetch a wet nurse whereupon Miriam brought her the child's mother.

Moses was brought up as the son of Pharaoh's daughter in the royal palace. Around age 40, Moses killed an Egyptian for beating a Hebrew slave and had to flee from Egypt. Moses spent the next 40 years on the backside of the Sinai Desert tending his father-in-law's flocks. His wife (Zipporah) bore him two sons. Moses climbed a near-by mountain to study a bush that burned but was not consumed. God spoke to Moses out of the burning bush and instructed him to return to Egypt to free the Hebrew slaves. Because Moses was slow of speech, God told him to take his brother, Aaron, along with him when he went in before Pharaoh.

God told Moses that Pharaoh would refuse to free

the Hebrews and thus bring upon his throne and upon Egypt God's wrath; and that after punishing Pharaoh and Egypt, God would bring the Hebrews out with a mighty hand thereby revealing to all nations his great power. God turned the Nile into blood, sent great swarms of flies and locusts throughout Egypt; covered the land with frogs and lice; destroyed the Egyptian crops with hail and fire; covered the Egyptians and their cattle with boils and disease; blanketed Egypt in total darkness for three days; and killed every firstborn in every Egyptian family. Pharaoh ordered the Hebrews out of Egypt and they departed laden with gold, silver, precious stones, clothing, food and livestock.

When Moses and the Hebrews approached the Red Sea, Pharaoh and his army pursued after them. God placed a pillar of fire between the Hebrews and the Egyptians, then parted the sea allowing the Hebrews to cross through the water on dry ground. Pharaoh and his army entered the sea in pursuit whereupon God released the restrained water and drowned the Egyptian army. The fleeing Hebrews numbered approximately six hundred thousand men of military age in addition to old folks, women and children.

Prior to the death of every firstborn in Egypt, God told Moses to have every Hebrew family kill a sacrificial lamb and to place some of the blood upon the lintel and two side posts of their door. God passed over the homes having doors smeared with sacrificial lamb's blood when slaying Egypt's firstborn. The Hebrew Feast of Passover commemorates this "passing over." God led the Hebrews through the wilderness using a pillar of cloud by day and a pillar of fire by night.

During the wilderness trek, the Hebrews complained periodically about lack of food and water. God watered them from dry rocks and fed them with manna (the bread from heaven which appeared with the morning dew). God also sent them flocks of quail for meat. When the people continued complaining about God's bounty and Moses' leadership, God sent plagues among them as chastisement for their grumbling.

God told Moses to climb up Mount Sinai to receive His law. When Moses had been out of sight for many days, the people fashioned a golden calf to worship and determined to return to Egypt. Moses returned and, in anger, cast down the two tables of stone upon which God had written His law, and about three thousand transgressors were killed at Moses' command by the Levites. Moses went back up the mountain to intercede for the people. God personally wrote the law again on two tables of stone.

The law given to Moses covered man's relation to God and man's relationship to man: worship God only; do not make any graven image; do not speak God's name in vain; remember the Sabbath Day and keep it holy; do not commit adultery; do not steal; do not murder; do not bear false witness; do not covet; and honor both father and mother. Exodus also partially describes ceremonial, civil and criminal law.

In accord with God's instructions given to Moses, the people built a worship tabernacle and the Ark of the Covenant. They also made garments for Aaron and the sons of Aaron whom Moses appointed to serve as priests. God appointed the tribe of Levi to serve in the tabernacle and to carry the tabernacle including the service items and the Ark when the people journeyed.

The book of Leviticus provides additional details concerning the Law of Moses including integration of dietary law, religious ceremonies, civil and criminal law. The ten main points of the law are referred to as God's Ten Commandments. The ceremonial law governed the animal sacrifices offered to atone for transgressions of the law and to honor God.

The ceremonial law also governed the Sabbath Day, Sabbath Year, the Year of Jubilee, and the annual feast days. No work was to be performed on the Sabbath Day. No crops were to be planted or harvested during the Sabbath Year (that which grew without planting could be eaten). The Year of Jubilee (every year following seven Sabbath Years) was dedicated to worship and feasting. All bond servants were freed and all real estate reverted back to the original owner/family.

The Day of Atonement covers the annual offering made by the high priest for the sins of all the people. The ceremonial law portrayed the future sacrifice to be offered up by Jesus Christ. The animal sacrifices by which sins were temporarily forgiven were but shadows of the divine sacrifice to come. The civil and criminal law was to be administered by the priests on behalf of the people. A rope was tied to the high priest before he entered the most holy place inside the outer veil on the Day of Atonement. Should the high priest be less than respectful, the rope could be used to retrieve his dead body.

The sacrificial offerings and fire upon the altar were specifically ordained by God to be presented as instructed by Moses. When two of Aaron's sons (Nadab and Abihu) offered strange fire, they were consumed by fire issuing from God.

Total blessing is promised by God to the people for following the Law of Moses. Five chastisements are pronounced upon the people if they dishonor their law covenant with God: (first), terror, consumption, sorrow of heart, poor crop yield, falling before their enemies, foreign rule, and fleeing when none is pursuing; (second), drought and famine; (third), wild beasts to eat their children and their cattle and to make their highways desolate; (fourth), death by the sword, pestilence, extended famine, perpetual hunger; (fifth), siege of their cities wherein they will eat their own children, total desolation of their homeland and their carcasses to be cast upon their idols, and long term dispersion throughout Gentile nations where they will be hated above all nationalities.

God promises that a remnant of the Hebrews will be spared when they confess their trespasses against Him; and they will be blessed in accordance with God's covenant with Abraham.

The book of Numbers contains the numbering of the Hebrew men able to go to war and the organizational order of the tribes when proceeding to battle. The standard bearers were to mark the encampment for each tribe. The fighting men numbered six hundred and three thousand, five hundred and fifty. The men had been trained for war during the wilderness journey. A cloud covered the tabernacle by day and the appearance of fire by night. When the cloud was taken away, the people journeyed and when the cloud appeared over the tabernacle, the people rested.

Throughout the journey recorded in Numbers, the people complained about food, about water, and about Moses' leadership. God chastised the people when they complained by sending various plagues among them. Even Aaron and Miriam challenged Moses concerning his Ethiopian wife. Miriam was chastised with leprosy for a season and Aaron was advised to keep silent.

The Hebrews journeyed to the borders of the land promised to Abraham and Moses sent spies to scout out the land (one man from each of the twelve tribes). The spies searched the land for forty days and saw fortified cities, inhabitants prepared for war, giants, and a fertile, well-watered land. Ten of the spies advised the people not to cross the borders. Two spies, Joshua and Caleb, urged the people to go in since God would fight for them. The people wanted to stone Joshua and Caleb. God told Moses that none of the fighting men alive at the time (except Joshua and Caleb) would cross over into the promised land, and that the people would wander a year for each day the spies searched the land (40 days = 40 years) until a new generation of fighting men were ready for war. The people then presumed to take the land but were promptly defeated and chased back into the wilderness. Moses led the people in the wilderness during the ensuing forty years.

Two hundred and fifty men, famous within the Hebrew congregation, rebelled against Moses and attempted to usurp the priesthood. The families supporting the rebellion stood by their tents. The earth opened under them and they went down alive into hell. The two hundred and fifty men attempting to offer incense were burned alive.

The next day, the congregation murmured against Moses and Aaron whereupon God sent a plague among them which killed fourteen thousand, seven hundred. The issue of Aaron's priesthood and his seed after him was settled by laying up a rod for each of the twelve tribes to determine whose rod would be selected by God. Aaron's rod blossomed and was placed in the Ark of the Covenant.

The ceremonial law provided food and clothing for the priests and for the Levites who served the priesthood and the people. Ten percent of the wealth of the congregation was reserved for the priests and Levites. Clothing was provided for them and they ate a portion of designated sacrificial offerings.

Miriam died in Kadesh in the Desert of Zin where there was no water. The congregation murmured again against Moses and Aaron. God told Moses to speak to a certain rock before the people and water would issue from the rock. Moses, tired of listening to the people whine, struck the rock twice with his staff whereupon water flowed out for the congregation and their beasts. God told Moses and Aaron that they would not enter the promised land because of their disobedience in striking the rock instead of speaking to it.

The Edomites forced the Hebrews to detour around Edom and Aaron died along the coast. He was buried in Mount Hor and his son, Eleazar succeeded him as High Priest. Israel took the land of King Arad, the Canaanite, and journeyed onward. The way was difficult and the people again complained about lack of food and water. God sent fiery serpents among them and many died. The people repented and God told Moses to fashion a serpent of brass and set it upon a pole and those bitten need only to look upon the serpent to live. Thereafter, the murmuring ceased among the Israelites and the new generation of fighting men prepared for war.

The Amorites refused to let Israel pass through their land whereupon Israel attacked the Amorites and took over their cities. Balak, King of Moab, made a pact with the Midianites to resist the Israeli advance. Balak hired Balaam, a seer, to curse Israel, but God rebuked Balaam through the mouth of his donkey. The men of

Israel began to cohabit with the daughters of the Moabites; to eat meat sacrificed to idols; and to bow down before the Moabite gods. God sent a plague among the Israelites wherein twenty-four thousand died. When the people repented and the plague ended, the new generation of Israeli warriors were numbered for battle (six hundred and one thousand, seven hundred and thirty).

The law of inheritance permitted unmarried widows to inherit land among their own tribe. A wife was bound by a vow which her husband heard and did not forbid. Certain cities were to serve as "cities of refuge" where a person could flee after an accidental killing. The accused would be brought into judgment to determine whether the killing was truly accidental.

If judged accidental, the person would be returned to the city of refuge until the death of the high priest serving at the time. Then, the accused could return home. If found outside the city of refuge prior to the death of the high priest, the accused could be slain by the "avenger of blood." The murderer was to be put to death without recourse.

Israel fought against the Midianites and took all their cities. Moses prepared for death and reviewed Israel's wilderness journeys. The promised land was to be divided between the tribes in proportion to population. Because the tribe of Levi served the priests and the people, the seed of Joseph's sons (Ephraim and Manasseh) replaced the tribe of Levi pertaining to division of the land.

The tribes of Reuben and Gad requested that Moses give them the former kingdoms of Sihon and Og east of Jordon. Moses agreed to their request providing both tribes continued to fight alongside their brethren until the promised land was conquered. Moses determined that the half-tribe of Manasseh (according to their request) should also settle east of Jordan in order to balance the inheritance east of Jordon with the inheritance west of Jordon.

The book of Deuteronomy addresses the generation of Israelites born during the forty years of wandering wherein all the fighting men perished (other than Joshua and Caleb) that refused to follow Moses into the promised land. For the benefit of the new generation, Moses reviews the exodus from Egypt; the wilderness journeys; the manna from heaven and water from rocks; the murmurings among the congregation against Moses and God; God's ensuing chastisements; and the battles Israel fought while journeying through the wilderness to the promised land. Moses further reviews the dietary, ceremonial, civil and criminal laws including the cities of refuge.

Deuteronomy declares the blessings to be enjoyed while honoring God's law as well as the chastisements to be suffered for disobedience. God forbids intermarriage with the Gentiles and instructs Israel to obliterate idol worship and to kill everything that breathes within the nations occupying the promised land. The duties of the priesthood and the Levites are restated along with feast days, Sabbath Day, Sabbath Year, Year of Jubilee, sacrificial offerings, and the required support from each Israelite for the priests and Levites.

The law of war is outlined. When warring with nations and peoples outside the promised land, Israel is to first offer peace in exchange for service and tribute. If such peace offer is refused, all enemy males are to be killed and everything else taken as the spoils of war including women and children. With regard to the Hittites, Amorites, Canaanites, Perizzites, Hivites, and Jebusites (the peoples occupying the promised land), everything that breathes is to be annihilated.

Before marching into battle, every Israelite warrior having betrothed a wife, or having an undedicated house or vineyard, or being fainthearted or fearful is to be weeded out and sent home. The descendents of Amalek are to be exterminated by Israel because Amalek's warriors pursued Israel in the wilderness and killed off the hindmost and the weak and feeble.

Moses prophesies to Israel that future generations of Israelis will turn away from God and worship idols thereby bringing upon themselves all the chastisements which follow disobedience and idolatry including eating their own children and dispersion among Gentile nations. Moses also prophesies that a remnant will remain faithful and thus inherit all the promises God made to Abraham, Isaac, and Jacob. When actually crossing over Jordan into the promised land, Moses instructs Israel to set up and plaster great stones and to inscribe upon the stones all the words of God's law. Half of the tribes are to gather upon Mount Ebal and the other half upon Mount Gerizim.

The Levites are then to proclaim in a loud voice all the blessings and curses pertaining to obedience or disobedience under God's law. The tribes upon Mount Gerizim are to say Amen to the pronounced blessings; and the tribes upon Mount Ebal are to say Amen to the pronounced curses. Moses teaches the people a song highlighting their experiences between the exodus from Egypt and their preparation to enter the promised land, including the choice between blessings and curses.

Because of his disobedience concerning the water of Meribah, God instructs Moses to view the promised land from Mount Nebo and to relinquish leadership to Joshua. Thereafter, God buried Moses and the location of Moses' grave remains unknown.

Chapter eight

The book of Joshua covers the period between the death of Moses and the death of Joshua. (1451 BC to 1427 BC). Joshua takes over as God's appointed replacement for Moses. Under Joshua's leadership, God continues to use the fighting men among the tribes of Israel to wage war against the nations occupying the land promised to Abraham. It is noteworthy that God had given the Canaanites, Hivites, Hittites, Amorites, Perizzites, and Jebusites, more than four centuries to repent after the obliteration of Sodom and Gomorrah.

By the time Joshua was instructed by God to conquer the promised land, God had given up on the nations to be destroyed by Israel. Their continued existence served no purpose other than to be a stumbling block which would cripple Israel spiritually. The truth of this assertion is mirrored by God's instructions to "pray no more for Ephraim for he is joined to his idols," and "mourn no more for Saul seeing that I have rejected him."

Joshua led Israel to the bank of the Jordon River. To display his support of Israel, God parted the water allowing the people to cross over the river at flood stage. Two memorials were erected to call to remembrance Israel's crossing over into the promised land. Joshua sent two spies into the fortified city of Jericho and the two young men were hidden by a harlot in her home.

The spies reported back to Joshua and the harlot, Rahab, was marked for safe passage into Israel along with her family. In another display of His power, God flattened the walls of Jericho after Israel conducted a quiet and somber march around the city (once each day for six days and seven times on the seventh day followed by a great shout).

Under Joshua, Israel conquered the promised land but failed to totally drive out all the inhabitants. God instructed Joshua to divide the land between the tribes of Israel according to the distribution ordered by Moses. The tribes were instructed to finish driving out all the prior inhabitants (whereas God had told Moses to "leave nothing alive that breathes").

Israel was to be a theocracy ruled over by God, himself. In his farewell address, Joshua reminded the people of the blessings and curses connected with their covenant with God to keep the laws given to Moses. Joshua lived a total of 110 years and was buried in Mount Ephraim. Israel honored the covenant with God all the days of Joshua and the days of the elders who had seen all the things God did to protect Israel.

The narrative in Joshua sets the stage for the book of Judges which records periodic Israeli apostasy, servitude, and sub-sequent deliverance from bondage. Israel is repeatedly subjected to servitude by remnants of those nations which they failed to totally destroy as instructed by Moses. Deliverance is provided under the leadership of various individuals appointed by God as "judges."

The book of Judges covers seven Israeli apostasies, seven servitudes to seven ungodly nations, seven deliverances and a total of thirteen judges during a period of approximately three centuries. Because Israel allowed the remnants of the heathen nations to become tributaries rather than totally destroying them, God used the heathen peoples to chastise Israel for presumptive disobedience to His revealed will.

Israel became content to dwell among the Canaanites, Hittites, Amorites, Perizzites, Hivites and Jebusites. Israel intermarried with the heathen peoples and worshiped their gods. Israel paid tribute to the king of Mesopotamia and served him eight years. Israel cried before God and he sent Caleb's grandson, Othniel, to lead the revolt against Israel's oppressors. Thereafter, Othniel judged Israel for forty years. Israel again forsook God and served Eglon, king of Moab for eighteen years.

Again Israel cried out to God and Ehud, a Benjamite, killed Eglon while leading Israel to victory over the Moabites. Israel enjoyed peace eighty years under Ehud's judgeship. Thereafter, the Philistines oppressed Israel and God raised up Shamgar, son of Anath, to free Israel from Philistine dominion.

Israel again slipped into worship of strange gods whereupon God allowed Jabin, king of Canaan, to rule ruthlessly over Israel for twenty years. Deborah, both prophetess and judge, supported by Barak, son of

Ahinoam, and blessed by God, led a revolt against Jabin totally defeating the Canaanites thereby ushering in forty years of peace for Israel.

Israel turned away from God again and became servants to the Midianites for seven years. Israel cried out to God again and Gideon, son of Joash, protected by God, led 300 warriors to victory over the combined forces of the Midianites and Amalekites making possible another forty years of peace within Israel. Following Gideon's death, Israel again practiced idolatry. Abimelech, Gideon's son by a concubine, headed a conspiracy to murder all of Gideon's other seventy sons assisted by the men of Shechem, his mother's kinsmen. Abimelech recruited vile men to assist in murdering his brothers and managed to rule over Israel for three years. During a civil war battle within Israel, Abimelech's skull was crushed by a millstone thrown by a woman from a besieged tower.

After Abimelech, Tola, the son of Puah judged Israel for twenty-three years followed by Jair, a Gileadite, who judged Israel for twenty-two years. Israel again turned to idolatry and worshiped the gods of Syria, Zidon, Moab, the Philistines, and the children of Ammon. The Philistines and the Ammonites put Israel to servitude for eighteen years. Israel cried before God again and God told them to go and cry unto their idols for deliverance. Nevertheless, God again showed mercy toward Israel and Jephtah, son of a harlot, was empowered by God to free Israel from servitude.

Jephtah judged Israel six years including a brief war between Gileadites and Ephraimites.

Following Jephtah, Ibzan of Bethlehem judged Israel for seven years; Elon, a Zebulonite judged for ten years; and Abdon, son of Hillel, judged for eight years. Then, Israel again turned away from God resulting in another forty years of oppression by the Philistines. The spirit of God rested upon Samson, a Nazarite from birth. Samson was blessed with God-given strength whereby he performed as a one-man army against the Philistines.

Samson began an intimate relationship with a ruthless woman named Delilah who betrayed him to the Philistines for money. Samson, after being nagged by Delilah, revealed to her that his great strength would fade should his Nazarite hair length be shortened. While asleep upon Delilah's knees, Samson's hair was cut short and God rejected him. The Philistines took him captive, put out his eyes, and forced him to grind like an ox. While grinding as a prisoner, Samson's hair began to grow again.

While feasting and making merry before their god, Dagon, the Philistines brought Samson into Dagon's house of worship to make sport of him. Samson was placed between two pillars supporting the house wherein all the lords of the Philistines and approximately three thousand men and women laughed at him. Samson prayed for strength to avenge himself and to die with the Philistines. He pulled mightily against the two pillars supporting the huge structure. The house fell upon Samson and all the Philistines therein such that Samson killed more Philistines at his death than he did during his judgeship spanning twenty years. After the death of Samson, the Children of Israel did as they pleased including bastardized priest and Levite service, rape, sodomy, murder, and civil war.

The book of Ruth tells the story of Ruth's devotion to Naomi, her mother-in-law, during widowhood. After the death of her husband, Elimelech, and her two sons, Naomi decided to return to Bethlehem-judah and Ruth refused to abandon Naomi. Ruth traveled to Bethlehem-judah with Naomi and gleaned in the fields of Boaz, a near kinsman of Naomi's deceased husband. Boaz became intrigued with Ruth and chose to redeem Elimelech's property and take Ruth for his wife. The son born to Boaz and Ruth was Obed, the father of Jessie. King David was the son of Jessie which places Ruth in the human bloodline of Jesus Christ (along with Rahab, the harlot who hid the spies inside Jericho).

The First Book of Samuel begins with the total corruption of Israel's priesthood under Eli and his two sons, Hophni and Phinehas. Eli's sons were exceeding wicked. They took more than the priests' share from the sacrifices offered by the people. They also indulged in sexual relations with women who came to worship in the temple. Before Samuel was born his mother was barren and she placed Samuel in the service of Eli as a sacrifice to God. Samuel grew up before Eli and God chose Samuel to be prophet and priest instead of Eli's sons. God rejected the descendents of Eli and marked them for suffering and early death. Israel rebelled against Philistine servitude and the Philistines killed thirty-four thousand Israelis including Hophni and Phinehas. When Eli heard that the Philistines had also taken the ark of the covenant, he fell off his seat backward and died from a broken neck.

There was a great slaughter and plague among the Philistines because they took the ark of the covenant. The ark was sent back to the Israelites by cart and oxen with a trespass offering of golden jewels upon the cart. The ark came to rest in the field of Joshua, the Beth-shemite. The men of Beth-shemesh looked into the ark and God sent a great slaughter among the Beth-shemites wherein fifty thousand and seventy perished. The ark was removed to Kirjath-jearim and received into the house of Abinadab where Eleazar, his son, watched over it for twenty years.

Under Samuel's advice the Israelites put away their idols and fought against the Philistines at Mizpeh and Eben-ezer. God gave Israel a great victory including the return of Israel's cities ruled over by the Philistines. When Samuel was old, his sons tried to take his place but they perverted judgment whereupon the elders of Israel demanded a king to rule Israel. God told Samuel to anoint a king over Israel but to solemnly protest and to warn the people concerning the manner in which kings would rule over them. Samuel anointed Saul, of the tribe of Benjamin, to be king. God sent thunder and rain during the wheat harvest to indicate his disgust with Israel's demand for a king.

Initially, Saul was humble and obedient to God's will as revealed to him through Samuel. Led by Saul and Jonathan, his son, Israel enjoyed several military victories over the Ammonites, Philistines, Edomites, Moabites, Amalekites, and kings of Zobah. Saul became arrogant and self-willed. He became impatient and intruded into the priest's office by offering sacrifices in the absence of Samuel.

Throughout his rein, Saul warred with the Philistines. Through Samuel, God instructed Saul to attack the Amalekites and totally wipe them out including their women, children, and flocks because they killed off the hindmost and weak among Israel during Israel's flight from Egypt. Saul saved Agag, king of the Amalekites, alive and also saved the best of the flocks. Because of his arrogant disobedience, God rejected Saul as king. Samuel executed Agag and secretly anointed David, son of Jessie, to replace Saul as king over Israel. Saul selected David to sooth him with harp music whenever he was troubled by an evil spirit.

A Philistine giant named Goliath mocked and challenged the men of Israel to fight him one-on-one. David, with nothing but a slingshot and faith in God, knocked Goliath down with a stone and then beheaded him with his own sword. Saul became jealous of David and suspected that David would replace him thereby cutting off his sons from inheriting his throne. David fled from Saul and Saul hunted him unsuccessfully for seven years. David gathered around him approximately four hundred men who were social outcasts and together they continued to flee before Saul. Twice, when he had the opportunity to kill Saul, David refused to harm him. David and his men scavenged for food and water and shared adventurous times. Saul and three of his sons were killed by the Philistines during a battle in Mount Gilboa

The Second Book of Samuel covers the time period between the death of Saul and the death of David. The men of Judah hailed David as king over Judah and there was war between the house of David and the house of Saul for another seven years. David prevailed over the sons of Saul and became king over all Israel. David brought out the ark of the covenant from the house of Abinadab and placed it inside a dedicated tabernacle in Zion, called "the City of David." God protected David and he subdued all the enemies of Israel. God blessed David and made a covenant with him to establish his kingdom forever, promising that David's seed would always sit upon his throne.

David became overwhelmed with lust for the wife of Uriah, the Hittite, when he saw her bathing herself. Uriah was with David's army fighting the Syrians and the Children of Ammon. David lay with Bathsheba, Uriah's wife, and she became pregnant. David attempted to pass off the pregnancy to Uriah by having him sent home where David wined and dined him and then instructed him to go home to his wife before returning to battle. Uriah refused to spend time with Bathsheba while his fellow warriors were joined in battle. David sent a letter by Uriah to Joab, captain of David's army, instructing Joab to place Uriah in the forefront of the fighting and then pull back so Uriah would be killed by the enemy. Uriah died in battle and David took Bathsheba as a wife.

Nathan, the prophet, told David that God was greatly displeased with his adultery, conspiracy to murder, and actual murder of Uriah. David repented whereupon God forgave his great sin but told David through Nathan that the sword would never depart from his house; that evil would rise up against him within his own family; that another would lay with his wives; and that the child conceived in adultery would die.

After the death of the bastard child, Bathsheba bore David a second son named Solomon. David's son, Amnon, raped his half-sister, Tamar, and his half-brother, Absalom, killed him. Thereafter, Absalom tried to take David's throne and David had to flee before Absalom and his followers. Absalom went in to David's concubines in the sight of the people. During a battle with David's army, Absalom was killed and David returned to Jerusalem. There was intrigue and murder within Israel's army and two minor rebellions which fizzled.

God sent a famine throughout Israel to chastise

the people for King Saul's genocide involving the Gibeonites. David delivered up seven of Saul's sons to the Gibeonites who hanged them thus ending the famine. David numbered the fighting men in Israel (one million, three hundred thousand) which displeased God because the numbering indicated reliance upon men rather than God. David was offered three choices for chastisement: seven years of famine; flee before his enemies for three months; or three days pestilence. David chose pestilence wherein seventy thousand men died.

The First Book of Kings continues the history of the Hebrew monarchy. Shortly before David's death, his son, Adonijah, supported by Joab, attempted to seize David's throne. Bathsheba and Nathan revealed the plot to David whereupon David named Solomon as his successor. Solomon established his kingdom by executing Joab, Adonijah, and Shimei (who had cursed David), and by removing Abaithar (who supported Adonijah) from the priesthood. God appeared to Solomon in a dream and told him to ask whatever he wanted. Solomon asked for wisdom to rightly judge Israel. His humility pleased God and God granted him both wisdom and great wealth. Solomon erected a temple for God and a great house for himself. Solomon ordered the ark of the covenant placed within the temple. Thereafter, God's glory filled the temple such that the priests could not stand to minister before the altar until the glory was lifted. Following Solomon's prayer dedicating the temple, God promised Solomon that he would always have seed to sit upon his throne providing he walked before God like David. Solomon's reputation for wisdom and great wealth spread throughout all nations and foreign rulers traveled to Jerusalem to see for themselves.

Solomon had seven hundred wives and three hundred concubines who turned his heart away from God during his old age. He built high places for idol worship and followed after strange gods. God raised up adversaries to plague Solomon including a servant named Jeroboam, the son of Nebat. After Solomon's death, Rehoboam (a foolish and arrogant son), tried to increase the burden required to support the royal court. Israel rebelled leaving only Judah and Benjamin loyal to the house of David.

The other ten tribes made Jeroboam king over them thereby splitting the nation into two kingdoms. The ten tribes making up the northern kingdom continued to call themselves "Israel" and the two tribes loyal to David's house called themselves "Judah." Jeroboam feared that temple worship in Jerusalem would threaten his throne. To discourage a reunion between Israel and Judah, Jeroboam erected an idol (golden calf) at Bethel and at Dan along with an alter upon which he burned sacrifices and incense. He also appointed a priesthood from among the least faithful in Israel.

Because of Jeroboam's great sin, a prophet told

him that his ailing son would die and that the house of
Jeroboam would be taken away as men take away dung
until it is all gone; and that his seed would be eaten by
dogs and scavenger birds. Judah also practiced idolatry
and homosexuality under Rehoboam. Judah was invaded
and sacked by Shishak, king of Egypt. Thus, both
Jeroboam and Rehoboam led their followers into evil
and idolatry. Judah was subsequently ruled by Abijam,
Asa, and Jehoshaphat. Abijam practiced evil like
Rehoboam, Asa and Jehoshaphat did that which was
right in God's sight thereby bringing God's blessings
upon Judah.

Jeroboam's son, Nadab practiced evil and reined
over Israel two years before being assassinated by
Baasha, son of Ahijah. And, there was war between Asa
and Baasha. Through the prophet Jehu, God told Baasha
that his house would perish like Jeroboam's. Elah
followed Baasha and reigned two years before being
killed by Zimri who took the throne and totally
destroyed the remaining seed of Baasha. Zimri did evil
before God and committed suicide following a failed
attempt to capture Gibbethon, a Philistine city. Tibni and
Omri competed for Zimri's throne thereby splitting
Israel into two monarchies. Omri vanquished Tibni and
practiced evil before God another twelve years. Omri
died and Ahab, his son, reigned over Israel.

Ahab was more evil than his father. He took
Jezebel, a Zidonian princess, as a wife and worshiped
Baal with her. He erected an altar and grove for Baal

worship and sanctioned the rebuilding of Jericho. Elijah, a zealous prophet, told Ahab there would be no rain nor dew for three years. Thereafter, Elijah hid by the brook, Cherith, and ravens brought him meat. When the brook dried up, God sent Elijah to Zarephath where a widow woman sustained him. When the widow's son died, Elijah prayed over him and God raised the boy from the dead.

God instructed Elijah to return to Ahab and end the drought. Elijah challenged Ahab and eight hundred and fifty prophets of Baal to a contest between Baal and God upon mount Carmel. Altars were erected to Baal and to God and sacrifices placed thereon. The prophets of Baal prayed to him until evening and cut themselves to get a response. Since Baal was just an imaginary god represented by a graven image, there was no response to the crying, praying and bleeding.

Then, Elijah had a trench dug around God's altar and poured water upon the sacrifice and filled the trench. Elijah prayed a short prayer and God sent fire that burned the wood, altar, sacrifice, stones, dust and water in the trench. The Israelite spectators fell on their faces before God. According to Elijah's word, all the prophets of Baal were executed by the brook Kishon. Elijah prayed for rain and a torrential rain watered the land.

Jezebel tried to kill Elijah and he fled to mount Horeb where God rebuked him for lack of faith and told him to return by way of Damascus and anoint Hazael king over Syria, and to anoint Jehu, son of Nimshi, king over Israel, and to appoint Elisha, the son of Shaphat as his successor; and that the idol worshipers who escaped the sword of Hazael would be slain by Jehu and Elisha.

Ben-hadad, king of Syria, demonstrated disrespect for God and attacked Israel twice. Ben-hadad was defeated both times and was appointed by God to utter destruction. Ahab made a covenant with Ben-hadad and let him live whereupon a prophet sent by God told Ahab his life would go for Ben-hadad's life and the people of Israel for the Syrians.

Ahab coveted a vineyard next to his palace owned by Naboth, a Jezreelite. Naboth refused to sell to Ahab and Jezebel arranged to have Naboth falsely accused and stoned to death. God sent Elijah to tell Ahab that dogs would eat Jezebel and lick up his blood also. Ahab repented, fasted and put on sackcloth after which God temporarily extended Ahab's life. Following three years of peace, Ahab enlisted the assistance of Jehoshaphat, king of Judah, and fought with Syria to take back the city of Gilead.

A random arrow struck Ahab's back and his blood pooled in his chariot. Israel withdrew from the battle and Ahab's chariot was driven back to Samaria where he died. Ahab's chariot was washed out at the pool of Samaria and the dogs licked up Ahab's blood. Jehoram, Jehoshaphat's son, sat as king of Judah and Ahaziah, Ahab's son ruled in Israel.

The Second Book of Kings covers a period of 308

years including the end of Elijah's ministry, Elisha's ministry and death, the carrying away of Israel into Assyria, and the captivity of Judah by Babylon.

Ahaziah, king of Israel, sent messengers to inquire of Baal-zebub, god of Ekron, whether he would recover from an injury and sickness. The messengers were met by Elijah who told them Ahaziah would surely die because he inquired of Baal-zebub rather than God. Ahaziah sent a captain with fifty men to apprehend Elijah and they were consumed with fire from God. Another captain with fifty men suffered the same fate. A third captain with his fifty fell on his knees before Elijah and pleaded with him to spare his life and the lives of his fifty men. Elijah appeared before Ahaziah and told him he would surely die because of his inquiry of Baal-zebub. Ahaziah died and Jehoram took his throne.

Elijah was translated into heaven and Elisha took over his ministry. Elisha performed many miracles including raising a young man from the dead. He was mocked by a group of children and forty-two of them were thereafter ripped to pieces by two female bears. Through Elisha, God healed Naaman, leader of the Syrian military forces, thereby displaying God's mercy to Gentiles. Syria besieged Samaria, whereupon the starving Israelites resorted to eating their own children thus fulfilling the prophecies by Moses more than six centuries earlier concerning future Israeli idolatry. Elisha prophesied that God would end the Syrian siege.

The Syrians heard sounds from God which

convinced them that Egypt and the Hittites were joining with Israel against them whereupon the Syrians fled leaving behind a huge supply of food, water, gold, silver and clothing. The monarchy in Israel continued for another one and a half centuries.

All of the monarchs who succeeded to the throne in the northern kingdom, Israel, continued to trespass against God in spite of continuous warnings by Hebrew prophets. Consequently, as foretold by Moses during the fifteenth century BC, the northern kingdom was taken into captivity by Assyria around 730 BC (now referred to as "the ten lost tribes of Israel").

The southern kingdom, Judah, lasted another hundred and forty-two years after the captivity of Israel. Although none of the monarchs reigning in Israel had followed after God, most of Judah's monarchs did (specifically Asa, Jehoshaphat, Joash, Amaziah, Uzziah, Jotham, Hezekiah, and Josiah). During the reign of Hezekiah, the Assyrians attempted to also take Judah captive but withdrew after the angel of the Lord killed one hundred and eighty-five thousand Assyrian men of war in a single night.

Josiah was the last monarch to follow after God prior to Judah being carried away captive into Babylon pursuant to the reign of Jehoahaz, Jehoiakim, Jehoiachin, and Zedekiah (wherein each monarch practiced evil before God). The Babylonians burned Jerusalem, broke down the city walls, pilfered and burned the temple, burned all the great houses, killed the balance of Judah's warriors, and carried the most skilled and educated citizens of Judah into Babylon.

King Nebuchadnezzar of Babylon appointed Gedaliah as governor over Palestine and the Jews who were allowed to remain there. Thereafter, the Jews revolted against Gedaliah and fled into Egypt. Jehoiachin (the last king of Judah) was released from prison in Babylon after thirty-seven years and fed at the royal table by Evil-merodach, successor to Nebuchadnezzar.

The First Book of Chronicles contains the genealogy of Israel from Adam to Solomon and provides some additional details covering the history of Israel under King Saul and King David.

The Second Book of Chronicles provides an additional history of King Solomon's reign; the split between the northern kingdom (Israel) and the southern kingdom (Judah) during the reign of Rehoboam, Solomon's heir; and the history of the Hebrew monarchies in Israel and Judah including the Assyrian captivity of Israel and the Babylonian captivity of Judah. Second Chronicles ends with a reference to the decree by the Persian king, Cyrus, allowing the remnant of Judah to return to Jerusalem to rebuild the temple.

The book of Ezra begins with the decree by Cyrus referred to in Second Chronicles (the Persians had overthrown the Babylonians during the Babylonian captivity of Judah) and covers the returning remnant of Judah to Jerusalem. The journey back to Israel's capital city (Jerusalem) by permission of the Persian kings

Cyrus and Darius is described as three separate expeditions over a period of ninety-two years.

The Persians, at times, were very tolerant of their Jewish population and allowed the Jews to both multiply and prosper. The first expedition led by Zerubbabel, the son of Shealtiel, and Jeshua, the son of Jozadak, included less than five thousand persons along with their servants and singers. The rest of the Jews inside the Persian Empire in 536 BC preferred to stay and enjoy peace and prosperity rather than trek back to a burned and barren homeland to worship the God of Abraham, Isaac, and Jacob. Cyrus returned to Zerubbabel and Jeshua all the remaining treasures and vessels of worship which the Babylonians had taken from the temple in Jerusalem.

The genealogy covering the followers of Zerubbabel and Jeshua is listed along with their horses, mules, camels, and asses. Seven months after departure from Persia, the first returning congregation was settled in Israeli cities; the altar was rebuilt in Jerusalem and sacrifices of thanksgiving offered thereon. Within the following year, the temple foundation was laid. The people inhabiting Israel's homeland tried to hinder the rebuilding of the temple by seeking to sabotage the work, withholding necessary supplies, and writing accusatory letters alleging Jewish treason directed to the Persian kings, Artaxerxes and Darius. The restoration work being done under the direction of Zerubbabel and Jeshua was temporarily halted and then allowed to continue upon discovery of the decree issued by Cyrus. King Darius commanded that the Jews be given all necessary supplies and that the work be not hindered. The prophets Haggai and Zechariah ministered to the Jews in Israel during this restoration period. During the sixth year of the reign of Darius, the temple restoration was completed and the Passover celebrated.

In 458 BC, Ezra, a priest, led a second expedition from Persia back to Jerusalem to reestablish the Jewish priesthood supported by the Levites. Under Ezra's priestly leadership, many of the Jews who returned from Persia forsook their heathen wives and those born of them in order to comply with the prohibition against idol worshiping wives ordained by God and commanded by Moses.

Chapter nine

The Book of Nehemiah begins with the third expedition from Persia to Jerusalem in 444 BC as organized by Nehemiah (cup-bearer to King Artaxerxes) to rebuild the city walls. King Artaxerxes approved Nehemiah's expedition and provided for necessary supplies. Two leaders of the Gentiles residing in Palestine, Sanballat and Tobiah, raised up opposition to the restoration of the city of Jerusalem and its defensive walls. The genealogy of the Jews performing the restoration work led by Nehemiah is recorded. Faced with ridicule, threats and armed opposition, Nehemiah and his workmen held weapons in one hand and worked with the other hand thereby rebuilding the walls of Jerusalem in spite of the intense opposition. The total number of Jews inside Israel pursuant to the three expeditions from Persia numbered approximately fifty thousand.

Under Nehemiah's and Ezra's leadership, the law of God was read and explained and the Feast of Tabernacles was celebrated followed by a solemn assembly. The Israelites fasted and repented of their evil deeds. The Levites and priests prayed to God and confessed the sins of the people while reciting the blessings and curses pronounced by Moses. The priests, Levites and elders among the people wrote and signed a covenant before God to separate themselves from the Gentiles residing in the land promised to Abraham; to walk in God's laws; to obey God's commandments, statutes and judgments; to honor the Sabbath days; to refrain from intermarriage; and to support the priests, Levites, and temple worship according to the writings of Moses.

The genealogy is recorded of the Jews who would dwell in Jerusalem (10% willingly or chosen by lot) and those who would dwell in Israel's cities. A separate genealogy is recorded pertaining to the priests and Levites who returned with Zerrubbabel. The rebuilt city walls were dedicated with sacrifices, joy, and thanksgiving. The temple was cleansed and the law of separation read to the people including the banning of Moabites and Ammonites forever from the congregation because they hired Balaam to curse Israel rather than meet them with bread and water.

After returning to Persia to serve King Artaxerxes as promised, Nehemiah again obtained leave to visit Jerusalem and found that the people were violating the Sabbath days; were not supporting the Levites and singers; were intermarrying with the heathen; and had given Tobiah (who opposed the restoration work) a chamber in the temple courts. Nehemiah evicted Tobiah and led a reform movement to restore proper tithing, to ban merchandizing during the Sabbath, and to halt intermarriage with heathen neighbors.

The Book of Ester is both a love story and an

example of God's protection of the remnant of Judah even during captivity for gross disobedience. Approximately 519 BC, the Persian king, Ahasuerus, decided to replace Queen Vasthi because she refused to obey the king's commandment when summoned to display her beauty for royal guests during a time of drinking and feasting. After consulting with his seven princes concerning a wife's proper obedience to her husband, Ahasuerus severed Vashti's role as queen and chose a new queen from among the fair young virgins within his kingdom. The new queen, Ester, was a Jew and daughter of the uncle of Mordecai, a Benjamite. Mordecai, being among the captive remnant of Judah, took Ester as his daughter after the death of her parents and kept watch around the court of the women's house to keep track of her. The king did not know Ester was Jewish nor her relationship to Mordecai until the Jews were threatened with genocide.

Mordecai discovered a plot to kill the king and warned Ester. Ester certified the plot to the king in Mordecai's name. Haman, an Agagite, was promoted to high honor by King Ahasuerus and the people bowed down to him except Mordecai. Haman was insanely angry and sought to destroy Mordecai and his people, the Jews, by order of Ahasuerus. During a sleepless night, records and chronicles were read to Ahasuerus including the plot to kill him reported by Mordecai. Ashsuerus ordered Haman to bestow great honor upon Mordecai. Queen Ester then revealed to the king her relationship to Mordecai and Haman's role in convincing the king to order the extermination of Mordecai and his people. The order had already gone forth and could not be reversed under Persian law.

Ahasuerus loved Ester above all the women in his harem and he issued a decree allowing the Jews to defend themselves. The king also ordered that Haman and his sons be hanged on the gallows Haman had built to execute Mordecai and that Mordecai be elevated to a position next to King Ahasuerus. In defending themselves, the Jews achieved a great victory over their enemies which is remembered and celebrated during the Feast of Purim.

The Book of Job addresses the question: why do the righteous suffer? Job lived in Mesopotamia in an area known as "the land of Uz" around 1520 BC. He exhibited a profound reverence for God and offered sacrifices and prayers daily for his sons and daughters. Job was exceedingly wealthy and donated willingly to the poor and needy. He was widely known, honored and respected. However, he was somewhat self-righteous and feared the loss of his status. Satan (the fallen angel and adversary of God) accused Job before God claiming that Job only respected God because of blessings and protection whereupon God allowed Satan to test Job by destroying everything Job possessed except his life.

Satan attacked Job's wealth, offspring, reputation and health. With his riches gone, his children dead and his body covered over with sore boils, Job sat down among ashes and scraped his boils with broken pottery. His wife reviled him and suggested he curse God and die. Job replied that he had received both good and evil and would trust God with his very life.

Job's friends came to mourn with him and each one offered lengthy philosophical monologues wherein Job was assumed to have committed some grievous sin which brought about his great suffering. When Job maintained his innocence, his comforters charged him with hypocrisy and deception. In his self-righteousness, Job cursed his birth and requested that God explain why he was suffering without cause.

God spoke out of a whirlwind asking Job to explain various aspects of creation and divine order. Job then confessed his error in questioning God. Thereafter, God instructed Job's accusing friends to offer atoning sacrifices after which Job would pray for them lest they be dealt with according to their folly. Job's wealth and status were restored. He fathered seven more sons and three daughters while enjoying a long and blessed life spanning four generations.

The Book of Psalms is more than just the praise and song book of devout Jews. Among the one hundred and fifty psalms are praises, prayers, thanksgiving, historical accounts and prophetic utterances including numerous prophecies concerning humanity's Messiah (Jesus Christ). King David is the best recognized author of Psalms although the contributions of others are acknowledged.

The Book of Proverbs is a collection of wise sayings, instructions, warnings, and divine references researched and organized by King Solomon. The primary concepts are avoidance of fools, respecting wise persons, and recognition of God.

The Book of Ecclesiastes is attributed to King Solomon and reflects his accumulated knowledge concerning human mortality, the illusion of wealth, the futility of striving after that which must be left to others, and the inevitable judgment by God. As an old man faced with the reality of unavoidable death, Solomon declares his great wealth to be worthless and his life spent in vanity "chasing after the wind."

The book called "The Song of Solomon" expresses the love and sexual attraction between husband and wife as well as the sorrow of separation and the joy of reunion. It is explicit in nature without being crude or offensive.

The balance of the Old Testament narratives is composed of the books of the major and minor prophets. There were four major prophets and twelve minor prophets. Two separate books were written by the prophet Jeremiah. The distinction between major and minor is the time period covered (past, present and future), and the sheer volume of prophetic messages. Isaiah, Jeremiah, Ezekiel and Daniel are the four major prophets.

Isaiah prophesied during the reigns of Azariah (Uzziah), Jotham, Ahaz, and Hezekiah, kings over

Judah. Isaiah's prophetic declarations are addressed primarily to Israel (the ten tribes taken captive by Assyria) and to Judah (the tribes of Benjamin and Judah). During Isaiah's ministry, Israel was already in captivity and the Babylonian captivity of Judah was approximately a century into the future.

The Book of Isaiah is composed of sixty-six chapters and two reoccurring themes both scattered and mixed together throughout Isaiah's sixty-six prophetic utterances spanning the entire scope of human existence on Earth. Isaiah uses past and current events to underscore prophecies coming to pass in the near future as well as prophecies to be fulfilled during coming centuries

Within a single chapter, past and current events plus short and long term prophecies are often blended together to shape a prophetic picture describing divine retribution for apostasy and idol worship, repentance, divine grace, forgiveness, restoration of innocence, and the judgment of nations which have oppressed Israel. Nonetheless, each individual chapter emphasizes one of Isaiah's two basic themes.

Chapters 1, 3, 5-10, 13-23, 36-39, and 46-47 focus upon the future judgment of Judah by God for disobedience, idolatry, greed and violence with appropriate references to the judgment of all nations, the reign of the "Holy One" (also called Wonderful, Counselor, The Mighty God, Everlasting Father, Prince of Peace, My Servant, The Branch, Son of David, The

Prince, and Anointed One) upon Earth, and the eternal kingdom of God. Chapters 2, 4, 11-12, 24-35, 40-45, 48-55, and 60-65 emphasize the coming Holy One (initially as a sacrificial lamb and subsequently as ruler over humanity), the future restoration of Israel as a nation and the Holy One's reign with occasional references to Israeli apostasy, idol worship, divine retribution and God's judgment upon Gentile nations. Chapters 56-59 reflect the patience, long-suffering, grace, tender mercy, and righteous judgments of God along with ethical instructions to avoid divine chastisement.

Chapter 14 includes a summary of Lucifer's (Satan's) fall from heaven and his ultimate demise. Chapter 24, verses 17-23 describe God's final judgment upon all nations and the dissolution of planet Earth. Chapters 42, 50, 52, 55, 61 and 63 contain the most specific prophecies concerning the Holy One except for chapter 53 which is totally dedicated to the Holy One as God's sacrificial lamb. There are numerous and very specific prophecies by Isaiah covering various events to occur in the distant future including the Holy One who first appeared more than seven centuries after Isaiah's time. For example, in chapter 45, Isaiah refers to the Persian king, Cyrus, by name more than a century before Cyrus' birth. The repetitive prophecy throughout Isaiah's writings that Israel, after a long dispersion among Gentile nations, would be united again as a nation (within the land promised to Abraham) was written down over twenty-five centuries before the nation of Israel was actually reborn "in a day" in 1948 A.D.

Jeremiah prophesied to Judah approximately sixty years after the death of Isaiah. The primary prophecies by Jeremiah relate to the time period between the 13th year of Josiah's reign over Judah and the Babylonian captivity of Judah with occasional references to past, present and future events (from the beginning of the universe to the Holy One's reign over Earth). Each of the fifty-two chapters comprising Jeremiah's prophecies are composed of one or more narratives relating to specific messages from God to Judah interspersed with warnings and promises directed to all humanity. When comparing the emotional aspect of Jeremiah's writings to Isaiah's, it can be summarized by saying that Isaiah's messages brimmed with fire and that Jeremiah's dripped with tears.

In chapter 1, God tells Jeremiah that before he was conceived and formed in the womb he had already been set apart by God and ordained as a prophet unto the nations. God further tells Jeremiah that Judah will be chastised by kingdoms situated north of Jerusalem. Chapters 1-22, 33-36, and 45 are concerned chiefly with Judah's apostasy, idolatry, greed, and repeated rebellion against divine guidance. Through Jeremiah, God warns Judah many times that severe chastisement is coming but also promises grace and mercy pursuant to sincere repentance.

Chapters 23 and 24 focus on the future restoration of Israel as a nation and the future reign of the Holy One over Earth with references to Judah's rebellion and coming chastisement. Chapters 25-28 continue the warnings pertaining to judgment of Judah's evil works and the imminent Babylonian captivity predicted by Jeremiah to span seventy years. Chapters 37-38 describe how Jeremiah's warnings are ignored and he is imprisoned in the king's court, removed to a deep hole filled with miry clay, and later returned to the court prison.

Chapters 29-32 record the initial Babylonian attack on Jerusalem by the armies of King Nebuchadnezzar, the transporting of the first Jewish captives from Jerusalem to Babylon, and Jeremiah's prophecies to the captives concerning the future return of a remnant to Jerusalem and the future restoration of Israel as a nation. Chapter 39 covers the major Babylonian attack upon Judah and the carrying away into Babylon of the balance of Judah's inhabitants other than the poor, unskilled and handicapped. Judah' king Zedekiah, was bound in chains, his eyes were punched out, and his sons killed along with most of the princes of Judah and their fighting men.

Jerusalem was sacked and burned and the walls battered down. Jeremiah was released from prison and allowed to return to his home. Chapters 40 and 41 record the appointment of Gedaliah, son of Ahikam, by Nebuchadnezzar as governor over the cities of Judah;

the secret rebellion against Gedaliah by Ishmael, son of Nethaniah (of the royal seed of Judah); and the slaughter of those loyal to Gedaliah working in the fields and vineyards.

Chapter 42 contains Jeremiah's prophecy that surviving Jews who flee into Egypt in fear of Babylonian retribution will be consumed by the sword, famine and pestilence; and that Jews remaining within the cities of Judah will receive divine protection. Chapters 43 and 44 detail Jeremiah's prophecies regarding the sorrow and death of those Jews fleeing from Judah into Egypt and the coming overthrow of the Egyptian Pharaoh.

Chapters 46-50 record Jeremiah's prophecies pertaining to God's judgment of Egypt, Philistia, Tyre, the Moabites, Ammonites, Edom, Damascus, Elam, and Babylon (Gentile powers that have oppressed the seed of Abraham). Through Jeremiah, God declares that these Gentile powers will be militarily defeated, slaughtered, and plundered. Chapter 51 gives a further detailed description of God's future judgment upon Babylon and the reasons for such judgment. Babylon is to be totally destroyed and not to rise again.

Chapter 52 retraces the overthrow and captivity of Judah during the reign of Zedekiah, king of Judah including the plundering and destruction of the Hebrew temple. The number of Jews transported to Babylon is stated as forty-six hundred; and Jehoiachin, the puppet king over Judah who rebelled against Babylon, is released thirty-seven years after his imprisonment and fed at the Babylonian king's table.

The Lamentations of Jeremiah consist of five separate expressions of grief by Jeremiah pertaining to the evil deeds by Judah and the ensuing chastisement by God wherein Judah suffers defeat, humiliation, horror and captivity during the Babylonian onslaught.

The prophet, Ezekiel, was among the Jews taken captive into Babylon and his prophecies are divided into forty-eight messages directed to all the seed of Abraham (chapters1-48). Ezekiel prophesied to Jews during the Babylonian captivity with references to all nations and to the past, present and future relation-ship between God and humanity. Like Isaiah, Ezekiel also addresses the adversary of God (Lucifer, the fallen angel, also called "Satan").

Chapter 1 relates Ezekiel's vision of the appearance and glory of God. Chapters 2 and 3 contain Ezekiel's commission from God to be a prophet. Ezekiel is also assigned by God to be a "watchman unto Israel" and is instructed to speak unto the people only when God puts words into his mouth. Ezekiel is commanded to warn the wicked on behalf of God regardless of whether those warned choose to listen and repent or to stop their ears.

In chapters 4-24 and 33, Ezekiel reminds his own generation as well as those born during the Babylonian captivity concerning the grievous transgressions committed by Jews against God and against other humans for which Jews have been and will be severely chastised. Ezekiel also reiterates God's promises that Gentile powers will likewise endure God's mercy or wrath according their deeds; that the nation of Israel will be restored to the status and glory enjoyed during the reign of King David; and that Jerusalem will be the center of worship during the Holy One's reign over Earth.

Chapters 25-32 contain Ezekiel's prophecies detailing the outpouring of God's wrath upon the Ammonites, Moabites, Edomites, Philistines, Tyre, Zidon, and Egypt. In chapter 28, Ezekiel addresses Satan, himself, the spiritual power behind the king of Tyre, and also refers to the future regathering of Israel under God's protection.

Chapters 34-37 include an additional warning to the Edomites dwelling in Mount Seir but are primarily descriptive of Israel's exodus from among Gentile nations and the majestic status to be enjoyed within the Holy One's kingdom.

In chapters 38 and 39, Ezekiel prophesies that a great battle involving many nations will be waged within the land promised by God to Abraham and to his seed, and that God will protect Israel by an overwhelming slaughter among the invaders wherein only one sixth of the combined armies moving against Israel will survive.

The surviving one sixth will flee leaving behind so many corpses that mass burials by the Israelis will consume seven months while enduring a stench   that stops the noses of inhabitants and travelers throughout the region. Ezekiel further prophesied that the abandoned weapons of war will be burned as fuel for seven years; and that after the mass burials, individual bones will be searched out and removed to decontaminate the land.

The central theme of chapters 40-48 is detailed instructions for post-captivity restoration of the Jewish temple and division of land among the tribes of Israel with references to the future temple as it will exist during the reign of the Holy One.

Daniel was among the princes of Judah and other educated Jews taken captive and transported to Babylon. The Book of Daniel is divided into twelve chapters which record a number of visions experienced by Daniel and interpreted by angels. Some brief personal history is narrated along with Daniel's interpretations of the dreams of Nebuchadnezzar (king of Babylon) but supernatural visions and angelic explanations connected therewith are the main focus.

Chapter 1 confirms that Daniel and three other royal captives were favored by the eunuch in charge of their care, diet and orientation regarding palace service and were allowed (following a test period lasting ten days) to eat pulse and drink water rather than violate Jewish dietary restrictions. Daniel, Hananiah, Mishael, and Azariah continued to appear better nourished than those who ate of the king's portion.

In chapter 2, Daniel interprets Nebuchadnezzar's dream wherein he saw a great image with a head of gold, silver arms and breasts, brass belly and thighs, iron legs, and feet of iron mixed with clay. The image visualized in the dream was smashed into dust by a stone not cut by man.

The wind carried the dust away and the stone became a mountain which filled the entire world. Nebuchadnezzar was disturbed by the dream but could not remember details. He commanded his wise men to both describe and interpret the dream, and they told him it was not possible whereupon Nebuchadnezzar ordered all of them executed. Being a wise man in the king's court, Daniel prayed to God for help in describing and interpreting Nebuchadnezzar's dream.

God revealed the matter to Daniel after which Daniel describes and interprets the dream and explains to Nebuchadnezzar that his kingdom is the head of gold --- that the silver kingdom will follow him being inferior but stronger --- that the brass kingdom will thereafter arise being even more inferior in quality but more powerful --- that a fourth world kingdom strong as iron will come to power which becomes divided thereby displaying a mixture of strength and weakness represented by the feet composed of iron and clay; that this kingdom will have multiple rulers who do not agree just like iron does not blend with clay ---- that God will establish a kingdom which shall subdue all earthly powers and shall endure forever. Nebuchadnezzar, after hearing Daniel's explanation, promoted him to ruler over the province of Babylon and appointed Hananiah (Shadrach), Mishael (Meshach) and Azaiah (Abed-nego) over the affairs of Babylon.

Chapter 3 describes events connected with a golden image set up by Nebuchadnezzar and his command that at the sound of special music all his subjects fall down and worship the image or immediately be cast alive into a hot furnace.

Shadrach, Meshach, and Abed-nego refused to worship the king's golden idol whereupon Nebuchadnezzar summoned them and gave them a second chance to worship the image or be cast into the fiery furnace. The three Hebrew princes replied that God is able to deliver them from the furnace; and, in any event, they would not worship the king's idol. Filled with rage, Nebuchadnezzar ordered the furnace to be heated seven times hotter and commanded members of his army to bind the three men and pitch them into the furnace. A burst of flames from the open furnace killed those warriors executing Nebuchadnezzar's urgent orders. To the king's astonishment, his intended victims walked freely among the flames joined by a fourth entity appearing celestial in form.

At Nebuchadnezzar's command, Shadrach, Meshach, and Abed-nego walked out of the furnace free from any injury and without any scent of fire upon their clothing. Thereafter, the king commanded that those speaking against the God of Shadrach, Meshach, and

Abed-nego be cut in pieces and their property to be converted into a dunghill.

In chapter 4, Daniel interprets another dream for Nebuchadnezzar wherein he saw a great and fruitful tree which provided food for all, shelter for animals and lodging for birds. A "watcher and a holy one" from heaven commanded to cut down the tree but to leave the stump; to give the dreamer the heart of a beast dwelling among wild animals; and to be wet with dew until such time that recognition be forthcoming that God rules over all kingdoms and appoints whomever He chooses to be kings notwithstanding character.

Daniel tells the king that he, Nebuchadnezzar, is the great and fruitful tree; that he will be driven from among his people and live among beasts of the field; that he will eat grass like an ox and be wet with dew until such time he understands that God is the supreme ruler in both heaven and earth and appoints over kingdoms as He sees fit --- after which he will return to his throne.

One year later, Nebuchadnezzar bragged about his personal accomplishments causing his dream to be fulfilled. He became insane and lived like a wild animal. He was drenched with dew and ate grass for food. His hair looked like feathers and his nails resembled the claws of a bird. When his regained his sanity, he honored and praised God and was able to return to his throne.

Chapter 5 covers the last days of the reign of

Belshazzar, son of Nebuchadnezzar. During a lavish feast, Belshazzar desecrated the sacred vessels his father had removed from the Jewish temple in Jerusalem. He and his guests drank wine from the temple vessels while praising their idols. Fingers of a man's hand appeared and wrote a message upon the palace wall in the sight of Belshazzar and his guests -- MENE, MENE, TEKEL, UPHARSIN. The Babylonian astrologers, Chaldeans, and soothsayers were brought in to decipher the message. When such wise men could not interpret the writing upon the wall (in spite of a huge reward promised to anyone who could), the queen suggested that Daniel be summoned.

Daniel reminded Belshazzar of the lesson God had taught his father concerning human vanity. Daniel pointed out that Belshazzar thereby knew God was able to abase the proud but had decided to praise idols while desecrating vessels hallowed by God. Thereafter, Daniel interpreted the writing and informed Belshazzar that he had been weighed in the balances and found to be wanting; that God had numbered his kingdom and finished it; and that his kingdom would be divided between the Medes and the Persians.

Belshazzar then commanded that Daniel be clothed with scarlet and a gold chain hung upon his neck and that he be promoted to third ruler in Belshazzar's kingdom. The same night, Belshazzar was killed and Darius, the Mede, being sixty-two years old, took over Belshazzar's throne.

Chapter 6 documents the events connected with appointments by King Darius of one hundred and twenty princes to rule over separate provinces within his kingdom. Darius further appointed three presidents to oversee the princes. Daniel was the most favored and first president such that Darius contemplated promoting Daniel to rule directly beneath the king. The princes and other presidents were jealous of Daniel and conspired to accuse him of wrongdoing before Darius. They persuaded Darius to sign a decree that no person in his kingdom be allowed to petition any god or man other than the king for thirty days; and that any person doing so be cast into the den of lions.

Thus, when Daniel continued to pray to God, the conspirators informed Darius and demanded that Daniel be thrown to the lions in accordance with the king's decree which could not be altered under the law of the Medes and Persians. Darius could not find a way to circumvent his decree and finally ordered that Daniel be cast into the den of lions. Darius told Daniel that the God Daniel served would deliver him. The king then spent the night in sorrow and fasting.

The next morning, Darius hurried to the den of lions and found Daniel alive and unharmed. He commanded that Daniel be taken out of the den and that his accusers and their families be fed to the lions. Darius also published a decree proclaiming the God of Daniel to be the Living God and that all his subjects fear and tremble before such a mighty and gracious God.

Chapter 7 describes the vision Daniel saw during the first year of Belshazzar's reign over Babylon. In the vision, four diverse beasts were seen arising from the great sea of humanity. The first beast looked like a lion with wings like an eagle. The wings were plucked and the creature was lifted up and its appearance transformed to resemble a man. The second beast appeared as a bear with three ribs between its teeth. The third beast was similar to a leopard with four heads and four wings on its back.

The fourth beast possessed great strength appearing grotesque and frightening with massive iron teeth and ten horns. It attacked and devoured among the other beasts and stomped the fragments. A little horn having eyes like a man and a bragging mouth came up among the ten horns and destroyed three of them. Thereafter, the "Ancient of Days" having snow white garments and hair like wool sat upon a flaming throne and fire issued from Him.

Millions ministered unto Him and millions stood before Him as His judgment commenced and the books were opened. The fourth beast was slain and his body cast into a flaming fire. The other three beasts were stripped of power but their lives were prolonged for an appointed time. Then, the "Son of Man" riding upon the clouds of Heaven came before the Ancient of Days and was given an eternal kingdom and dominion over all the earth.

Daniel was grieved and troubled and asked one

near the Son of Man to explain the vision. The one standing by revealed to Daniel that the four beasts represent four kings who will come to power but will be conquered by the saints of God, and the saints will possess the kingdoms forever. Daniel desired more information concerning the fourth beast and was informed that the kingdom of the fourth beast would be diverse and powerful enough to devour, tread down, and divide the whole earth.

The ten horns represent ten kings reigning over ten divisions of earth within the fourth kingdom. The little horn coming up among the ten horns will assume authority and conquer three of the ten kings while speaking against God and exhausting the saints in an attempt to change times and laws during his limited reign. God will take the little horn's kingdom and give all kingdoms to His saints whose dominion will be everlasting.

Chapter 8 contains Daniel's vision during the third year of King Belshazzar wherein Daniel saw by the River Ulai a ram with two horns and perceived that the higher of the two horns had come up last. The ram pushed north, south and west conquering as he went and became great. A male goat with one large horn attacked the ram, broke his two horns and stomped upon him.

The goat became stronger until its large horn was broken and replaced by four lesser horns. A little horn sprang up from one of the lesser horns and became exceedingly powerful pushing southward and eastward toward the city of Jerusalem -- even approaching the host of heaven and casting down some of the host along with stars to be trampled underfoot. The daily sacrifice was taken away, the temple defiled, and truth cast away while his own host expanded and prospered. Daniel heard one saint ask another saint how long the abominable desolation would continue and the answer given was twenty-three hundred days after which the temple would be cleansed.

     While Daniel pondered the vision and what it revealed, one appearing as a man stood before him and he heard a voice from the river directing someone named Gabriel to explain the vision. Daniel was afraid and fell upon his face as Gabriel approached him, set him upright, and interpreted the vision. The angel explained that the ram with two horns represents the kings of Media and Persia, and that the male goat with the notable horn represents the king of Grecia --- that four kings will succeed him but be unable to match his greatness; that toward the end of these four kingdoms, a fierce king full of wisdom and who understand deep mysteries will arise and conquer through the power of another entity; that this fierce king will prosper and destroy even the mighty and holy people while worshiping himself, and through peace destroy multi-- tudes; that he shall defy the Prince of princes thereby being totally vanquished.

     Gabriel further told Daniel to not publish the vision --- that it contained truth but the events disclosed were many days into the future. Daniel was astonished by the vision. He fainted and was sick for days after which he went about the king's business.

Chapter 9 records Daniel's prayer in which he confesses the sins for which the Jews were taken captive and seeks God's forgiveness on behalf of the people. While serving within the palace during the first year of the reign of Darius, King of Media-Persia, Daniel studied the prophecies of Jeremiah and concluded that the captivity of Judah would span seventy years.

During a time of prayer and supplication, Gabriel again appeared before Daniel and told him that he was greatly beloved and that his prayer had been heard. Gabriel explained to Daniel that seventy weeks (meaning 7 times 70 years totaling 490 years) were set aside to finish Judah's chastisement, to make an end of sins, to make reconciliation for iniquity, to bring in everlasting righteousness, to seal up the vision and prophecy, and to anoint "the most Holy."

Gabriel further disclosed that from the command-ment to restore and build Jerusalem to the coming of Messiah the Prince would be sixty-nine weeks after which Messiah would be cut off but not for himself; that the street and wall would be rebuilt during difficult times; that the prince to come will destroy the city and sanctuary again --- that he will seek to destroy with a flood of persecution and unto the end of the war there will much desolation; and that the destroying prince will make a covenant for one week but will breach it halfway through the week causing the sacrifices and oblations to cease until his power is taken away.

Chapter 10 and 11 record Daniel's vision of God's glory including interaction between angels, acknowledgment of Daniel's faithfulness, and God's revelations to Daniel concerning the future military engagements between Media-Persia and Grecia; the breaking up of the ensuing Greek Empire; subsequent wars involving Egypt and Syria; and the desecration of the temple in Jerusalem by a Syrian invader (Antiochus Epiphanes).

Chapter 11 concludes with God's revelation to Daniel pertaining to the "time of the end" and describing a kingdom which will arise and be ruled by an incredibly wicked king who will exalt and magnify himself above every god and blaspheme the true God.

He will be allowed to prosper until an appointed time while disregarding the god of his fathers and any desire for women, but rather will honor the god of forces with gold, silver, and precious stones within strongholds from which his forces will destroy at will, rule over many, and divide the land according to his purpose. He will establish his place within the temple in Jerusalem to be worshiped. At the appointed time, he shall be dethroned and cast down.

Chapter 12 continues God's revelation to Daniel covering the time of the end wherein there will be a period of unprecedented persecution of the Jews. Michael, Israel's heavenly Prince, will protect a remnant of Jews whose names have been recorded in the Book of Life.

Daniel also receives a brief preview of the resurrection and is commanded to seal up the words and the book until the "time of the end" during which knowledge and travel will be increased. Daniel's writings end with a vision of two heavenly figures. One asks the other to reveal how much time will pass before the end of the wonders revealed and the answer given is time, times and a half during which the power of the holy people will be scattered and the wonders will be finished.

Daniel did not understand the answer and was informed that the words are closed and sealed until the end of time; that many will be purified; that the wicked will continue on and not understand although the wise will perceive the truth; that from the time the daily sacrifice shall be taken away and the abomination that causes desolation set up shall be twelve hundred and ninety days; and that those who endure through the thirteen hundred and thirty-five days will be blessed. Finally, Daniel is instructed to go on his way and rest, and that he will stand among the resurrected at the end of time.

Chapter ten

The twelve minor prophets are Hosea, Joel, Amos, Obadiah, Jonah, Micah, Nahum, Habakkuk, Zephaniah, Haggai, Zechariah, and Malachi. Of these only Haggai, Zechariah, and Malachi delivered their prophecies after the remnant of Judah returned from Babylon to the land promised by God to Abraham and to his seed after him.

Hosea prophesied during the same time period as Amos in Israel, and Isaiah and Micah in Judah. Hosea's messages are directed to both Israel and Judah, and to the reunited nation of Israel during the latter days. Chapter 1 covers God's instructions to Hosea to take a whore as his wife to better appreciate the whorish nature of Israel.

Hosea's two children, Jezreel and Lo-ammi, by Gomer (the whore taken to wife) are pre-named by God to signify reprisal upon the house of Jehu for the mass murder of King Ahab's descendants, and God's mercy to be extended to Judah while Israel is taken captive.

God also gives Hosea a glimpse of the future of reunited Israel under divine protection. Hosea's messages and prophetic pronouncements recorded in chapters 2-14 intermingle three major themes --- condemnation of Israel's and Judah's past and present apostasy, idolatry and depravity --- the coming chastisement by God involving affliction, oppression and dispersion among the nations --- the future blessing and restoration of Israel.

Joel was a contemporary of Elisha during the reign of King Joash over Judah, and Joel warned the people concerning future chastisement by God for wickedness and perversion. Joel prophesied the regathering and blessings to be enjoyed by Israel and the destruction of Gentile powers during the "day of the Lord."

Chapter I describes plagues and drought pursuant to disobedience and idolatry. Chapter 2 foretells the gathering of nations against Israel during the latter days; the outpouring of God's spirit upon his people; and the destruction wrought by God upon armies surrounding Jerusalem. Chapter 3 prophesies God's judgment upon the nations gathered together for war in the valley of Jehoshaphat along with references to God's mercies extended to reunited Israel and God's judgment upon Israel's oppressors.

Amos prophesied during the reign of Jeroboam II over Israel (the northern kingdom) and directs his prophetic warnings to both Israel and Judah (the southern kingdom). Amos also foresees God's hot wrath being directed toward specific Gentile nations within the Middle East.

Chapters 1 and 2 predict divine judgment upon Damascus, Gaza, Edom, Tyrus, Ashdod, Ashkelon, Ekron, the Ammonites, and the Moabites, along with Judah and Israel for perverse wickedness. Chapters 3-8 focus upon specific evils for which Israel and Judah will be punished and their refusal to confess such sins and to repent. Chapter 9 foretells the dispersion of Israel among the Gentile nations; the regathering of Israel during the latter days; and God's future blessings upon restored Israel.

Obadiah prophesied during the reign of King Ahaziah over Judah and he predicted the future destruction of Edom because the Edomites (descendants of Esau) stood by and rejoiced when Judah was oppressed, attacked and looted; and because the Edomites assisted in the looting and stood by the crossroad to cut down those fleeing from Judah. Obadiah prophesies that Edom will be completely destroyed during "the day of the Lord" and that the house of Jacob will be exalted over the Gentiles.

Jonah prophesied to the city of Nineveh during the reign of King Joash over Judah. God instructed Jonah to travel to Nineveh and warn the inhabitants of imminent destruction because of their great wickedness. Jonah did not relish the mission of prophesying to a Gentile city, especially if the warning would result in the city repenting and avoiding the prophesied judgment. Jonah took refuge in a ship sailing from Joppa whereupon God sent a fierce storm that threatened to sink the vessel. When all aboard trembled and prayed to their gods, Jonah told the sailors to cast him overboard so that the storm would pass over.

When Jonah was tossed into the raging sea, a great fish prepared by God swallowed Jonah and he swirled around in the stomach of the fish. After three days and nights, Jonah repented of his disobedience. Thereafter, the fish vomited up Jonah along the coast of Nineveh and God repeated his instructions to Jonah pursuant to which Jonah delivered God's warning that Nineveh would be destroyed within six weeks.

All the people of Nineveh (over 120,000) including the king fasted and repented in sackcloth and ashes. God spared the city and when Jonah sulked, God pointed out to him that mercy is appropriate following repentance by a spiritually ignorant population.

Micah was a contemporary of Isaiah and his prophecies were directed primarily to Samaria, the capital city of Israel, with references to Judah and to reunited Israel. Micah also prophesied concerning the birth and rejection of Messiah, the judgment of Gentile nations, and the future kingdom of Messiah. Micah's prophecies have been divided into seven chapters.

Chapters 1-3 contain warnings pertaining to the apostasy and idolatry of both Israel and Judah but also include a glimpse of Israel's restoration as a nation ruled by Messiah. Chapter 4 makes reference to the future Babylonian captivity of Judah but principally describes the peace, security and prosperity to be enjoyed by Israel following restoration as a nation.

Chapters 5-7 contains prophecies concerning the birth of Messiah in Bethlehem; an intervening but indeterminate time period; judgment upon heathen populations; and the glory of Israel in the future kingdom.

Nahum's prophecy is directed to Nineveh approximately a century and a half after Nineveh repented and turned to God to avoid the destruction prophesied by Jonah. The Book of Nahum consists of three chapters. Chapter 1 states that God is long-suffering, merciful and slow to anger but will not ignore wickedness; and that beauty is reflected by good tidings and peace. Chapters 2 and 3 describe the evils practiced in Nineveh and foretell the devastation that will accompany the coming judgment upon Nineveh as proclaimed by God.

Habakkuk's questions, and his answers received by prophetic vision, were voiced before Judah was taken captive by the Babylonians. Habakkuk raised the perplexing question --- why is judgment upon the wicked slow in coming in view of God's holiness and divine justice?

God answers that many woes have already been determined upon evil doers and gives Habakkuk a preview of the horror and slaughter Judah will endure while being subdued by the Babylonians. God further reveals to Habakkuk the future repentance and re-gathering of Israel within a kingdom filled with the knowledge and glory of the Lord; and that the just shall live by his faith.

Zephaniah ministered to Judah during the revival led by Josiah, king of Judah, approximately forty years before Judah was taken captive by Babylon. Zephaniah recounts the evil deeds for which Judah will be judged by God, and prophecies regarding the coming captivity; the calling out of a faithful remnant from captivity; judgment upon all nations; and the future restoration of Israel within a righteous and glorious kingdom.

Haggai ministered approximately 520 BC to the remnant of Judah who returned to the land promised by God to Abraham following the seventy years of captivity foretold by Jeremiah. Through the mouth of Haggai, God expressed his displeasure that the people delayed the restoration of the temple and focused on building their own houses while planting and harvesting crops.

Haggai verbally chastised the priests and the people for misplaced priorities and pointed out that they had sown much and reaped little because the temple had been neglected and because the priests had not purified themselves according to the law given to Moses.

Haggai encouraged the priests and the people to complete the restoration of the temple and to adhere to the law of purification. Haggai prophesied that God will destroy the power of heathen nations and will fill the temple with glory.

Zechariah was a contemporary of Haggai and he prophesied to Judah during the same time window. Zechariah's prophecies are much broader in scope and describe ten symbolic visions with reference to the return of a remnant of Judah from captivity; the restoration of the temple; and rebuilding of Jerusalem. Zechariah foresees the first coming of Messiah and subsequent rejection by his people; the lengthy dispersion of Jews among hostile nations; the regathering of Israel as a united people during the latter days; the judgment by God upon all nations; the second coming of Messiah; and the future kingdom of Messiah wherein Jerusalem will be the center of worship. The Book of Zechariah has been divided into fourteen chapters.

Chapters 1-3 briefly look back upon the captivity of Judah; the return of a remnant after seventy years from captivity; and God's displeasure with nations at ease while Judah has endured chastisement. Then, the time reference is shifted into the future gathering of Israel from among all nations and the status of Israel within a future kingdom ruled by Messiah (the BRANCH).

Chapter 4 proclaims the ministry of God's Holy Spirit and the future appearance of two witnesses anointed to display God's power over all the earth. Chapters 5-7 look back at divine judgment for perpetual wickedness and the dispersion of Israel among the Gentiles. Chapter 8 looks forward again to the glorified status of Israel within the future kingdom wherein Jerusalem will be the center of worship. Chapters 9 and 10 look both backward and forward concerning the captivities of Israel and Judah, and God's judgment upon Gentile powers; the future coming of Jerusalem's King (Messiah) riding upon the foal of an ass; and the future deliverance of united Israel prior to Messiah's reign over Earth.

Chapter 11 pictures symbolically the initial rejection by Jews of their prophesied Messiah; the price paid for Messiah's betrayal (thirty pieces of silver); the wrath of God pursuant to Messiah's rejection; the end of the covenant between God and Israel based upon the law given to Moses; and the future oppression of Jews by ruthless Gentile powers.

Chapter 12 predicts that Jerusalem will be the center of a great battle wherein God will destroy the besieging armies and Israel will acknowledge the second coming of Messiah with mourning and supplication, and shall look upon him whom they pierced.

Chapter 13 describes the rejection by Israel of all idols, false prophets, and evil spirits thereby cleansing the land promised by God to Abraham; the acknowledgment of the wounding of Messiah's hands; the final persecution of Jews wherein only one third will survive by divine intervention, and the reconciliation between God and the seed of Abraham.

Chapter 14 describes God's protection of the Jewish remnant even though God gathers all nations against Jerusalem pursuant to which the armies will be smitten with a plague causing virtually instant death (nuclear radiation). The Lord shall stand upon the Mount of Olives and the mount shall cleave in twain to provide an escape route for Israel. Thereafter, the nations will be completely subdued and the kingdom of Messiah shall be established with Jerusalem being the center of Messianic worship.

Malachi was the last post-captivity prophet and is the final narrative making up the Old Testament Scriptures. Malachi stressed God's love for Israel but condemned the formality rather than the sincerity of worship as practiced by the restored remnant. The priests were allowing blind, lame, sick, and torn animals and polluted bread to be sacrificed upon the altar dedicated to God. The people were giving mere lip service to the law given by God to Moses and had neglected the tithing required to support the priests and Levites.

Malachi prophesied concerning God's chastisement for insincere worship and intermarriage with heathen populations; God's recognition of those who remain faithful while surrounded by hypocrisy; God's judgment upon the proud and the wicked; the future kingdom ruled by Messiah; and the coming of a messenger having the power and spirit of Elijah who would announce the arrival of Messiah before the great and fearful day of the Lord.

Before commencing with the summaries of the twenty-seven narratives making up the New Testament Scriptures, a backward look at the Old Testament Scriptures should bathe our eyes with tears and our hearts with shame. Until we look beyond ourselves and accept the inescapable fact that neither we nor a series of random, purposeless events created the universe and all the wonders, beauty, and life we behold with our eyes and our senses, we are beyond help with no future and no hope. Only when we allow ourselves to be freed from pride, arrogance, lust and rebellion can we begin to perceive the God of all creation who created humans and bestowed upon us an everlasting love that encompasses awareness, chastisement and eternal redemption ---- salvation at a cost far beyond our ability to calculate value.

There are among us those who deny the existence of God and believe there is no Being possessing greater intelligence than they, themselves; those who believe there is a God but live their brief life on Earth as if God does not hold their very existence in his hands; those who have convinced themselves that they are divine and that God is everywhere around them; and those who have unconditionally accepted God as a supreme being existing outside of time and space, and have further accepted the atoning sacrifice God provided to redeem fallen humans back to Himself. Every individual having reached the age of accountability must answer the question --- does God exist?

If we believe there is a God, and that we cannot begin to comprehend His power and majesty, then every revelation from God and the sordid human history recorded within the Holy Bible make perfect sense and demonstrate why only the sacrifice which God provided by offering up Himself in the person of Jesus Christ can save us from our just punishment and bestow upon us eternal life as recorded in the New Testament Scriptures.

For those of us who have unconditionally accepted God and recognize His power to act and to judge as He pleases, the Old Testament Scriptures are both enlightening and indispensable concerning God's relationship to humans.

The first twelve chapters within the Book of Genesis reveal three central truths which become the mainstream issues throughout the entire body of inspired Scriptures. First, God created the universe and all life therein including humans. Humans were created as perfect living beings endowed with immortality and a free will to choose between eternal life within the created bodies given to them by God, and the physical death of their flesh by exercising their free will to disobey God.

The spiritual life which God breathed into the first humans, and is passed on to every human born thereafter, exists apart from the physical body and thus cannot be extinguished. Second, humans chose to rebel against God by breaking His single commandment thereby bringing upon themselves physical death and a spiritual existence separated from God. Third, God pronounced the sentence of physical death in the future of humanity but promised that one given birth by a woman would triumph over evil.

One man, Abraham, exercising simple faith in God, was chosen by God to become the father of many nations and his seed predestined to become the human bloodline through which God would bless humanity.

The entire balance of Old Testament Scriptures traces the history of Abraham's descendants as God interacts with them. It is paramount to understanding God's warnings and promises to humanity that the passing of time, as we mark time, does not drive the mills of God's wrath, mercy and grace.

Between the final utterance by Old Testament prophets and the preaching of John the Baptist, there are four centuries of silence between God and humanity. Because our physical lives are so brief we tend to desire God to act in accordance with our concept of time. God's "fullness of time" is revealed only as God chooses to do so as reflected in His statement to Moses --- "I AM THAT I AM" -- (Exodus, 3:14 partial).

Chapter eleven

The writings of Matthew, Mark, Luke, and John (the Four Gospels) are four separate accounts of the life, ministry, death, and resurrection of Jesus Christ (referred to as both Son of God and Son of man). All four gospels were written within a single lifetime following the resurrection of Jesus --- between approximately 34 AD and 96 AD. Matthew and John were two of the twelve apostles.

Mark and Luke believed the teachings of Jesus and were associates of the apostles and of Paul and Barnabas. Matthew points to Jesus as fulfilling the Messianic Scriptures. Mark pictures Jesus as the lowly servant acting in a straightforward manner and exercising the power of God. Luke portrays Jesus as the Son of God obedient even unto death. John presents Jesus as God who became "His Word" and dwelled among humans to give us access to spiritual light and truth. Each of these authors describe various sermons, teachings, explanations, and warnings spoken by Jesus along with many miracles (healing people with all types of sickness, disease, and disability). Each author reports the ministry, life, death, burial, and resurrection of Jesus; and relates the words and deeds pertaining to Jesus which tend to complement the author's emphasis. Consequently, each separate biography adds or omits sayings and events as compared to the other three authors. The Gospel according to St. Matthew is followed by a brief summation covering Mark, Luke, and John pertaining to only that which has not been adequately captured by Matthew.

The Gospel according to St. Matthew is divided into twenty-eight chapters and is dated 37 AD. Chapter 1 presents the genealogy of Abraham downward to Jesus Christ and counts fourteen generations between Abraham and David, fourteen generations from David to the Babylonian captivity, and fourteen generations between the beginning of the Babylonian captivity and the birth of Jesus Christ to a virgin named Mary espoused to Joseph, the son of Jacob, of the house of David.

The angel of the Lord appeared to Joseph in a dream and told him Mary was pregnant with the seed of God --- to take her to wife and to name the child Jesus, and that Jesus would save the people from their sins. Joseph married Mary but did not have sexual relations with her until after Jesus was born. Isaiah prophesied the virgin birth of Jesus Christ in 742 BC (Isaiah 7:14).

Chapter 2 records the visit by wise men (Magi) who followed a bright star from the east to worship the infant, Jesus. King Herod, advised by the chief priests and scribes, attempted to locate Jesus through the Magi to kill Him. Being warned by God in a dream, Joseph and Mary fled into Egypt and the Magi did not return to Herod. Thereafter, Herod ordered the death of all the children two years old and young-er within the regions of Bethlehem --- as prophesied by Jeremiah in 606 B.C. (Jeremiah 31:15). Chapters 3 and 4 relate the call to repentance by John the Baptist; the baptism of Jesus by John; the descending of the Spirit of God upon Jesus in the form of a dove; the voice of God introducing Jesus as His beloved Son; the temptations of Jesus by Satan in the wilderness; the imprisonment of John and the departure of Jesus into Capernaum where He began to preach "repent, for the kingdom of heaven is at hand" (Matthew 4:17).

Chapter 4 narrates the call of four apostles by Jesus (Peter, Andrew, James and John) who followed as He preached the "gospel of the kingdom" and healed all types of sickness, disease, and disability (including demon possession) and attracted large crowds that sought Him out, coming from Galilee, Decapolis, Jerusalem, Judaea and from beyond the Jordan River.

Chapters 5-7 (the sermon on the mount) contain the teachings of Jesus concerning love and Christian stewardship: the kingdom of heaven belongs to the poor in spirit; they that mourn shall be comforted; the meek shall inherit the earth; those who hunger and thirst after righteousness shall be filled; the merciful shall obtain mercy; the pure in heart shall see God; peacemakers shall be called the children of God; those who are reviled and persecuted for the cause of righteousness shall inherit the kingdom of heaven; those reviled, persecuted and spoken evil of for the cause of Christ shall receive great rewards in heaven; Christian stewards are the light of the world and the salt of the earth whose good works others will see and give glory to God.

Christ came to fulfill the law and not to destroy it. He that is angry at another without cause is a murderer in his heart. Make reconciliation for offenses before offering sacrifice to God. Those calling another a fool are in danger of hell fire. Do not haggle with an adversary but seek quick agreement. To lust after a woman is to commit adultery in your heart. It is better to live maimed, blind and crippled than to have your whole body cast into hell. Do not enter into divorce except for sexual infidelity. Do not swear nor speak idle words. Love your enemies and do good to those who hate and curse you. Do not resist evil but rather turn the other cheek. Do not turn away those needing a loan or a handout. Do not give to the needy to be praised by others. Do not fast and pray with the heart of a hypocrite.

Do not speak long prayers for the ears of those around you because God knows what you need before you pray. Do not pray using vain repetitions because God does not favor such prayers. When praying, give honor to God and submit to His will; ask for your daily bread and freely forgive others when seeking forgiveness; ask for deliverance from evil temptations; and acknowledge that to God belongs the kingdom, power and glory forever.

Do not be concerned with earthly wealth but

rather lay up treasures in heaven through love, good works, forgiveness, and mercy. Do not be anxious about food, drink, clothing, and shelter but consider that God feeds the birds and arrays the lilies in the field. Do not worry about tomorrow but first seek the kingdom of God and His righteousness and He will supply your needs.

Do not judge others lest you be judged accordingly. Do not resent in others what you excuse for yourself. Give not what is holy unto dogs nor cast pearls before hogs. Treat others like you want to be treated. Avoid false prophets and teachers who can be identified by their words and deeds. Heaven is only entered by those obeying the will of the Father. Build your house upon a rock foundation rather than sand lest a flood carry you away. The path to hell is broad and the gate to heaven is narrow.

Chapter 8 describes Jesus healing a leper; the servant of a Roman officer (having faith); and Peter's mother-in-law. Thereafter, many sick, diseased, and demon possessed people were brought before Jesus whereupon He cast out the devils by His word, and healed the sick and diseased. Jesus rebuked the professing disciples who were not willing to leave everything behind and follow Him. Jesus and His disciples boarded a ship and while Jesus slept the ship was engulfed by a sudden storm. The frightened disciples awoke Jesus whereupon Jesus rebuked the storm and the sea became calm. Upon departure from the ship, Jesus was met by two men possessed by devils and the devils recognized Jesus, then asked Him if He had come to torment them before their time. Jesus gave the devils permission, upon being cast out, to enter into a nearby herd of feeding hogs. The possessed hogs stampeded down a steep slope and drowned in the sea. The hog keepers fled into the city and explained the loss of their herd after which many people came out from the city and asked Jesus to leave their coasts.

Chapter 9 documents additional miracles performed by Jesus including healing a palsied man, restoring sight to two blind men, casting out a demon, healing a woman with a blood disease, and raising a young woman from the dead. The unbelieving priests, scribes and Pharisees belittled Jesus for healing on the Sabbath day and declared that Jesus cast out devils by the power of Satan. Jesus called Matthew to follow Him and dined at his house with publicans and sinners. The Pharisees asked Jesus why He ate with such people. Jesus replied that He came not to minister to the righteous but to save sinners. Jesus continued to preach throughout Galilee and to heal from sickness and disease those who came to Him. Jesus looked upon the people with great compassion as they fainted along the way and were scattered as sheep without a shepherd.

Chapter 10 contains the names of the twelve apostles: Peter, Andrew, James, John, Philip, Bartholomew, Thomas, Matthew, James (son of Alphaeus), Thaddaeus, Simon (the Canaanite), and Judas Iscariot.

Jesus sent all twelve to Jewish cities, towns and villages to preach the "kingdom of heaven is at hand," to heal the sick and lepers, to cast out devils, and to raise the dead. Jesus instructed them to take nothing with them but to stay in the homes of those who gladly received them, and to shake the dust from their feet when leaving a population that would not receive them nor listen to their words.

Jesus warned them that they would be persecuted, hated, and scourged for His sake, and that God's Spirit would speak through them when they were delivered up before kings and governors. Jesus also stated that His mission to save humanity would not bring peace but rather a sword; that, for His sake, families would be divided to the point of delivering up each other for execution; that His followers would be insanely hated beyond logic or reason; and that those who maintain their faith in Him will be saved from hell.

Jesus further told His disciples: the servant is not greater than his master; if they call Me Satan's child, what will they call you?; there is nothing hid that will remain secret; what you hear in darkness, proclaim in the light; do not fear those who can only kill you, but rather fear God who can cast you into hell; God considers even the fall of sparrows, and has numbered the hairs on your head; those who will not publicly state their belief in Me, I will deny before My Father in heaven; your life is not within your power, therefore, always be prepared to meet God; and you will be rewarded for whatever you give to others in My name.

Chapter 12 records Jesus' statement that He is Lord of the Sabbath day in answer to the accusations voiced by the Pharisees when his disciples picked and ate corn with unwashed hands, and when Jesus healed on the Sabbath day a man with a withered hand. When Jesus cast a devil out of a man made blind and dumb by the evil spirit, the Pharisees again declared that Jesus cast out devils by the power of Satan, to which Jesus answered: "If Satan cast out Satan, he is divided against himself; how then shall his kingdom stand?" (Matthew 12:26). Jesus also warned the Pharisees concerning witnessing the miraculous works of God and proclaiming such works to be evil in origin. Such blasphemy, Jesus stated, will never be forgiven. Jesus further warned that words make known our inner thoughts, and that we will be judged by our words.

When the scribes and Pharisees asked for a sign to verify His statements, Jesus replied that no sign would be given other than that pertaining to Jonah; that like Jonah spent three days and nights inside the whale, He would be in the center of the earth three days and nights; that those refusing to believe His words would be accused in the judgment by evil generations who had not heard Him; that attempts at self-reformation are worthless; and that those doing the will of God, the Father, are His earthly family.

Chapter 13 contains parables spoken by Jesus to illustrate the mysteries concerning the kingdom of heaven. He said that seed scattered by a farmer in all directions fell by the road; into stony ground; among thorns; and upon fertile soil. Seed which fell along the road was eaten by birds; seed falling into stony ground sprouted but withered in the sun due to shallow roots; seed among thorns was choked out by spreading thorns; and seed falling into fertile soil sprouted and multiplied many times over. The disciples asked Jesus why he spoke to the people in parables. He answered that the people did not yet perceive His mission because of their traditional mind-set, and that which they were seeing and hearing had been withheld from many prophets and righteous men.

Jesus explained to His disciples that the seed represented the gospel of the kingdom which some heard but allowed Satan to snatch the truth away; others gladly received the word but became overwhelmed by temptation; some allowed the cares of earthly life and lust for wealth to choke out the word; and some heard and understood and brought forth a harvest by teaching the word to others.

Jesus spoke another parable wherein He said that the kingdom of heaven can be compared to a man who planted wheat in his field, and that under cover of night his enemy came and sowed tares among the wheat. The crop sprouted and the tares became visible whereupon the man's servants asked if they should dig up the tares. The man replied that trying to remove the tares might uproot the wheat. He instructed the servants to let the crop grow until the harvest at which time the tares could be separated and burned while the wheat was gathered into the barn.

Jesus explained to His puzzled disciples that He, the Son of man, is sowing good seed in the field (the world), and that Satan is sowing the tares; the good seed represents the children of God and the tares the followers of Satan; the harvest is the end of the world and the reapers are the angels. Those who believe the gospel shall enter into the kingdom of heaven, and those who believe not will be cast into the fire.

Jesus further compared the kingdom of heaven to the tiny mustard seed which grows into a sheltering tree; to leaven hidden within a batch of dough; to a treasure buried in a field which a man discovers and sells all that he has to buy the field; to a pearl of great value for which one gives all he possesses; and to a net cast into the sea and drawn to shore filled with mixed creatures both good and bad. Jesus returned to His hometown, Nazareth, but did not perform many miracles because the people there perceived Him as only the son of Joseph and Mary.

Matthew, chapter 14 describes the murder of John the Baptist by Herod, the tetrarch, to please his wife and stepdaughter following a session of drinking and erotic dancing. Jesus sought solitude by departing by ship to a desert area but the people followed Him on foot from out of the cities. Jesus felt compassion for them and healed the sick and diseased that thronged Him.

Many among the multitude had traveled a long way without food and Jesus told His disciples to feed them. The disciples could find only five loaves of bread and two fishes. Jesus instructed the people to sit down on the grass and then He blessed the loaves and fishes and gave divided portions to the disciples who distributed the food to the people. After approximately five thousand men plus women and children had eaten all they wanted, the disciples gathered up twelve baskets of leftovers.

The disciples departed by ship and Jesus went into a mountain area alone to pray. During the night, the disciples' ship was tossed about by the wind. Jesus came to them walking upon the water causing the disciples to tremble. Jesus revealed Himself, and Peter asked permission to walk upon the water whereupon Jesus told him to proceed. Peter walked toward Jesus but became fearful of the restless sea and began to sink. Jesus rescued him and rebuked him for lack of faith. The wind calmed and the ship landed at Gennesaret where Jesus healed the diseased persons brought before him.

Chapter 15 contains the rebuke of the Pharisees by Jesus when they again challenged His disciples for eating with unwashed hands. Jesus told them: you nullify the law of God by your tradition; you are blind men trying to lead the blind; you give God only lip service; and, it is not what goes into the mouth that defiles a man, but rather that which proceeds out of the mouth. Jesus explained to His disciples that the mouth speaks a person's true thoughts --- murder, adultery, fornication, thievery, lies and blasphemy.

A Gentile woman begged Jesus to cast a devil out of her daughter. Jesus replied that He was sent only to the lost sheep of Israel whereupon the woman replied that dogs eat from the children's table. Jesus commended her faith and made her daughter whole. Again, the people brought to Jesus the lame, blind, dumb, sick and disabled and He healed them. The people followed Jesus three days without eating. Jesus again told His disciples to feed the multitude and they scrounged up seven loaves plus a few small fishes. Jesus blessed the food and His disciples divided the loaves and fishes among the people after which they took up seven baskets of leftovers. Approximately four thousand men were filled beside women and children.

In chapter 16, Jesus asked His disciples whom they believed Him to be. Peter answered, "Thou art the Christ, the Son of the living God." (Matthew 16:16) Jesus replied that God had revealed the truth to Peter, and that Peter's profession of faith was the rock upon which Jesus would build His church; that hell would not overcome the church; that the church would preach the kingdom of heaven; and, that the disciples should not yet make known His identity.

Jesus further warned His disciples that He would have to endure much punishment in Jerusalem inflicted by the chief priests, elders, and scribes; and that He would be executed and rise again on the third day. Peter replied that Jesus should not accept suffering and death, but Jesus said to him, "Get thee behind Me, Satan: thou art an offense unto Me: for thou savourest not the things that be of God, but those that be of men." (Matthew 16:23)

Jesus then told His disciples that: those desiring to follow Him must deny themselves; one wanting to save his life will lose it; one willing to lose his life for My sake shall find it; a man profits nothing regardless of how much he owns if he loses his soul; every person will be rewarded in proportion to works; and that the Son of man would soon be seen in His glory.

Chapter 17 details the transfiguration of Jesus as witnessed by Peter, James, and John upon a mountain wherein the face of Jesus radiated as the sun and His clothing appeared as white light. Moses and Elijah appeared and conversed with Him.

Peter suggested building three tabernacles, one for Jesus, one for Moses, and one for Elijah. God spoke to them from a cloud saying, "This is my beloved Son, in whom I am well pleased; hear ye Him." (Matthew 17:5) When the three disciples heard God speak, they fell upon their faces and were afraid.

Jesus came near and told them not to fear whereupon they opened their eyes and saw only Jesus. He instructed them not to reveal what they had just witnessed until after His resurrection from the dead. The disciples asked, "Why then say the scribes that Elijah must first come?" Jesus replied, "Elijah truly shall first come and restore all things. But I say unto you, that Elijah is come already, and they knew him not, but have done unto him whatsoever they listed." (Matthew 17:11-12) Then the disciples understood that Jesus was referring to John the Baptist.

The disciples asked Jesus why they were unable to cast the devil out of a certain child. Jesus replied that if they had faith equal to a grain of mustard seed, nothing would be impossible for them to accomplish. Jesus again told them, "The Son of man shall be betrayed into the hands of men: and they shall kill Him, and the third day He shall be raised again." (Matthew 17:22-23)

In chapter 18, Jesus tells His disciples: "Except ye be converted, and become as little children, ye shall not enter into the kingdom of heaven." (Mat-thew 18:3). Jesus declared that He came to seek that which was lost --- like a shepherd will leave his flock to find a single lost sheep; that where two or three are gathered in His name, He is in the midst of them; that one should never cease forgiving another; and that God forgives those who are willing to forgive others.

Chapters 19 and 20 relate additional details concerning the teachings of Jesus. The Pharisees ques-tioned Jesus concerning the reasons for divorce under the law given to Moses. Jesus replied that Moses allowed a "writing of divorcement" because of the hardness of the husband's heart; that God does not approve of divorce; that any man who divorces his wife for any reason, except for fornication, and marries another commits adultery; and that any man who marries a divorced woman causes her to commit adultery.

A rich man asked Jesus what he must do to have eternal life. Jesus referred him to the Ten Commandments. The man claimed to have lived according to the commandments from his youth and inquired what else he should do. Jesus told him to sell all he owned, give the proceeds to the poor, and to follow after him thereby laying up treasure in heaven.

The rich man was unwilling to do so because his possessions were enormous. Jesus said to His disciples, "Verily I say unto you that a rich man shall hardly enter into the kingdom of heaven. And again, I say unto you, it is easier for a camel to go through the eye of a needle, than for a rich man to enter into the kingdom of God." (Matthew 19:23-24) The disciples were amazed whereupon Jesus answered, "With men this is impossible; but with God all things are possible." (Matthew 19:26)

The disciples asked Jesus what reward will be given because they forsook everything to follow after Him. Jesus replied that, when He sat upon the throne of His kingdom, they would sit upon twelve thrones judging the twelve tribes of Israel; "But many that are first shall be last; and the last shall be first." (Matthew 19:30) Jesus told His disciples a parable wherein the owner of a vineyard went into the marketplace during each watch of the day to hire laborers and agreed to give each one a penny for his time. At the end of the day, each man received a penny according to the order in which he was hired. The men who worked all day complained to the vineyard owner and said that they should have received more than those who worked just one hour.

The owner replied that he had agreed with each man for a penny and therefore had paid as agreed; and that his money was his to do with as he saw fit. Then Jesus said, "So, the last shall be first, and the first last; for many be called, but few chosen." (Matthew 20:16)

On the way to Jerusalem, Jesus told His disciples: "Behold, we go up to Jerusalem; and the Son of man shall be betrayed unto the chief priests and unto the scribes, and they shall condemn Him to death, and shall deliver Him to the Gentiles to mock, and to scourge, and to crucify Him: and the third day He shall rise again."

The mother of James and John came and worshiped Jesus and requested that her sons be appointed to sit on the right hand and on the left hand of Jesus in His kingdom. Jesus replied that she and her sons did not understand what they were asking; and questioned whether James and John could drink of His cup and be baptized with Him.

James and John responded that they were able to do so. Jesus said, "Ye shall drink indeed of My cup, and be baptized with the baptism that I am baptized with: but to sit on My right hand, and on My left, is not Mine to give, but it shall be given to them for whom it is prepared of my Father." (Matthew 20:23) Jesus further admonished: "And whosoever will be chief among you, let him be your servant; even as the Son of man came not to be ministered unto, but to minister, and to give His life a ransom for many." (Matthew 20:27-28) Two blind men sitting by the road to Jericho cried for healing as Jesus passed by. Jesus was moved with compassion; stopped and restored their sight.

In chapter 21, Jesus rides into Jerusalem mounted upon the colt of an ass and the multitude preceding Him place their outer clothing and palm branches in His path while shouting, "Hosanna to the son of David: Blessed is He that cometh in the name of the Lord; Hosanna in the highest." (Matthew 21:9)

Jesus entered the temple and drove out the moneychangers and merchants and said, "It is written, My house shall be called the house of prayer; but ye have made it a den of thieves." (Mat-thew 21:13) The chief priests and scribes were enraged when they saw the things Jesus did and heard the people shouting praises to Him. They demanded to know whether Jesus understood the people were hailing Him as Messiah. Jesus answered, "Yea; have ye never read, Out of the mouth of babes and sucklings Thou hast perfected praise?" (Matthew 21:16)

Going from Bethany back to Jerusalem, Jesus was hungry. He passed by a fig tree and looked for figs among the leaves. Jesus found no figs and said to the tree, "Let no fruit grow on thee henceforth forever."

(Mat-thew 21:19) The fig tree withered away.

The disciples were amazed whereupon Jesus said, "Verily I say unto you, if you have faith and doubt not, ye shall not only do this which is done to the fig tree, but also if ye shall say unto this mountain, Be thou removed, and be thou cast into the sea; it shall be done. And, all things, whatsoever ye shall ask in prayer, believing, ye shall receive." (Matthew 21:21-22) Thereafter, while Jesus was teaching in the temple, the elders and chief priests demanded to know who had given Him the authority to act and teach. Jesus asked them whether John the Baptist was a true prophet.

When they answered they could not tell, Jesus replied, "Neither tell I you by what authority I do these things. But what think ye? A certain man had two sons; and he came to the first and said, Son, go work today in my vineyard. He answered and said, I will not: but afterward he repented and went. And he came to the second, and said likewise. And he answered and said, I go sir: and went not. Whether of the twain did the will of the father?" When they acknowledged that the first son performed the will of his father, Jesus said unto them, "Verily I say unto you, That the publicans and harlots go into the kingdom of God before you. For John came unto you in the way of righteousness, and ye believed him not: but the publicans and harlots believed him: and ye, when ye had seen it, repented not afterward, that ye might believe him. Hear another parable:

There was a certain householder, which planted a vineyard, and hedged it round about, and digged a wine press in it, and built a tower, and let it out to husbandmen, and went into a far country. And when the time of the fruit drew near, he sent his servants to the husbandmen, that they might receive the fruits of it. And the husbandmen took his servants, and beat one, and killed another, and stoned another. Again he sent servants more than the first: and they did unto them likewise. But last of all he sent unto them his son, saying, They will reverence my son. But when the husbandmen saw the son, they said among themselves, This is the heir; come, let us kill him, and let us seize on his inheritance. And they caught him, and cast him out of the vineyard, and slew him. When the lord therefore of the vineyard cometh, what shall he do unto those husbandmen?"

They said the lord should destroy those wicked men and let the vineyard out to other husbandmen. Jesus said to them, "Did ye never read in the scriptures, The stone which the builders rejected, the same is become the head of the corner: this is the Lord's doing, and it is marvelous in our eyes? Therefore, I say unto you, the kingdom of God shall be taken from you, and given to a nation bringing forth the fruits thereof. And whosoever shall fall on this stone shall be broken: but on whomsoever it shall fall, it will grind him to powder." (Matthew 21:27-44)

In chapter 22, Jesus also said that the kingdom of

heaven is like the wedding dinner a king prepared for his son. When all preparations were completed, the invited guests were called by the king's servants but some gave idle excuses for not attending the marriage. Others abused and killed the servants. The king's soldiers then killed the murderers and burned their cities. Because those invited were not worthy, the king ordered his servants to go into the streets and invite strangers to the wedding. Afterward, the king noticed a man not wearing a wedding garment and asked him why he entered having no wedding garment, but the man was speechless. The king ordered him to be bound and cast out into the darkness where there is wailing and grinding of teeth. So it is, said Jesus, "that many are called but few are chosen."

In an effort to find a cause whereby they could accuse Jesus before the Roman governor, the Herodians asked Jesus whether the Roman taxes were legal. Jesus referred to a penny and asked them whose image was engraved thereon. They replied that the image was Caesar's. Jesus told them to give to Caesar what belonged to him and to God that which honors Him.

The Sadducees came to Jesus and said that a man having six brothers took a wife and died childless. According to Moses, in order to raise up seed to his brother, the first brother took the widow to wife but also died childless. Each remaining brother followed Moses' commandment but all died leaving no offspring; and thereafter, the woman died. The Sadducees then asked

Jesus which brother would be husband to the woman in the resurrection. Jesus replied, "Ye do err, not knowing the scriptures, nor the power of God. For in the resurrection they neither marry, nor are given in marriage, but are as the angels of God in heaven. But as touching the resurrection of the dead, have ye not read that which was spoken unto you by God, saying, 'I am the God of Abraham, and the God of Isaac, and the God of Jacob?' God is not the God of the dead, but of the living." (Matthew 22:29-32)

The people were astonished by the words from Jesus. Then the Pharisees came and asked Jesus which is the greatest commandment within the law. Jesus said, "Thou shalt love the Lord thy God with all thy heart, and with all thy soul, and with all thy mind. This is the first and great commandment. And the second is like unto it, Thou shalt love thy neighbor as thyself. On these two commandments hang all the law and the prophets." (Matthew 22:37-40)

Jesus asked the Pharisees, "What think ye of Christ? Whose son is he?" They answered, "David's son." Jesus replied, "How then doth David in spirit call him Lord, saying, 'The Lord said unto my lord, Sit thou on my right hand, till I make thine enemies thy footstool?' If David then call him Lord, how is he his son?" (Matthew 22:42-45) The Pharisees could not answer and ceased to question Jesus.

Chapter 23 contains Jesus' condemnation of the scribes and Pharisees as miserable hypocrites, a generation of vipers destined for hell; and the lament of Jesus over Jerusalem, "O Jerusalem, Jerusalem, thou that killest the prophets, and stonest them which are sent unto thee, how often would I have gathered thy children together, even as a hen gatherest her chickens under her wings, but ye would not! Behold, your house is left unto you desolate. For I say unto you, Ye shall not see Me henceforth, till ye shall say, Blessed is He that cometh in the name of the Lord." (Matthew 23:37-39)

In chapter 24, Jesus tells his disciples about the coming destruction of the temple, stone by stone, and the signs pointing to His return and the end of the world. Jesus told them that many shall come and claim to be Christ; that wars and earthquakes will multiply along with pestilence and famine; that His followers will be tortured and killed and hated above all people; that because evil will abound, including great signs and wonders, the love and faith of many will be abandoned; that the gospel of the kingdom shall be preached throughout the world for a witness to all nations; and then the end shall come.

Jesus further forewarned that the abomination of desolation prophesied by Daniel, the prophet, will precede the greatest of all persecutions; that there will only be time to run; that people should pray that their flight avoids winter and the Sabbath day; and that God will shorten the time of such persecution in order that some flesh might be saved.

Jesus also said that following this great tribulation,

the sun and moon will be darkened, the stars will fall from heaven, and the heavens will shake; that all people upon earth will mourn when they see the Son of man returning with great power and glory; that a mighty trumpet shall sound and the angels shall gather His elect from everywhere upon earth; that as a fig tree grows tender branches and leaves heralding summertime, when such things come to pass, the end is near; that as sudden destruction caught Noah's generation unaware, so shall it be when the Son of man returns; and that only My Father knows the day and hour the end shall come.

In chapter 25, Jesus compared being prepared for His return to ten virgins with lighted lamps waiting for the bridegroom to appear. Five virgins took along extra oil for their lamps and five did not. While waiting, all ten fell asleep. At midnight, the coming of the bridegroom was announced and the virgins got up and trimmed their lamps, but the lamps of the five who brought along no extra oil had gone out. They tried to borrow oil from the five who brought oil with them, but were advised to go buy for themselves lest all the lamps run out. While the five were gone to buy, the bridegroom came and the door was shut. When the unprepared virgins returned they were denied entry because the wedding had commenced.

Jesus spoke another parable wherein He said the kingdom of heaven is like a man going on a trip who called his servants and gave them money, according to their abilities, to invest during his absence --- five talents to one, two talents to one, and one talent to another. The servant receiving one talent buried it, and the others invested wisely. Upon their lord's return, the servants who invested returned twice what they had been entrusted with. The lord rewarded them with greater authority. The servant who was entrusted with one talent admitted that he believed the lord was a hard man, reaping that which he had not sowed; that he had kept the talent safely buried in order to return it without risk. The lord was furious and ordered that the one talent be given to the servant returning ten talents; and that the unprofitable servant be cast into outer darkness filled with wailing and gnashing of teeth.

Jesus warned that when He sits upon the throne of His glory He will separate the nations as a shepherd divides his sheep from the goats ---- with the sheep on His right hand and the goats on His left: "Then shall the King say unto them on His right hand, Come, ye blessed of My Father, inherit the kingdom prepared for you from the foundation of the world: For I was an hungred, and ye gave Me meat: I was thirsty, and ye gave Me drink: I was a stranger, and ye took Me in: naked, and ye clothed Me: I was sick, and ye visited Me: I was in prison and ye came unto Me.

Then shall the righteous answer Him, saying, Lord, when saw we Thee an hungred, and fed Thee? or thirsty, and gave Thee drink? When saw we Thee a stranger, and took Thee in? or naked, and clothed Thee? Or when saw we Thee sick, or in prison, and came unto

Thee? And the King shall answer and say unto them, Verily I say unto you, Inasmuch as ye have done it unto one of the least of these My brethren, ye have done it unto Me.

Then shall He say also unto them on the left hand, Depart from Me, ye cursed, into everlasting fire, prepared for the devil and his angels: For I was an hungred, and ye gave Me no meat: I was thirsty, and ye gave Me no drink: I was a stranger, and ye took Me not in: naked, and ye clothed Me not: sick, and in prison, and ye visited Me not. Then shall they also answer Him, saying, Lord, when saw we Thee an hungred, or athirst, or a stranger, or naked, or sick, or in prison, and did not minister unto Thee? Then shall He answer them, saying, Verily I say unto you, Inasmuch as ye did it not to one of the least of these, ye did it not unto Me. And these shall go away into everlasting punishment: but the righteous into life eternal." (Matthew 25:34-46)

Chapter twelve

Matthew, chapter 26 relates the conspiracy among the chief priests, scribes, and elders to convince the Romans to execute Jesus. Two days before the Passover, Jesus again tells His disciples that He will be betrayed and crucified. While Jesus was seated in a friend's house, a woman poured a very expensive ointment upon His head. The disciples voiced their opinion that such a precious ointment could have been sold and distributed to the poor. Jesus answered, "Why trouble ye the woman? For she hath wrought a good work upon Me. For ye have the poor always with you; but Me ye have not always. For in that she hath poured this ointment on My body, she did it for My burial. Verily I say unto you, Wheresoever this gospel shall be preached in the whole world, there shall also this, that this woman hath done, be told for a memorial of her." (Matthew 26:10-13)

Judas Iscariot agreed with the chief priests to betray Jesus for thirty pieces of silver, and waited for his chance to do so. Jesus sent His disciples ahead to prepare a place to eat the Passover supper. As they ate, Jesus told them that one of them would betray Him. Each disciple asked who the betrayer would be. When Judas Iscariot asked if he would betray Him, Jesus told Judas that he had spoken of himself.

Jesus took bread and divided it among the disciples, saying, "Take, eat; this is My body." And he took the cup, and gave thanks, and gave it to them, saying, "Drink ye all of it; For this is My blood of the new testament, which is shed for many for the remission of sins. But I say unto you, I will not drink henceforth of this fruit of the vine, until that day when I drink it new with you in My Father's kingdom." (Mat-thew 26:26-29)

After ending supper by singing a hymn, Jesus and His disciples went into the Mount of Olives where Jesus said, "All ye shall be offended because of Me this night: for it is written, I will smite the shepherd, and the sheep of the flock shall be scattered abroad."

Peter answered that even if all others will be offended, he would never be offended. Jesus said to Peter, "Verily I say unto thee, That this night, before the cock crow, thou shalt deny Me thrice." Peter said unto him, "Though I should die with Thee, yet will I not deny Thee." Likewise also said all the disciples. (Matthew 26:31-35)

When they entered the Garden of Gethsemane, Jesus said, "Sit ye here while I go and pray yonder." He took with Him Peter, James, and John, and began to be sorrowful and very heavy. Then He said, "My soul is exceedingly sorrowful, even unto death: tarry ye here and watch with Me."

And He went a little farther and fell upon His face, and prayed, "O My Father, if it be possible, let this cup pass from Me: nevertheless not as I will, but as Thou wilt." And He cometh unto the disciples, and findeth them asleep, and saith unto Peter, "What, could ye not watch with Me one hour? Watch and pray, that ye enter not into temptation: the spirit indeed is willing, but the flesh is weak."

He went away the second time, and prayed, saying, "O my Father, if this cup may not pass away from Me, except I drink it, Thy will be done." And He came and found them asleep again: for their eyes were heavy. And He left them and went away again, and prayed the third time, saying the same words.

Then cometh He to His disciples, and saith unto them, "Sleep on now, and take your rest: behold, the hour is at hand, and the Son of man is betrayed into the hands of sinners. Rise, let us be going: behold, he is at hand that doeth betray Me." (Matthew 26:36-45)

Judas had told the multitude, that came with him to arrest Jesus, that he would single out Jesus with a kiss. When the mob began to lay hands on Jesus, one disciple drew a sword and cut off the ear of one of the high priest's servants. Jesus said, "Put up again thy sword into his place: for all they that take the sword shall perish with the sword. Thinkest thou that I cannot now pray to My Father, and He will presently give Me more than twelve legions of angels? But how then shall the scriptures be fulfilled, that thus it must be?" (Matthew 26-52-54)

As all the disciples fled the scene, Jesus was taken

prisoner and led before Caiaphas, the high priest where solicited false witnesses testified against Jesus, but their testimony was not in agreement. Finally, two false witnesses came and testified that Jesus claimed to be able to destroy the temple of God and rebuild it in three days.

Jesus remained silent. The high priest demanded that Jesus say whether he is Christ, the Son of God. Jesus answered, "Thou hast said: nevertheless I say unto you, Hereafter shall ye see the Son of man sitting on the right hand of power, and coming in the clouds of heaven." (Matthew 26:64)

The high priest tore at his clothing and declared Jesus had spoken blasphemy; that no further witnesses were needed because all those assembled heard the blasphemy. The conspirators pronounced Jesus worthy of death. They beat Jesus mercilessly, spit in His face, and mocked Him. Peter was approached three times and accused of being a disciple of Jesus. He denied with an oath, coupled with cursing and swearing, that he did not even know Jesus. When Peter heard the cock crow, he went out and wept with self-contempt.

Chapter 27 documents how Jesus was accused before the Roman governor, Pontius Pilate. The subjugated Jews were forbidden by Rome to carry out a death sentence. When Jesus remained silent before His accusers, Pilate deemed Him innocent of any wrongdoing and wanted to set Him free.

The Romans had consented to release one

prisoner in recognition of the Passover. Pilate offered the mob Barabbas, a notable prisoner, or Jesus. The people screamed for Barabbas. Pilate's wife urged him to free Jesus, but Pilate feared an uprising among the Jews which he knew would be reported to Caesar. Pilate washed his hands before the riotous mob and said, "I am innocent of the blood of this just person: see ye to it."

Then answered all the people and said, "His blood be on us and on our children." (Matthew 27:24-25) Pilate released Barabbas. He had Jesus scourged and gave permission to crucify Him. Judas repented and tried to return the thirty pieces of silver to the chief priests and elders. Upon being derided, Judas threw the silver onto the temple floor and departed and hanged himself. The priests gathered up the silver and purchased the potter's field in which to bury strangers (prophesied by Zechariah 487 BC).

Pilate's band of soldiers took Jesus into the common hall; stripped Him; mocked Him; wrapped a scarlet robe about Him; and pressed a crown of thorns upon His head. They placed a reed in His right hand, hailed Him as king of the Jews, spit upon Him, and took the reed and beat upon His head. Then, the soldiers put His own clothes back on Him and took Him away to crucify Him. A man of Cyrene, named Simon, was compelled to carry Jesus' cross. At a hill called Golgotha, there the soldiers crucified Jesus between two thieves, and cast lots for His garments (prophesied by King David more than 1,000 years BC). Jesus refused the gall and vinegar offered to deaden His senses, and the people sat down to watch Him.

Pilate had a statement nailed to the top of Jesus' cross: THIS IS JESUS THE KING OF THE JEWS. The chief priests, scribes, elders, and Jewish rabble continued to mock Jesus, saying, "----- If thou be the Son of God, come down from the cross --- He saved others; Himself He cannot save --He trusted in God: let Him deliver Him now, if He will have Him: for He said, I am the Son of God." The two thieves also derided Him. (Matthew 27:38-44)

From noon until three in the afternoon, a thick darkness fell upon all the land. Around three pm, Jesus cried out, "Eli, Eli, lama sabachthani?" (My God, my God, why hast thou forsaken Me?). Some spectators thought Jesus was calling for Elijah. Again, He was offered vinegar while others suggested waiting around to see if Elijah would appear. Jesus again cried aloud and then died upon His cross. The veil of the temple was ripped down the middle from top to bottom; the earth quaked and rocks split apart. Some graves of the faithful opened up and their resurrected bodies were seen in Jerusalem three days later. Upon beholding all that happened, the Roman soldiers and some of those gathered around to jeer at Jesus realized that He truly is the Son of God and were filled with fear.

Joseph, of Arimathaea, received permission from Pilate to take down and bury the body of Jesus in the tomb Joseph had carved for himself. He wrapped the corpse of Jesus in a clean linen cloth; rolled a great stone over the tomb entrance; and departed.

Mary Magdalene and another woman named Mary sat nearby. The chief priests and Pharisees convinced Pilate to assign a Roman guard to secure the tomb lest the disciples steal away the body and claim that Jesus arose from the dead. The tomb was sealed and Roman soldiers rotated guard duty.

Chapter 28 documents the resurrection of Jesus. Around dawn, the first day following the end of the Passover celebration, being also the first day of the week, Mary Magdalene and the other Mary went to see the tomb. The earth shook as the angel of the Lord descended from heaven, rolled away the stone from the tomb entrance, and then sat thereon. For fear of the angel, the Roman guards trembled and became as dead men. And the angel said unto the women, "Fear not ye: for I know that ye seek Jesus which was crucified. He is not here: for He is risen as He said. Come, see the place where the Lord lay. And go quickly, and tell His disciples that He is risen from the dead: and, behold, He goeth before you into Galilee; there shall ye see Him: lo, I have told you." (Matthew 28:5-7)

As the women ran to tell the disciples, Jesus met them and told them, "Be not afraid: go, tell My brethren that they go into Galilee, and there shall they see Me." (Matthew 28:10) Some of the Roman guards reported to the chief priests what they had seen. The chief priests and elders gave huge sums of money to the soldiers to say that Jesus' disciples took away His body while they slept; and promised the soldiers if Pilate heard the story, they would persuade Pilate on their behalf.

Jesus appeared to His disciples on a mountain in Galilee and said to them, "All power is given unto Me in heaven and in earth. Go ye therefore, and teach all nations, baptizing them in the name of the Father, and of the Son, and of the Holy Ghost: teaching them to observe all things whatsoever I have commanded you: and, lo, I am with you always, even unto the end of the world." (Matthew 28:18-20).

The Gospel according to St. Mark adds that John the Baptist was clothed with camel's hair and a girdle of skin about his loins and that he ate locusts and wild honey. John preached the baptism of repentance for the remission of sins and said, "There cometh one mightier than I after me, the latchet of whose shoes I am not worthy to stoop down and unloose. I indeed have baptized you with water: but he shall baptize you with the Holy Ghost." (Mark 1:7-8)

Mark states the "unpardonable sin" with more detail, "Verily I say unto you, All sins shall be forgiven unto the sons of men, and blasphemies wheresoever they blaspheme: But he that shall blaspheme against the Holy Ghost hath never forgiveness, but is in danger of eternal damnation; Because they said, He hath an unclean spirit." (Mark 3:28-30) Mark reports that John and some other disciples saw a man casting out devils in Jesus' name and the disciples forbid him to do so because he did not follow after Jesus. But Jesus said, "Forbid him not: for there is no man which shall do a miracle in My name, that can lightly speak evil of He. For he that is not against us is on our part. For whosoever shall give you a cup of water to drink in My name, because ye belong to Christ, verily I say unto you, he shall not lose his reward." (Mark 9:38-40)

Mark writes that, "Jesus sat over against the treasury, and beheld how the people cast money into the treasury: and many that were rich cast in much. And there came a certain poor widow, and she threw in two mites, which make a farthing. And He called unto Him His disciples, and saith unto them, Verily I say unto you, that this poor widow hath cast more in, than all they which hath cast into the treasury: For all they did cast in of their abundance; but she of her want did cast in all that she had, even all her living." (Mark 12:41-44) Mark identifies Peter as being the disciple who drew his sword and cut off the ear of the high priest's servant during the arrest of Jesus.

Concerning the resurrection of Jesus, Mark adds: "Now when Jesus was risen early the first day of the week, He appeared first to Mary Magdalene, out of whom He had cast seven devils. And she went and told them that had been with Him, as they mourned and wept. And they, when they had heard that He was alive, and had been seen of her, believed not. After that He appeared in another form unto two of them, as they walked, and went into the country. And they went and told it unto the residue, neither believed they them. Afterward He appeared unto the eleven as they sat at meat, and upbraided them with their unbelief and hardness of heart, because they believed not them which had seen Him after He was risen. And He said unto them, Go ye into all the world and preach the gospel to every creature. He that believeth and is baptized shall be saved; but he that believeth not shall be damned. And these signs shall follow them that believe; In My name shall they cast out devils; they shall speak with new tongues; they shall take up serpents; and if they drink any deadly thing, it shall not hurt them; they shall lay hands on the sick, and they shall recover. So then after the Lord had spoken unto them, He was received up into heaven, and sat on the right hand of God. And they went forth, and preached everywhere, the Lord working with them, and confirming the word with signs following. Amen." (Mark 9-20)

The Gospel according to St. Luke records the most details concerning the birth of both Jesus and John the Baptist. Luke writes that a priest, Zacharias, and his wife, Elizabeth, were old and childless; that the angel, Gabriel, appeared to Zacharias and told him Elizabeth was going to bear him a son, and that Zacharias should name the boy, John; that John would be favored by God and filled with the Holy Ghost from birth; that he would not drink wine nor strong drink; and that he would minister displaying the spirit and power of Elijah to make ready a people prepared for the Lord. Zacharias asked for a sign and Gabriel told him that he would be unable to speak until the child was born.

Luke names Gabriel as the angel who appeared to Mary and told her that, remaining a virgin, she would bring forth a son and should name Him JESUS; "He shall be great, and shall be called the Son of the Highest: and the Lord God shall give unto Him the throne of His father, David: And He shall reign over the house of Jacob for ever; and of His kingdom there shall be no end."

Then said Mary unto the angel, "How shall this be, seeing I know not a man?" And the angel answered and said unto her, "The Holy Ghost shall come upon thee, and the power of the Highest shall overshadow thee: therefore also that holy thing which shall be born of thee shall be called the Son of God. And behold, thy cousin Elizabeth, she hath also conceived a son in her old age: and this is the sixth month with her, who was called barren. For with God nothing shall be impossible." (Luke 1:32-37)

Luke further writes that when Mary visited with Elizabeth, the child in Elizabeth's womb leaped for joy at Mary's greeting, and Elizabeth was filled with the Holy Ghost. Luke also records the joyous and prophetic sayings of Elizabeth, Mary and Zacharias pertaining to the birth of Jesus and John.

Luke records that Joseph and Mary traveled from Nazareth to Bethlehem in compliance with a tax levied by Caesar Augustus, and that Mary gave birth to Jesus in

Bethlehem; that she wrapped him in swaddling clothes and laid him in a stable manager because she found no other way to shelter him. Luke writes: "And there were in the same country shepherds abiding in the field, keeping watch over their flock by night. And, lo, the angel of the Lord came unto them, and the glory of the Lord shone round about them: and they were sore afraid. And the angel said unto them, 'Fear not: for, behold, I bring you good tidings of great joy, which shall be unto all people.

For unto you is born this day in the city of David a Savior, which is Christ the Lord. And this shall be a sign unto you; Ye shall find the babe wrapped in swaddling clothes, lying in a manger.' And suddenly there was with the angel a multitude of the heavenly host praising God, and saying, Glory to God in the highest, and on earth peace, good will toward men.

And it came to pass, as the angels were gone away from them into heaven, the shepherds said one to another, 'Let us now go even unto Bethlehem, and see this thing which is come to pass, which the Lord hath made known unto us.' And they came with haste, and found Mary and Joseph, and the babe lying in a manger." (Luke 2: 8-14)

Jesus was circumcised, being eight days old, and was brought into the temple by Mary and Joseph to present Him to the Lord; and Jesus was recognized by Simeon, as promised to Simeon by the Holy Ghost; and by Anna, a prophetess, and they worshiped Him.

Luke also recounts that when Jesus was twelve years old, Mary and Joseph inadvertently left Him behind at Jerusalem. They traveled for a day prior to missing Him whereupon they returned to Jerusalem and found Him in the temple conversing with doctors and astonishing the people with His understanding and answers. Upon hearing that Mary and Joseph had been searching for Him, Jesus said, "How is it that ye sought for Me? Wist ye not that I must be about My Father's business?" (Luke 2:49) Luke records the genealogy of Mary backward to Adam.

Luke contains some additional parables spoken by Jesus. A man had two sons and the younger asked for his portion of the father's wealth which he then squandered in a far country upon harlots and riotous living. With his fortune spent and in the midst of a famine, the foolish youth was hired to feed swine, and was so hungry he considered eating the husks falling from their mouths. He decided to return home and ask his father to take him in as a hired servant. When the father saw him coming, he ran to meet him, hugged his neck, kissed him and commanded his servants to array him in the best robe; to put a ring on his finger, shoes on his feet and to prepare a feast with merriment because his son that was lost was found alive.

The elder son was angry and refused to celebrate. The father entreated him and told him he was heir to all; and that it was a time to be glad and make merry because his brother was dead and is alive again, and was lost and is found.

A steward was accused by his master of wasteful management and commanded to give an account of his stewardship. He could not do laborer's work and was too proud to beg. He decided to discount debts owed by his master's customers hoping to be received into their homes. The unfaithful steward was commend-ed because he had done wisely, for the children of this world are, in their minds, wiser than the children of light. However, one cannot serve both God and Satan, and being unfaithful in the things of another, who will give you what is your own?

A beggar covered with sores sat by a rich man's gate wanting nothing but the crumbs falling from the inside table, and dogs came and licked his sores. The beggar died and was carried by angels to Abraham's bosom. The rich man died later and was buried. Finding himself suffering in the flames of hell, he looked across the great gulf between hell and paradise and spotted Lazarus being comforted by Abraham. He called to Abraham to send Lazarus to him with a little water to cool his tongue.

Abraham reminded him that he had basked in wealth while Lazarus suffered; and that Lazarus could not cross the great gulf to come to him. The rich man then pleaded with Abraham to send Lazarus to warn his five brothers lest they also find themselves in hell. Abraham replied that they should listen to Moses and the prophets. The rich man said his brothers would repent if one from the dead testified to them. Abraham told him that if his brothers refused to listen to Moses and the prophets, they would not be persuaded by one risen from the dead.

A Pharisee and a publican went to the temple to pray. The Pharisee cited his own righteousness whereas the publican smote his breast and prayed to God for mercy upon a sinner. Jesus said that the publican went away justified rather than the Pharisee; that the humble shall be exalted and the exalted humbled.

Luke records the repentance of one of the thieves crucified with Jesus, and Jesus' promise to meet him in paradise. Luke provided more details concerning the discourse between Jesus and His disciples pursuant to His resurrection, and the instruction to them to wait in Jerusalem to be endued with power from God.

The Gospel according to St. John portrays Jesus as the divine man: "In the beginning was the Word, and the Word was with God, and the Word was God. The same was in the beginning with God. All things were made by Him; and without Him was not any thing made that was made. In Him was life; and the life was the light of men. And the light shineth in darkness; and the darkness comprehended it not. There was a man sent from God, whose name was John. The same came for a witness, to bear witness of the Light, that all men through Him might believe. He was not that Light, but was sent to bear witness of that Light. That was the true Light, which lighteth every man that cometh into the world. He was in the world, and the world was made by Him, and the world knew Him not. He came unto His own, and His own received Him not. But as many as received Him, to them gave He power to become the sons of God, even to them that believe upon His name: Which were born, not of blood, nor of the will of the flesh, nor of the will of man, but of God. And the Word was made flesh and dwelt among us, (and we beheld His glory, the glory as of the Only Begotten of the Father,) full of grace and truth." (John:1-14)

John describes a marriage celebration attended by Jesus, His mother, and His disciples. The wine ran out and Mary relayed the concern to Jesus whereupon Jesus told her His hour had not yet come. Mary told the servants to do whatever Jesus asked of them. He told the servants to fill six stone pots (holding between 18 and 27 gallons each) with water and present them to the governor of the feast. When the head waiter tasted the water which Jesus turned into wine (over 100 gallons), he was astounded by the taste and fragrance.

John also writes that Nicodemus, a member of the Jewish high court, sought out Jesus at night (fearing to be seen in his presence) and praised Jesus regarding His many miracles. Jesus told him that, unless he was born again, he would not enter the kingdom of God.

Nicodemus thought He meant physical rebirth and Jesus explained that it is the spirit of humans that must be reborn, and that rebirth is like the blowing of the wind; and Jesus stated: "And as Moses lifted up the serpent in the wilderness, even so must the Son of man be lifted up: That whosoever believeth in Him should not perish, but have everlasting life. For God sent not his Son into the world to condemn the world; but that the world through Him might be saved. He that believeth in Him is not condemned: but he that believeth not is condemned already, because he hath not believed in the name of the Only Begotten Son of God." (John 3:14-18)

John records a meeting between Jesus and a woman from Samaria wherein Jesus sat upon Jacob's well around noon and asked the woman to draw some water in her container for Him. She asked why a Jew would have dealings with a Samaritan. He replied that if she knew who was asking for a drink, she could have asked of Him and He would have given her living water which would become a well within her springing up into everlasting life. The woman then asked for such water and Jesus told her to go and get her husband, and then return. The woman replied that she had no husband. Jesus told her that she answered truly since she had been married five times, and was not married to the man she was living with. She left her water pot, went into the city, and told the people she had spoken with Christ. Many Samaritans came forth and believed in Him and He spent two days in Samaria.

John records that Jesus described Himself as the bread of life: "Verily, verily, I say unto you, He that believeth on Me hath everlasting life. I am that bread of life. ---- I am the living bread which came down from heaven: if any man eat of this bread, he shall live forever: and the bread that I will give is My flesh, which I will give for the life of the world. --- Whoso eateth My flesh, and drinketh My blood, hath eternal life; and I will raise him up at the last day. --- He that eateth My flesh, and drinketh My blood, dwelleth in Me, and I in him." (John 6:47-56, portions thereof) "I said therefore unto you, that ye shall die in your sins: for if ye believe not that I am He (the Christ), ye shall die in your sins. --- And because I tell you the truth, ye believe Me not. --- Your father Abraham rejoiced to see My day: and he saw it, and was glad."

Then said the Jews unto him, "Thou art not yet fifty years old, and hast Thou seen Abraham?" Jesus said unto them, "Verily, verily, I say unto you, Before Abraham was, I am." (John 8:24-58, portions thereof)

"I am the door of the sheep. All that ever came before Me are thieves and robbers: but the sheep did not hear them. I am the door: by Me if any man enter in, he shall be saved, and shall go in and out, and find pasture. --- I am the Good Shepherd; the Good Shepherd giveth His life for the sheep. --- As the Father knoweth Me, even so know I the Father: and I lay down My life for the sheep." (John 10:7-15, portions thereof)

John witnessed and recorded the raising of Lazarus from the dead as presented in the first chapter of this book. John was also present at the Passover supper when Jesus washed the disciples feet as an example of love and service to one another; and thereafter said, "Let not your hearts be troubled: ye believe in God, believe also in Me. In My Father's house are many mansions: if it were not so, I would have told you. I go to prepare a place for you. And if I go and prepare a place for you, I will come again, and receive you unto Myself; that where I am, there ye may be also." --- Philip saith unto Him, "Lord, shew us the Father, and it sufficeth us."

Jesus saith unto him, "Have I been so long time with you, and yet hast thou not known Me, Philip? He that hath seen Me hath seen the Father; and how sayeth thou then, Shew us the Father? Believeth thou not that I am in the Father, and the Father in Me? The words that I speak unto you I speak not of Myself: but the Father that dwelleth in Me, He doeth the works. Believe Me that I am in the Father, and the Father in Me: or else believe Me for the very works sake." (John 14:1-11, portions thereof)

Jesus further explained, "He that hateth Me hateth My Father also. If I had not done among them the works which none other man did, they had not hath sin: but now have they both seen and hated both Me and my Father. But this cometh to pass, that the word might be fulfilled that is written in their law, They hated Me without a cause. But when the Comforter is come, whom I shall send unto you from the Father, even the Spirit of Truth, which proceedeth from the Father, He shall testify of Me: And ye also shall bear witness because ye have been with Me from the beginning."

(John 15:23-27)

The book called "The Acts of the Apostles" contains a brief history of the founding of the Church described by Jesus, the inclusion of Gentiles in the Church, the conversion of Paul the Apostle, and a cross section of Paul's ministry. The book is divided into twenty-eight chapters. Chapter 1 refers to the interaction between Jesus and His disciples; a summation of those who saw Jesus after His resurrection; the ascension of Jesus; and the choice, by lot, of a replacement for Judas Iscariot. Chapter 2 details the outpouring of the Holy Spirit upon the followers of Jesus gathered together in Jerusalem on the day of Pentecost; the first recorded sermon by Peter preaching Jesus to be Christ fulfilling the Scriptures as testified to by his mighty works and resurrection from the dead; and three thousand souls being added to the Church through repentance, acceptance of Jesus as the Son of God, and baptism in His name. It is also noted that the early Church banded together, sold all their goods and possessions, and divided the proceeds among themselves according to each one's needs; and that the Lord added daily to the Church those being converted through the preaching of the Gospel.

Chapter 3 describes the healing through Peter and John of a man crippled from birth followed by Peter's second sermon declaring that Jesus fulfilled the covenant and the prophecies pertaining to Christ, and that forgiveness of sins is through believing upon Him.

Chapter 4 records the first persecution of the followers of Jesus by Jewish religious leaders. Peter and John preached with great power and testified to the resurrection of Jesus, and many thousands were converted and filled with the Holy Ghost. The high priest and his supporters threatened Peter and John and forbade them to speak in Jesus' name. Peter and John, filled with the Spirit of God, continued to preach with boldness and believers gathered about them in prayer were also filled with the Spirit.

Chapter 5 records that a married couple sold some property and held back part of the price but pretended to contribute the full price into the Christian common fund. Peter told them they had lied to the Holy Ghost whereupon the couple died.

The Apostles performed many miracles and healed all manner of sickness and disease including casting out demons. The Jewish religious leaders locked the apostles in the common prison but during the night the angle of the Lord brought them out leaving the prison secure and locked. The next day, when officers came to fetch the apostles, they found the prison locked and guarded and discovered that the apostles were teaching in the temple. Again, the apostles were arrested and brought before the ruling council. The apostles preached Christ as Lord and Savior before the council whereupon they were beaten, warned again not to speak in the name of Jesus, and then set free. The apostles rejoiced because they were counted worthy to suffer for

Jesus' sake, and they continued to preach and teach daily in His name in homes of believers and in the temple.

Chapters 6 and 7 document the friction which arose between the Greeks and the Hebrews concerning daily care for Greek widows; the appointment by the apostles of devout men full of faith and the Holy Ghost (including Stephen, a deacon) to oversee distribution according to need; the arrest and false accusations brought against Stephen by suborned witnesses; the sermon before the council by Stephen wherein he reviewed the history of Israel's persecution and killing of the prophets culminating in the betrayal and murder of Jesus; the bloody attack upon Stephen and his death by stoning while he saw a vision of Jesus and prayed for God's forgiveness of his murderers; and the witnessing of Stephen's martyrdom by Saul of Tarsus (also called Paul).

Chapter 8 describes the persecution of Christians by Saul; Philip's ministry in Samaria; the desire of Simon, a sorcerer, to purchase the power to baptize with the Holy Ghost; Peter's rebuke of Simon; the personal ministry to an Ethiopian eunuch, by Philip; the baptism of the eunuch by Philip; and the spiritual transporting of Philip by the Holy Ghost to Azotus where he preached, and then continued preaching throughout the cities lying between Azotus and Caesarea.

Chapter 9 relates Saul's vision on the road to Damascus wherein Saul was blinded by a heavenly light and heard Jesus personally speaking to him; Saul's conversion from Church persecutor to Paul, the apostle to the Gentiles; Paul's sight restored and his baptism by Ananias (a follower of Jesus); Paul's early ministry at Damascus, and the plot to kill him; Paul's preaching at Jerusalem, and his return to Tarsus. Chapter 9 also documents Peter's healing of Aeneas (a man with palsy), and a woman named Dorcas being raised from the dead by God through Peter.

Chapters 10 and 11 detail Peter's vision wherein God reveals to him that Gentiles are also to be ministered to; Peter's visit to the house of Cornelius, a Gentile, and Peter's preaching to him and his household pursuant to which they all believed and were filled with the Holy Ghost; Peter's defense before certain Jewish believers pertaining to his preaching to Gentiles; the preaching of Paul and Barnabas at Antioch (where the followers of Jesus were first called Christians); the prophecy by Agabus, a Christian, concerning a coming drought; and the donations sent by the believers in Antioch to Christians in Judaea (delivered by Paul and Barnabas).

Chapter 12 records the murder of James (the brother of John) and the imprisonment of Peter by King Herod. Peter was chained and heavily guarded within the prison by Roman soldiers. The Church prayed without ceasing for Peter and the angel of the Lord transported Peter out of the prison and into the city whereupon Peter went to a house where many were gathered together praying for him.

Thereafter, the angel of the Lord smote Herod with worms and Herod died, but the word of God grew and multiplied. Paul and Barnabas returned from Jerusalem to Antioch and took with them John (whose surname is Mark).

Chapters 13 and 14 describe the calling out of Paul and Barnabas by the Holy Ghost to preach at Seleucia, Cyprus, and then Paphos where a sorcerer named Elymas opposed their preaching to Sergius Paulus, a deputy of the country. At Paul's word, Elymas became blind and he sought someone to lead him by the hand, and the deputy became a believer. Paul and Barnabas returned to Antioch and John (Mark) went to Jerusalem.

After two Sabbaths of preaching in the synagogue at Antioch whereby many Jews and religious proselytes believed, Jewish opposition increased mightily whereupon Paul and Barnabas directed their ministry to the Gentiles who gladly received them.

At Iconium, a mob led by Jews purposed to stone Paul and Barnabas so they moved on to Lystra, Derbe, and Lycaonia. At Lystra, Paul healed a man crippled from birth and the people were barely restrained from worshipping them. Then came a band of Jews from Antioch who persuaded the people to stone Paul and they dragged him outside the city thinking him to be dead. When believers gathered around Paul, he stood up and returned to the city, departing the next day with Barnabas to Derbe where they preached the gospel and taught the believers, then returned to Lystra, Iconium, and Antioch encouraging believers and ordaining elders in the churches before traveling on to Pamphylia. They preached also in Perga and Attalia and sailed to Antioch where they rested a long time and related to the brethren all that God had done with them and how the Gentiles listened and believed.

Chapter 15 reports the doc-trinal dispute among Christians concerning observance of the law of Moses and the issue of circumcision. Some Jewish elders believed that to be saved Christians must keep the law given to Moses and also must be circumcised. Paul and Barnabas, among others, believed that Christians are not bound by the law of Moses.

The apostles and elders came together to consider the question and thereafter gave Paul and Barnabas a letter stating that Gentile converts should abstain from meats offered to idols, from eating blood or strangled crea-tures, and from fornication. Paul and Barnabas determined to revisit each city where they had preached and see how the brethren fared. Barnabas wanted to take along John Mark but Paul disagreed because John had left them at Pamphylia. Barnabas and John sailed to Cyprus. Paul selected Silas and they traveled through Syria and Cilicia confirming the churches.

Chapters 16-19 focus on Paul's bonding with a young convert named Timothy; the missionary travels of Paul, Silas and Timothy to Phrygia, the regions of Galatia, Mysia, Troas, Philippi, and Thyatira; Paul's casting out of a woman a spirit of divination, the subsequent beating of Paul and Silas, their imprison-ment and conversion of their Philippian jailor; the founding of the church at Thessalonica; Jewish opposition at Thessalonica and Berea; additional missionary ministry at Athens and Corinth; the miracles of healing and casting out of devils by Paul; and the great uproar at Ephesus triggered by craftsmen producing images of the heathen goddess, Diana.

Chapters 20-23 relate Paul's preaching and teaching at Macedonia, Troas, Miletus, and Ephesus; Paul being forbidden by the Holy Spirit to go to Jerusalem; Paul's visit to Jerusalem where he was seized and bound in chains; Paul's defense before his accusers and his claim to be a Roman citizen by birth; Paul's further defense before the Jewish court; the Jewish plot to kill Paul made known to the Roman chief captain who then sends Paul safely to Caesarea to be questioned by Felix, the governor.

Chapters 24-26 record Paul's defense before Felix wherein he is accused by the Jewish high priest and elders and bound over by Felix awaiting the arrival of the Roman chief captain; Paul's second defense before Felix causing Felix to tremble; Paul's ensuing imprisonment with liberal privileges for two years; Paul's hearing before Porcius Festus (who replaced Felix) and Paul's appeal as a Roman citizen to Caesar; the visit to Caesarea by King Agrippa and his wife, Bernice, to salute Festus; the referral of Paul by Festus to King Agrippa (great-grandson of Herod the Great);

and Paul's defense before Agrippa causing him to say to Paul, "Almost thou persuadest me to be a Christian." (Acts 26:27).

Chapters 27 and 28 describe the transfer of Paul to Rome by ship wherein the ship flounders at Melita and breaks apart; the escape of all aboard the ship due to Paul's warnings and encouragement; Paul's ministry to the Melita island natives including healing the sick and diseased; Paul's arrival in Rome where he was allowed to dwell in his own hired house under Roman guard; the ministry by Paul to all who came to him, both Jews and Gentiles; and continued Jewish opposition to Paul causing him to concentrate on Gentiles.

The Book of Romans is a letter written by Paul to the Christians at Rome expressing his intention to visit them soon, and explaining to them the contrast between God's relationship to humanity under the law given to Moses and God's new covenant of mercy, grace and redemption based upon the sinless life, sacrificial death, and resurrection of Jesus Christ.

Paul writes that there is no excuse for not acknowledging God because He has revealed Himself through that which He created; that those ignoring God are vain and wise within themselves, becoming exceedingly foolish idol worshipers practicing all manner of evil including homosexual abominations; that where there is no law, there is no sin; that God's law given to Moses condemned all humanity and pointed out the need for a sacrificial lamb because fallen humanity is incapable of keeping God's holy law.

Paul points out that the purpose of the law is to point us to Christ through Whom we can be redeemed back to God being reborn spiritually and becoming new creatures in Christ and without fault before God; that we will not be sinless living on earth in our physical bodies of flesh and blood, but that our sins will be abhorred in our minds and not be imputed to us because of Jesus Christ's sacrifice of himself in our place; that we will not practice sin because such behavior is completely contrary to our new spiritual being; that there is no difference between Jews and Gentiles pertaining to the need for redemption because all have sinned and are condemned under the law; and that circumcision, being commanded under the law, is of no avail because we are justified before God by our faith in Jesus Christ without regard to the law.

The Book of First Corinthians is the first of two letters written by Paul to the church at Corinth which had become plagued with doctrinal divisions, judgmental bias, protectionism toward immorality, chaotic order of church service, confusion concerning the resurrection, jealousy among church leaders, corruption of spiritual gifts, and a gluttonous approach to communion service. Paul's letter is oriented toward teaching rather than preaching, and answering questions directed to him concerning Christian lifestyle and stewardship.

Paul writes that Christianity is not divided into

followers of Paul, Cephas, Opollos, etc., but Christ is the one who was crucified and in whose name believers are baptized; that redemption is not rooted in human wisdom, but God has ordained that through the foolishness of preaching believers in Christ shall be saved.

Paul teaches that Christ is the foundation upon which believers can lay up a reward for themselves through faithful stewardship; that believers can lose their reward but not salvation because we are saved by grace and not by works; that believers should not be puffed up and judgmental toward each other, but rather suffer wrongdoing instead of going to court before unbelievers; that sexual immorality and other wickedness within the church is not to be tolerated; and that those who have dedicated themselves to preaching the gospel are worthy of financial support by believers. Paul also writes that communion service in remembrance of Jesus sacrificing Himself is not a time for feasting and drinking, but rather receiving a bite of bread and a sip of wine in commemorating His body and blood until He returns.

Regarding spiritual gifts and orderly worship service, Paul writes that prophetic utterances, speaking in other tongues and interpretation thereof, a word of wisdom, working of miracles, and exercise of other spiritual gifts must not be chaotic in order for both believers and unbelievers to be edified within the church; that in the absence of Godly love, all that can be willingly sacrificed coupled with spiritual gifts profits nothing.

Concerning the resurrection, Paul explains that physical death involves the body and not the spirit; that Christ overcame death and the grave for us; that upon our resurrection from the dead, we are clothed with a body that is pleasing to God; and that believers who are in their physical bodies when Jesus returns will be changed within the twinkling of an eye and be joined by those who have died believing in Christ --- and then corruption will have put on incorruption, and mortal will have put on immortality.

Paul's second letter to the church at Corinth is known as Second Corinthians and focuses primarily upon God's mercy and grace versus legal justification based on works as the basis for human redemption. He begins by emphasizing his deep and abiding love for the Corinthian believers and his concern that some are being led astray from salvation by grace through faith, and confused by those desiring to burden the simple exercise of faith in Christ with the keeping of the law given to Moses.

Paul writes that the gospel of Jesus Christ is holy, spiritual, and glorious and not legal; that the gospel is not improved upon or made perfect by those preaching it; that he is not seeking the praise of men but is filled with joy when he suffers for the cause of Christ; that all believers in Christ are new creatures reconciled to God by the purity and perfection of Christ suffering the penalty for our sins and taking every transgression upon Himself; that believers are ambassadors for Christ walking by faith and not by sight; and that believers should not be unequally yoked together with unbelievers for there is no agreement between the temple of God and idols or between Christ and Satan.

Paul encourages the church at Corinth to help support their fellow Christians lacking financial resources, in accordance with their ability to share, and not grudgingly because God loves a cheerful giver. Paul further writes that the church must avoid false apostles and deceitful workers who present themselves as apostles of Christ, and that the church should not to be surprised by their claims because Satan, himself, is often transformed into an angel of light.

The Book of Galatians is the letter from Paul to the church at Galatia where the two-pronged false doctrine of grace mixed with law as the foundation for redemption, and the believer made perfect by adherence to the law, was being taught.

Paul writes that if a man comes preaching any gospel other than salvation by grace through faith, let him be accursed; that he was not given the gospel of grace by man nor taught it by man, but it came by a revelation from Jesus Christ; that no one is justified by the works of the law but by their faith exercised in Jesus Christ; that those whose hope is in the law are cursed under the law for failing to do all the things written in the law; that the just shall live by faith; that the law is not of faith so that justification under the law requires continuous obedience which has never been accomplished other than by Jesus Christ; that it is evident that no one shall be justified by the law before God.

Paul reasons that if righteousness came by keeping the law, then Christ died in vain; that Abraham believed God and his faith was accepted by God as righteousness; and that the promises made by God to Abraham were not annulled by the law which was given to Moses four hundred and thirty years later.

The Book of Ephesians is the letter from Paul to the church at Ephesus containing encouragement, spiritual teaching, and description of Christian stewardship. Paul writes that from the foundation of the world it was determined that Jesus would redeem humanity back to God; that Jesus is seated at God's right hand having dominion over all principalities and power and above every name in this world and the world to come; that all things are under His feet; that He is the head of all things pertaining to the church which is His body, that it is Jesus after Whom the whole family in heaven and earth is named; that within the body of Christ (the sum of all believers) are apostles, prophets, evangelists, pastors and teachers to minister to and to edify the entire body; that, in the fullness of Christ, believers should not be deceived and swept away by false doctrine and by the craftiness of Satan.

Paul exhorts that we treat each other with love, respect, and meekness of spirit being kind and tenderhearted toward one another and forgiving one another as God, for Christ's sake, has forgiven us; and that we should be thankful to God for all things in the name of our Lord and Savior, Jesus Christ.

The Book of Philippians is a letter from Paul to the church at Philippi saluting the faithfulness of the members and requesting their prayers and financial support. He states that the hardships he has endured and his bonds which are evident in Rome have furthered the gospel of Christ; and that he is committed to magnifying Christ in both life and death.

Paul encourages the members to avoid strife and division by having the mind of Christ who was humble and obedient even to the sacrifice of Himself in accordance with the will of God; to be vigilant concerning evil workers, especially those of the circumcision mixing law with grace; to not sacrifice truth for the sake of unity; and to be faithful to such things which bring honor and glory to Jesus Christ.

Chapter thirteen

The Book of Colossians is a letter from Paul to the church at Colosse warning against man-made doctrines and false teachings which follow after tradition rather than after Jesus Christ.

Paul stresses that Jesus is the image of the invisible God and that by Him all things are created and brought into being, and that only through His body and blood can anyone's sins be forgiven; that Jesus made our peace with God through the blood of His cross thereby presenting us holy and without fault before His throne; that circumcision of our hearts rather than our flesh is pleasing to God; that we should not judge in regard to meat, drink, holy days, new moons, and Sabbaths which were merely a shadow of things which have now appeared.

Paul further warns that we should not allow our own will worship to confuse the grace whereby we are justified by teaching abstinence instead of being dead with Christ to the rudiments of this world; that we, as new creatures in Christ, set our affections on things above and not on earth being dead to the world and our life hid with Christ in God; and that all humans are set free in Christ allowing the peace of God to rule in our hearts while giving praise and thanks to God in all our words and deeds.

The First Book of Thessalonians is one of two letters written by Paul to the church at Thessalonica setting forth the essence of Christian lifestyle and to comfort members concerning those dead in Christ. Paul calls to remembrance the forsaking of idol worship for the truth that is in Christ Jesus through whom we are presented faultless before God. He writes that we should praise God by our outward behavior as well as our inner devotion; that the gospel of Christ consists not of that which is pleasing to man but that which is ordained of God; and that we should extend brotherly love to each other, warn those who are unruly, comfort the feeble-minded and weak, be patient toward all men, not render evil for evil, rejoice always and pray without ceasing.

Concerning those dead in Christ, Paul writes: "But I would not have you to be ignorant, brethren, concerning them which are asleep, that ye sorrow not, even as others who have no hope. For if we believe that Jesus died and rose again, even so them also which sleep in Jesus will God bring with Him. For this we say unto you by the word of the Lord, that we which are alive and remain unto the coming of the Lord shall not prevent them which are asleep.

For the Lord Himself shall descend from heaven with a shout, with the voice of the archangel, and with the trump of God: and the dead in Christ shall rise first: Then we which are alive and remain shall be caught up together with them in the clouds, to meet the Lord in the air: and so shall we ever be with the Lord. Wherefore comfort one another with these words." (I Thessalonians 4:13-18)

The Second Book of Thessalonians is Paul's letter to the church at Thessalonica addressing the confusion among the members concerning the period of great tribulation and the day of Christ.

Paul explains that before the man of sin (Antichrist) is revealed, the Holy Spirit must allow it to be so, and such lifting of the Holy Spirit will not occur prior to a falling away of believers (apostasy); that the one coming with the power of Satan will, through lying signs and wonders, deceive those who have rejected the truth and love unrighteousness; and that the son of perdition will exalt himself above God and sit in the temple of God demanding to be worshiped, but will be destroyed by Jesus with His word and the power of His appearing.

Paul further encourages the church to remain faithful and to withdraw from those behaving foolishly and refusing to work; to not become weary with well doing; and to avoid those ruled by their flesh, but to reprove them as brethren and not as enemies.

The Book of First Timothy is the first of two letters written by Paul to Timothy (his beloved son in the faith) concerning church order, sound doctrine and member discipline. Paul advises Timothy to avoid fables, endless genealogies, and all subjects contrary to the gospel of Christ which gender strife rather than edification; that the law was not made for the righteous but for the lawless and disobedient; that Christ came into the world to save sinners; and that some still attempt to teach the law which they understand not and thus corrupt the gospel of Christ.

Paul also advises that supplications, prayers, intercessions, and thanksgiving be the heart of church worship; that there is one God and one mediator between God and man, which is Jesus Christ; and that women adorn themselves with that which expresses godliness, and to not usurp authority over men, nor to teach, but rather to learn in silence.

Concerning qualifications for bishops and deacons, Paul writes that they must be blameless, vigilant, sober, well behaved, apt to teach, given to hospitality, not a brawler, not given to much wine, not covetous, not greedy, and have no more than one wife, ruling their own houses well, keeping their children under subjection, and having a good reputation from without the church. Their wives also must be grave, not given to gossip, sober, and faithful in all things.

Paul warns Timothy that in the latter days some will lose their faith being swayed by false teachings, Satanic doctrines, and hypocritical liars which forbid marriage and eating of certain meats; and that he should turn away from such falsehoods standing fast in that which he knows to be sound doctrine approved by God. Paul also advises Timothy to treat an elder like a father and younger men as brethren, older women like a mother and younger women as sisters with purity; to honor and care for widows who need charity; and to drink a little wine for his stomach's sake and to soothe his frequent infirmities.

Paul's second letter to Timothy suggests that Paul knew his martyrdom was near. He writes that he is ready to be offered and that the time of his death is at hand; that he conquered his persecutions and maintained his faith thereby having a reward reserved for him in heaven. Paul again cautions Timothy that he will have to battle against false doctrines, corruptions of the gospel of Christ, and Satanic snares; that with the passing of time, humans will become more foolish and more perverse while professing godliness but denying the power of God; that evil doers will become exceedingly wicked deceiving both themselves and others; and that Timothy will be faced with rejection, ridicule, and persecution which will be directed to all believers in Jesus Christ.

The Book of Titus is Paul's letter to another "son in the faith" and is quite similar to his first letter to Timothy wherein he sets forth the qualifications for bishops and reviews the foundations of the gospel of Christ in concert with faithful stewardship. Paul advises Titus to avoid foolish questions, genealogies, contentions and striving about the law; and to obey secular authority consistent with the teachings of Jesus Christ.

The Book of Philemon is a brief letter from Paul to his friend, Philemon, whose slave had robbed him and fled to Rome. While in Rome, Onesimus, the runaway, was converted by Paul to Christianity. Paul sent him back to Philemon with his personal letter beseeching Philemon to receive Onesimus back as a brother rather than as a slave, and that whatever Onesimus owed should be charged back to Paul.

The Book of Hebrews declares that Jesus Christ has fulfilled the whole purpose of the law through His sinless life, sacrificial offering of Himself as "the Lamb of God," His glorious resurrection, and His subsequent presentation of all who accept Him as being covered by His righteousness before God, and as being totally justified by His obedience even unto death; and that Jesus now sits at the right hand of God interceding for believers as their High Priest.

Hebrews teaches that God's acceptance of Judaism, as confirmed under the law given by God to Moses, ended with Jesus' sacrificial death whereby He suffered the penalty for all humans required under the law thus setting us free from the law and its prescribed penalties for disobedience; and that Jesus ushered in the new covenant under which the law became null and void making possible the redemption back to God of all believers who accept Jesus as the sacrificial lamb for their personal sins.

Hebrews warns that there remains no path of repentance and forgiveness for those who, having received the word of truth and having been enlightened by the Holy Ghost, refuse to accept Jesus Christ as the one and only sacrifice God will accept for the remission of their sins. Furthermore, Hebrews confirms that Jesus is the brightness of God's glory and the express image of His person; that He took upon Himself the flesh of man and was tempted in all things wherein we are tempted, yet without sin; and that through His obedience unto death, we are made guiltless.

Personal faith in that which is unseen is emphasized in Hebrews, especially in chapter 11; and such faith in Jesus Christ and His finished work of redemption, apart from the law, is the common thread that binds all thirteen chapters together.

The Book of James teaches that the manner in which a person behaves and interacts with others is a direct reflection of morals and values shaped by inner faith. James cautions that the tongue is an unruly evil filled with deadly poison, and that whoever offends not in words is able to control the entire body; that we should not boast of tomorrow because our life is in God's hands; that we should be doers as well as hearers of God's word; and that it is through our own lusts that we are tempted and drawn into sin. James writes: "Is any among you afflicted? let him pray. Is any merry? let him sing psalms. Is any sick among you? let him call for the elders of the church; and let them pray over him, anointing him with oil in the name of the Lord: And the prayer of faith shall save the sick, and the Lord shall raise him up; and if he have committed sins, they shall be forgiven him." (James 5:13-15)

The First Book of Peter is one of two letters written by the apostle, Peter, to Christian Jews and Gentiles scattered throughout Pontus, Galatia, Cappadocia, Asia, and Bithynia encouraging them to maintain the faith in both word and deed so as to silence the ignorance of foolish men. Peter writes that Jesus is the Shepherd and Bishop of our souls who bore our sins in His own body and by Whose stripes we are healed; that Jesus, being without sin, was reviled and persecuted but did not despise nor threaten His tormentors thereby leaving us an example to follow; and that we should be joyful when reproached for our faith in Christ, and exercise sincere love toward each other.

Second Peter is addressed to all Christians and refers to the grace, peace, and knowledge of God that is in Jesus Christ through which we have escaped the corruption of the world and have become the recipients of the exceedingly great and precious promises of God; and that we should with all diligence exhibit faith, virtue, knowledge, temperance, patience, kindness, charity and godliness.

Peter writes that his martyrdom is near and warns us to be watchful for false prophets and false teachers who will, with damnable heresies and veiled lies, lead many astray; and that no prophecy of the scripture is of any private interpretation.

Peter further admonishes that with the passing of time the second coming of Christ will be scoffed at, but that the day of the Lord will come when least expected wherein the heavens shall pass away with a mighty sound and the elements will melt with fervent heat and Earth will be dissolved; and that there will be new heavens and a new Earth filled with righteousness.

The Books of First, Second, and Third John are three letters written by the apostle, John, around 90 AD. The first letter is directed to "born again" believers and confirms that John saw, heard, and touched Jesus Christ through whom we have fellowship with the Father; that God is light and in Him is no darkness; that if we walk in God's light, we have fellowship with each other and the blood shed by Jesus Christ keeps us free from sin; that if we say we do not sin, we are liars who deny God's word, but if we confess our sins, we are forgiven because Jesus Christ intercedes for us; that if we love the things of the world, the love of God is not in us; and that if we love Christ we will keep his commandments to maintain our faith in Him, to love one another and to treat others as we desire to be treated.

John writes that any prophecy or teaching that denies that Jesus Christ is God's Son, come in the flesh, is of the spirit of antichrist, that many false prophets are in the world; and that all those who profess and believe in Jesus Christ cannot sin (sin is not imputed) because they are born of God.

Second John is a personal letter from John to a woman (the elect lady and her children) expressing his joy that her children are believers, and stressing God's commandment to love one another; that deceivers are in the world; and that she should not receive such into her house nor bid them God speed to avoid sharing their evil deeds.

Third John is another personal letter from John to Gaius (one of the beloved brethren) wishing him prosperity and good health. John informs Gaius, a man of integrity, faithful to Christ, and member of a certain church, that he (John) had written to the church but had not been received there due to the evil influence of Diotrephes who refused to receive the brethren himself and cast out those who would receive them. John recommends Demetrius and states his desire to visit soon with Gaius face to face.

The Book of Jude is a letter from Jude, the brother of James, to the brethren encouraging them to stand firmly in the faith thereby contending with false prophets and teachers who deny the grace of God and Jesus Christ. Jude compares such evil doers to those slain by God in the wilderness for unbelief, to angels who left their first estate, and to the people of Sodom and Gomorrah.

Jude calls to remembrance the warnings of the apostles concerning such filthy dreamers who despise dominion and speak evil of dignities whereas Michael, the archangel, would not bring a railing accusation against Satan, himself. Jude advocates loving and supporting each other in Jesus Christ who is able to sustain believers and present them faultless before God with great joy.

The Book of Revelation was written by the apostle, John, approximately 96 AD during his banishment to the isle of Patmos because of his faithfulness to the gospel of Jesus Christ. John experiences a vision wherein Jesus appears to him in glorified form and instructs him to write letters to the seven churches in Asia (in Ephesus, Smyrna, Pergamos, Thyatira, Sardis, Philadelphia, and Laodicea) giving praise, warning, and rebuke to each individual church in accordance with the church's spiritual standing.

John was caught up in the spirit to witness "things which shall be hereafter" and saw in his vision the glory of God seated upon His throne surrounded by heavenly living creatures, angelic beings, and elders. A rainbow arched around the throne and there were lightning, thundering, and voices, and seven lamps of burning fire. In the right hand of the Glorious One upon the throne was a book written within and on the back side sealed seven times over. An angelic voice thundered through heaven asking who is able to open the book and loose the seals. The awesome silence was broken only by weeping. Then, before the throne appeared a Lamb bearing the wounds of slaughter having seven horns and seven eyes who took the book from God's right hand whereupon millions of angels, the living creatures, and the elders fell down before the lamb with worship, praise and singing.

As the Lamb loosed the seals, John saw the things which are coming upon the world: four horsemen bringing false peace --- war--- famine and pestilence --- death and hell thereby destroying one fourth of the world's population; a mighty earthquake dislocating mountains and islands; the heaven rolling together as a scroll; the sun becoming black and the moon appearing as blood; burning masses from space pelting the earth; and humans hiding in holes, caves, dens and among the rocks trying to hide from the wrath of God and of the Lamb.

John heard angels sealing twelve thousand individuals from each tribe of Israel, and he saw a great multitude of people from among all nations who suffered martyrdom during the period of great tribulation gathered before the throne with angels, elders and the living creatures giving honor, praise and glory to God.

When John saw the Lamb open the seventh seal, there was silence in heaven for approximately thirty minutes followed by lightning, thundering, and an earthquake in Earth.

Then, hail and fire mingled with blood fell on Earth and one third of trees and grasses burnt up; a great mountain burning with fire fell into the sea destroying a third of ships and a third of marine life; a huge flaming mass (named wormwood) fell upon the rivers and fountains of water poisoning a third of those waters; the sun, moon, and stars were smitten so that a third of the day and a third of the night were without light; mutant locusts swarmed from within Earth having stingers that cause torment for five months; and four fallen angels were freed from darkness to lead an army of two hundred million to kill one third of Earth's remaining population. Thereafter, a mighty angel swore by the living God that there should be time no longer.

After this, John saw two appointed witnesses and heard an angel proclaim their power to smite Earth with plagues according to their choosing for twelve hundred and sixty days before being killed by Satan and subsequently resurrected by God and summoned into heaven.

John stood upon land and saw a hellish beast rise from the sea having seven heads and ten horns with ten crowns and blasphemy written on the seven heads. One of the heads suffered a fatal wound which healed causing the world to wonder after and to worship the beast who blasphemed God and all that dwell in heaven.

The beast was given power to continue for forty-two months to make war, to blaspheme, and to rule over all Earth's remaining population whose names are not written in the Lamb's Book of Life. Another beast appeared on Earth having two horns and speaking like a dragon and exercising all the power exhibited by the first beast and working great wonders including calling down fire from heaven. This beast also required everyone to receive a mark in the right hand or forehead without which no one can buy nor sell; and the mark is the number of the name of the beast and the number is six hundred and sixty-six.

John saw an angel flying in the midst of heaven

preaching the everlasting gospel and proclaiming that God should be honored, praised and feared because the time of his judgment is come. Then, a second angel announced the fall of Babylon, and a third angel warned against taking the mark of the beast which confers everlasting punishment in fire and brimstone.

After seeing and hearing additional wonders attributing glory, praise and honor to God, John saw and heard God's wrath continue in Earth: a noisome and grievous sore appeared upon all who worshiped the beast; the sea became as the blood of a dead man and everything died therein; the rivers and fountains of water became blood; the sun scorched everything living; and then total darkness descended upon Earth.

When the armies of the nations gathered together on the battlefield of Armageddon, an unprecedented earthquake caused islands and mountains to disappear and the great city was divided into three parts; great hailstones (each about the weight of a talent) fell upon Earth; and humans blasphemed God because of the hail for the plague was exceedingly great.

An angel carried John away in the spirit and showed him a woman riding upon a scarlet colored beast having seven heads and ten horns. The woman was clothed in purple and scarlet color and adorned with gold, silver and precious stones and held a cup full of the abominations and filthiness of her fornications; and on her forehead was written "Mystery Babylon The Great, the Mother of Harlots and Abominations of the

Earth;" and she was drunken with the blood of saints and the blood of the martyrs of Jesus Christ.

John marveled at the sight and the angel explained that the beast is Satan's false prophet and the woman is the great city which reigns over the kings of the earth; that the seven heads are seven mountains upon which the great whore sits; that there are seven kings of which five have fallen, that one king is, and the seventh is yet to appear; that the beast ridden by the whore was alive and is now dead but shall ascend from the bottomless pit; that the ten horns are ten kings without kingdoms who shall receive power one hour with the beast, having one mind and giving their power and strength to the beast to make war with the Lamb but they shall not prevail; that the ten horns will turn on the whore leaving her desolate, naked, and burned with fire; and that the waters where the whore sits are peoples, multitudes, nations, and tongues.

John saw heaven open and Jesus leading forth the armies of heaven to take control of Earth. The beast and the false prophet were taken and cast alive into a lake of fire burning with brimstone. Those following after the beast were slain by the spoken word of Jesus and devoured by ravenous birds.

A mighty angel chained Satan and locked him in the bottomless pit where he would not deceive the nations for one thousand years during which time Jesus Christ and those who believed in and accepted him will reign upon Earth. Thereafter, Satan will be loosed for a brief period and shall gather a great army to make war against Jesus and his saints whereupon the armies will be devoured by fire coming out of heaven. Satan is cast into the lake of fire where the beast and false prophet are, and will be tormented day and night forever.

The seas, death and hell deliver up all their dead to stand before God, and the books are opened. All those who died in their sins, having rejected the sacrificial death and resurrection of Christ are formally judged according to their works and cast into the lake of fire along with death and hell.

Thereafter, John saw a new heaven and a new Earth without seas, and the holy city, new Jerusalem, descending out of heaven. The city measures twelve thousand furlongs in height, width and breadth having twelve foundations and the glory of God and of the Lamb provide light without need for the sun and moon.

Proceeding from the throne of God and of the Lamb is the crystal pure river of life lined on both sides with the tree of life bearing twelve different fruits and yielding fruit each month. "And the spirit and the bride say, Come. And let him that heareth say, Come. And let him that is athirst come. And whosoever will, let him take the water of life freely." (Revelation 22:17)

The foregoing summaries covering all sixty-six books within the Holy Bible are obviously not intended to substitute for a careful and thoughtful reading of the Holy Scriptures which fill up approximately twelve hundred pages in a small print edition. The author's purpose is rather to present a brief summary of each book so that readers who are unfamiliar with the text can more easily follow the difficult narratives and hopefully better understand Biblical prophecies.

When comparing Christianity to all other world religions, it is worth remembering that only Jesus Christ is believed by over two billion people to be alive and making intercession for them before God. Moreover, only the God detailed within the Holy Bible actually walked upon Earth and communicated directly to humanity in human form (Jesus Christ) while healing all manner of sickness and disease; raising the dead; opening blind eyes and deaf ears; restoring withered and crippled limbs; controlling the wind and waves; and feeding thousands with a handful of bread and fish. Jesus performed many of these wondrous works before tens of thousands of eye witnesses; and His most vicious and jealous enemies did not deny He did such things. Rather, those hating Him for personal reasons simply said He performed such works by supernatural evil powers. Their solution to preserving their own self-worship was to find a way to murder Jesus

Only Jesus willingly offered Himself up before God as humanity's sacrificial lamb. Only Jesus was seen and heard by hundreds of people over a period of forty days after He rose from the dead. Only Jesus is returning to Earth from Heaven to rule over Planet Earth for a thousand years. Only faith in Him can save mankind.

The age of the Dispensation of Grace and Mercy will end with the rapture of living individuals who have accepted Jesus Christ as the divine sacrifice for their personal sins. Concurrent with this event, the dead in Christ will be resurrected, and together, the redeemed will put on immortality and a new body not subject to death. The word rapture is used to describe the events foretold in these Scriptures:

"But I would not have you to be ignorant, brethren, concerning them which are asleep, that ye sorrow not, even as others which have no hope. For if we believe that Jesus died and rose again, even so them also which sleep in Jesus will God bring with Him. For this we say unto you by the word of the Lord, that we which are alive and remain unto the coming of the Lord shall not prevent them which are asleep. For the Lord Himself shall descend from heaven with a shout, with the voice of the archangel, and with the trump of God: and the dead in Christ shall rise first: Then we which are alive and remain shall be caught up together with them in the clouds, to meet the Lord in the air: and so shall we ever be with the Lord. Wherefore comfort one another with these words." (I Thessalonians, chapter 4, verses 13-18)

"Now this I say, brethren, that flesh and blood cannot inherit the kingdom of God; neither doth corruption inherit incorruption. Behold, I shew you a mystery; We shall not all sleep, but we shall all be changed, in a moment, in the twinkling of an eye, at the last trump: for the trumpet shall sound, and and the dead shall be raised incorruptible, and we shall be changed. For this corruptible must put on incorruption, and this mortal must put on immortality. So when this corruptible shall have put on incorruption, and this mortal shall have put on immortality, then shall be brought to pass the saying that is written, Death is swallowed up in victory. O death, where is thy sting? O grave, where is thy victory? The sting of death is sin, and the strength of sin is the law. But thanks be to God, which giveth us the victory through our Lord Jesus Christ. Therefore, my beloved brethren, be ye steadfast, unmovable, always abounding in the work of the Lord, forasmuch as ye know that your labor is not in vain in the Lord." (I Corinthians, chapter 15, verses 50-58)

When is the rapture going to occur? The day, hour and year is known only to God. However, the approach of this momentous event is looming ever closer. There are no Old Testament or New Testament prophecies that must be fulfilled prior to the rapture. The last pre-rapture prophecy was fulfilled in 1948 when Israel again became a nation after 1,878 years of dispersion and persecution among the nations (70 A.D. to 1948). The prophecy recorded in the book of Daniel has also been fulfilled: "But thou, O Daniel, shut up the words, and seal the book, even to the time of the end: many shall run to and fro, and knowledge shall be increased." (Daniel, chapter 12, verse 4; written 534 B.C.)

Today's world population is the most mobile in the history of humanity, being able to circle Earth within three days; and more people are traveling today than any prior generation. Humanity has acquired more know-ledge during the last hundred years than in the previous fifty-nine centuries. A mere 149 years ago, the Civil War was raging in the United States. The primary mode of transportation was horse drawn vehicles or on horseback. 300 years ago, the United States did not exist. In less than 150 years, human knowledge has advanced from horse and buggy to the space shuttle. It is certainly an understatement that many are running to and fro and knowledge has been increased.

A statement made by Jesus Christ concerning the end of humanity on Earth has already occurred:

"And this gospel of the kingdom shall be preached in all the world for a witness unto all nations, and then shall the end come." (Matthew, chapter 24, verse 14; Jesus Christ answering questions from apostles)

Missionaries have spread the Gospel of Christ to the least civilized areas of the globe. Radio and television blanket Earth with Christian broadcasts around the clock. The gospel of the kingdom is truly being preached to all nations. Jesus also said that humanity would be behaving like the people of Noah's day and like the inhabitants of Sodom and Gomorrah

(Luke, chapter 17, verses 26-30). The United States is the most Christian nation on Earth, yet homosexuality is displayed on prime time television. Homosexuals have no more shame than the people of Sodom and Gomorrah. We have homosexual demonstrations in our streets and parks. We are passing laws to give them rights to teach our children, to fondle their partners in public, to flout same sex marriages, and to lay the cost of their sexually transmitted AIDS problems upon the public treasury. We are condoning all types of homo-sexual behavior like it is a God given right, whereas the Biblical remedy for homosexual activity is public execution:

"If a man also lie with mankind, as he lieth with a woman, both of them have committed an abomination: they shall surely be put to death; their blood shall be upon them." (Leviticus, chapter 20, verse 13; see also Romans, chapter 1, verses 24-32)

Not only are we attempting to exterminate the population of our nation by same sex copulation, we are murdering our children in the womb and calling this infanticide "pro-choice." We have a clever approach to this premeditated murder. We just deny that the baby being murdered exists. Unborn children have been classified by law as being a non-person, just a blob of tissue that is a non-living entity within the womb. We soothe the mother with this Satanic lie while the murderer invades her womb and prematurely turns the baby so his/her body can be partially extracted from the birth canal head first.

Then, a surgical instrument is used to open a hole in the back of the baby's head so the infant's brain can be extracted. The child is then fully removed from the mother and discarded. After all, it's not a baby, it's just a glob of tissue. Of course, all abortions are not partial birth in nature. We murder our children at various stages of life, ranging from a developing fetus to partial birth. O God! Surely hell is the just and deserving habitation for abortionists.

The classification of unborn children as non-persons and having no life of their own until actual birth has taken place is absolute nonsense, and invented solely to escape the penalty for murder. Should the abortionist accidentally allow the baby to slip free of the birth canal before murdering the infant, the abortion laws would not apply and a charge of intentional homicide would be valid under criminal law. However, someone other than the abortion team would have to witness and report the incident, which is highly unlikely.

When does life begin during the reproductive process? An objective answer must take into account the scientific definition of life described as the abilities to initiate movement, to feed and to reproduce. When conception occurs, a living being is created from the fertilization of the female egg by copulation with a male or by artificial insemination. The fertilized egg has a life of its own because it moves, it feeds, and it reproduces through the process known as mitosis. The developing embryo continues to move and feed and reproduce until it progresses through the fetal stage and can be freed from the womb. Inside the womb, the baby is dependent upon the mother's blood stream for feeding, and outside the womb, the baby is dependent upon the mother's milk or some substitute therefor.

If the criteria for life is not being dependent upon the mother, or a mother substitute, for continued existence, then all babies outside the womb are non-persons; just globs of tissue. It is worthwhile reflecting that Jews were first classified as non-persons before being murdered by the Germans.

Another indication that the rapture is near is the capability of humans to destroy all life on Earth. Heads of state who would not hesitate to use nuclear weapons are in the process of acquiring them. India and Pakistan have threatened nuclear war. Israel has nuclear capability now, and Arab nations are frantically seeking nuclear weapons. North Korea is manufacturing a nuclear arsenal. Terrorists are being funded to buy or steal nuclear firepower. The actual use of such weaponry is looming on the horizon. The prophecy recorded in Zechariah is shortly going to be fulfilled:

"And this shall be the plague wherewith the Lord shall smite all the people that have fought against Jerusalem; Their flesh shall consume away while they stand upon their feet, and their eyes shall consume away in their holes, and their tongue shall consume away in their mouth." (Zechariah, chapter 14, verse 12; written

487 B.C.)

This prophecy paints a picture of nuclear war in the Middle East, especially when viewed in light of a similar prophecy in Ezekiel:

"And it shall come to pass in that day, that I will give unto Gog a place there of graves in Israel, the valley of the passengers on the east of the sea: and it shall stop the noses of the passengers: and there shall they bury Gog and all his multitude: and they shall call it the valley of Hamon-gog. And seven months shall the house of Israel be burying of them, that they may cleanse the land. Yea, all the people of the land shall bury them; and it shall be to them a renown the day that I shall be glorified, saith the Lord God. And they shall sever out men of continual employment, passing through the land to bury with the passengers those who remain upon the face of the earth, to cleanse it; after the end of seven months shall they search. And the passengers that pass through the land, when any seeth a man's bone, then shall he set up a marker by it, till the buriers have buried it in the valley of Hamon-gog. And also the name of the city shall be Hamonah. Thus shall they cleanse the land." (Ezekiel, chapter 38, verses 11-16; written 587 B.C.)

It is today no mystery why so much care will be given to searching out and burying individual bones in order to cleanse the land. It is because such bones will be radioactive.

Although the timing of the rapture is known only

to God, the sequence of events following the rapture are prophesied with specific time references, up to and including the death of all species on Earth. It is critical to understanding these prophecies that we take note that Satan will exert considerably more power over the activities of humanity after the faithful Christians are raptured. This is because Christians, filled with the Spirit of God, are no longer standing in his way: "And they worshiped the dragon (Satan) which gave power unto the beast (Antichrist): and they worshiped the beast, saying, Who is like unto the beast? who is able to make war with him? And there was given unto him a mouth speaking great things and blasphemies; and power was given unto him to continue forty and two months. And he opened his mouth in blasphemy against God, to blaspheme His name, and His tabernacle, and them that dwell in heaven." (Revelation, chapter 13, verses 4-6; Patmos vision, 96 A.D.)

The Apostle, John, after surviving being dipped into a pot of boiling oil, was banished to the isle of Patmos, where, in 96 A.D., he saw a vision wherein Jesus Christ showed him the sequence of events which will occur   following the rapture of those "dead in Christ" and those "alive in Christ;"

1. The appearance of Satan "in the flesh" (the beast) following a war wherein Israel will exit as a world power;   2. The rise of an individual (the false

prophet) who will organize all forms of worship into Satanism; 3. The beast elevated to global dictator in connection with a peace treaty to end all conflict in the Middle East and around the world; 4. The mark of the beast without which no one may buy or sell, and all who refuse the mark will be hunted down and tortured to death; 5. Two prophets oppose the beast and shake the world with a series of devastating plagues and 144,000 individuals will be preaching the wrath of God upon the kingdom of the beast and salvation to those martyred during the reign of Satan; 6. The battle of the nations (Armageddon) just prior to the return of Jesus Christ to Earth as "King of kings and Lord of lords;" 7. Satan bound and powerless during the reign of Christ on Earth (one thousand years); 8. Loosing of Satan and the final battle between God and Satan; 9. The death of all corrupted species on Earth and the "new creation" in conjunction with judgment of all who have rejected God's plan of redemption (Jesus); 10. Eternal banishment of Satan's followers into the lake of fire.

The reign of Satan in the form of Antichrist (the beast) will last seven years. The reign of Christ on Earth will last one thousand years; and time without end (eternity) will commence thereafter. The trinity of Satan (the dragon, the beast, and the false prophet) will spend eternity in the lake of fire joined by all of Satan's disciples (those who by choice selected Lucifer [Satan] as spiritual father, lord and master). Those humans who will occupy the lake of fire forever will be there by conscious choice. Because, when given the opportunity to choose between God and Satan, they chose the prince of darkness rather than the Sacrificial Lamb; they chose the lust of the flesh, the lust of the eyes and the pride of life rather than undefiled love, divine grace and tender mercy. They will be there because they deemed the free gift of redemption to be less desirable than the pleasures of sin for a season.

You say you don't believe in hell, or Jesus Christ, and all that crap. Well, do you suppose your lust, pride, and arrogance will put out the lake of fire, or nullify the final judgment, or quiet the whining of lost souls time without end? In any event, the choice is yours to make as a free moral agent, created in God's own image. And, you are not the first deluded soul to insist upon your right to follow Satan into eternity:

".......We have made a covenant with death, and with hell are we at agreement; when the overflowing scourge shall pass through, it shall not come unto us: for we have made lies our refuge, and under falsehood have we hid ourselves." (Isaiah, chapter 28, verse 15)

"The earth mourneth and fadeth away, the world languisheth and fadeth away, the haughty people of the earth do languish. The earth also is defiled under the inhabitants thereof; because they have transgressed the laws, changed the ordinance, broken the everlasting covenant. Therefore hath the curse devoured the earth, and they that dwell therein are desolate: therefore the inhabitants of the earth are burned, and few men left."

(Isaiah, chapter 24, verses 4-6)

Perhaps you are among the lukewarm, the "divine vomit," who, having accepted the sacrifice of Jesus Christ are, like Lot among the people of Sodom and Gomorrah, keeping company with the children of Satan. At a time when you think not, in the twinkling of an eye, the rapture will occur and you will be left behind to seal your testimony with your own blood. While you were watching pornography on the idiot box, evolutionists were teaching our children that they evolved from apes.

While abortionists and homosexual advocates were being elected to control the legislative and judicial branches of our government, you found more important things to do than cast your vote for God fearing candidates. You supported blasphemy and anti-Christian themes on television by watching the programs and enriching the sponsors by buying their products and services. You encouraged motion pictures belittling God and Christian values by paying to watch the productions. You were occupied with the lust of the flesh and status elevation rather than participating in Christian steward-ship, and pooling resources with other Christians to defeat Antichrist forces within our churches, schools, and government. You gave lip service to Christ, but were silent before his enemies:

"I know thy works, that thou art neither cold not hot: I would thou wert cold or hot. So then because thou art lukewarm, and neither cold nor hot, I will spew thee out of My mouth." (Revelation, chapter 3, verses 15-16)

When the rapture occurs, the people who remain on Earth will be aware that certain Christians are missing, but will be unaware of the true reason therefor. Excuses will be offered to explain away the missing individuals who will represent a small percentage of Earth's human population. Life on Earth will continue and the raptured Christians will soon be old news as those left behind are captivated by emergence of a new celebrity (the Antichrist). This magnetic personality will provide believable solutions to previously insolvable problems and will orchestrate global peace including a treaty with Abraham's seed (Israel).

Pursuant to being accepted as dictator over all humanity, the Antichrist will use the absolute power given him to wage a genocide campaign against all Jews and to hunt down the "divine vomit" (left behind, lukewarm Christians) who will recognize the Antichrist as Satan in the flesh (the beast). The treaty with Israel will be violated and the beast will proclaim himself to be almighty god. Peace will revert to global war ushering in pestilence, famine, and decimation of Earth's population.

These events are revealed to John during the portion of his Patmos vision pertaining to "the things which shall be hereafter." A scroll, written on both sides and sealed with seven seals, is being unsealed by "the Lamb of God" (Jesus). The angels are in attendance along with four divinely ordained living creatures (the four beasts), and twenty-four "elders" from among the raptured and the redeemed remnant of Israel.

"..............the Lamb opened one of the seals, and I heard, as it were the noise of thunder, one of the four beasts saying, Come and see. And I saw, and behold a white horse: and he that sat on him had a bow; and a crown was given unto him: and he went forth conquering, and to conquer. And when He had opened the second seal, I heard the second beast say, Come and see. And there went out another horse that was red: and power was given to him that sat thereon to take peace from the earth, and that they should kill one another: and there was given unto him a great sword. And when He had opened the third seal, I heard the third beast say, Come and see. And I beheld, and lo a black horse; and he that sat on him had a pair of balances in his hand. And I heard a voice in the midst of the four beasts say, A measure of wheat for a penny, and three measures of barley for penny; and see thou hurt not the oil and the wine. And when He had opened the fourth seal, I heard the voice of the fourth beast say, Come and see. And I looked, and behold a pale horse: and his name that sat on him was Death, and Hell followed with him. And power was given unto them over the fourth part of the earth, to kill with sword, and with hunger, and with death, and with the beasts of the earth." (Revelation, chapters 4, a portion of verses 1-11; chapter 6, verses 1-8, Patmos vision, 96 A.D.)

The nuclear war described in Zechariah, chapter

14, verse 12; and in Ezekiel, chapter 38, verses 1-23; chapter 39, verses 1-16 will set Israel apart from other nations to such an extent that the Antichrist will have to negotiate a peace treaty with the Jews in order to bring about the false peace which vaunts him into power as global dictator. This false peace will last forty-two months (the first half of the reign of Satan on earth). The peace will be broken when the beast (Antichrist) sets out to exterminate the seed of Abraham:

"And woe unto them that are with child, and to them that give suck in those days! But pray ye that your flight be not in winter, neither on the sabbath day: for then shall be great tribulation, such as was not since the beginning of the world to this time, no, nor ever shall be. And except those days should be shortened, there should no flesh be saved: but for the elect's sake those days shall be shortened." (Matthew, chapter 24, verses 19-22; Jesus Christ prophesying to his disciples)

"And there followed him a great company of people, and of women, which bewailed and lamented him. But Jesus turning unto them said, Daughters of Jerusalem, weep not for Me, but weep for yourselves, and for your children. For, behold, the days are coming, in the which they shall say, Blessed are the barren, and the wombs that never bare, and the paps which never gave suck. Then shall they begin to say to the mountains, Fall on us; and to the hills, Cover us. For if they do these things in a green tree, what shall be done in the dry?" (Luke, chapter 23, verses 27-31; spoken by

Jesus on the way to his sacrificial death)

In 538 B.C., the angel, Gabriel, explained the treachery of Satan in the flesh (Antichrist) to Daniel the prophet. The time references were given in "weeks of years" (one week equals seven years; or a total period of time equal to seventy times seven years):

"Seventy weeks are determined upon thy people and upon thy holy city, to finish the transgression, and to make an end of sins, and to make reconciliation for iniquity, and to bring in everlasting righteousness, and to seal up the vision and prophecy, and to anoint the most Holy. Know therefore and understand, that from the going forth of the commandment to restore and to build Jerusalem unto Messiah the Prince shall be seven weeks, and threescore and two weeks: the street shall be built again, and the wall, even in troublous times. After threescore and two weeks shall Messiah be cut off, but not for Himself: and the people of the prince that shall come shall destroy the city and the sanctuary; and the end thereof shall be with a flood, and unto the end of the war desolations are determined. And he shall confirm the covenant with many for one week: and in the midst of the week he shall cause the sacrifice and the oblation to cease, and for the overspreading of abominations he shall make it desolate......." (Daniel, chapter 9, verses 24-27; spoken by Gabriel, 538 B.C.)

Four hundred and eighty-three years (sixty-nine weeks of years) elapsed between the decree allowing the remnant of Judah and Benjamin to return to Jerusalem, and the death of Christ, exactly as predicted by Gabriel. One week of years (seven years) still remain to be fulfilled as referenced by Gabriel to Daniel in 538 B.C. This period of seven years will be fulfilled during the reign of the Antichrist, and the clock will begin ticking again pursuant to the rapture of faithful Christians from Earth. The first three and one half years of Antichrist's reign will be peaceful, and the final three and one half years will be filled with terror, torture, murder, war, and genocide:

"And one said to the man clothed in linen, which was upon the waters of the river, How long shall it be to the end of these wonders? And I heard the man clothed in linen, which was upon the waters of the river, when he held up his right hand and his left hand unto heaven, and sware by Him who liveth forever that it shall be for a time, times, and a half; and when he shall have accomplished to scatter the power of the holy people, all these things shall be finished. And I heard, but I understood not: then said I, O my Lord, what shall be the end of these things? And he said, Go thy way, Daniel: for the words are closed up and sealed till the time of the end. Many shall be purified, and made white, and tried; but the wicked shall do wickedly; and none of the wicked shall understand; but the wise shall understand. And from the time that the daily sacrifice shall be taken away, and the abomination that maketh desolate set up, there shall be a thousand two hundred and ninety days." (Daniel, chapter 12, verses 6-11)

The abomination that maketh desolate is the violation of the Jewish temple by Antichrist wherein Satan, in the flesh, occupies the temple and proclaims himself to be almighty god. This occurs at the midpoint of his seven year reign, and coincides with his efforts to kill every Jew, and to torture to death all who refuse to take his mark and to worship him as god. He will wage war against Israel, and roving death squads will hunt down the "divine vomit" (those lukewarm Christians left behind at the rapture, but knowing enough to reject Satan's mark and to refuse to worship him):

"And he had power to give life unto the image of the beast, that the image of the beast should both speak, and cause that as many as would not worship the image of the beast should be killed. And he causeth all, both small and great, rich and poor, free and bond, to receive a mark in their right hand, or in their foreheads: And that no man might buy or sell, save he had the mark, or the name of the beast, or the number of his name. Here is wisdom. Let him that hath under standing count the number of the beast: for it is the number of a man; and his number is six hundred threescore and six." (Revelation, chapter 13, verses 15-18; Patmos vision, 96 A.D.)

To understand the rotating references to Satan, Antichrist, and the false prophet, it is helpful to remember that Satan is the spiritual power sustaining his incarnation in the body of the individual identified as the Antichrist, whereas the false prophet is the Satanic substitute for the Holy Spirit. The false prophet, acting as the world's spiritual figurehead, calls upon all humanity to worship the beast (Antichrist).

During the last forty-two months (3 1/2 years, 1,260 days) of Antichrist's reign, two witnesses oppose him and, like Moses opposing Pharaoh, call upon God to plague the kingdom of Antichrist and his followers. This period is also referred to as the "great tribulation." The population of Earth must endure both the wrath of God and the terror perpetuated by Antichrist. The devastating plagues pursuant to the ministry of the two witnesses will be similar in nature to the plagues suffered by Egypt during the time of Moses, but of much greater intensity. The mayhem, torture and murder wrought by Antichrist will be of such magnitude that the majority of Jews will be killed, and over half of non-Jews will be slaughtered.

One hundred and forty-four thousand Jewish male virgins will be protected by God and serve as evangelists during the great tribulation. Millions will be martyred rather than worship Satan:

"After this I beheld, and lo, a great multitude, which no man could number of all nations, and kindreds, and people, and tongues, stood before the throne, and before the Lamb, clothed with white robes and palms in their hands; And cried with a loud voice, saying, Salvation to our God which sitteth upon the throne, and unto the Lamb........And one of the elders answered, saying unto me, What are these which are arrayed in white robes? and whence came they? And I said unto him, Sir, thou knowest. And he said unto me, These are they which came out of great tribulation, and have washed their robes, and made them white in the blood of the Lamb. Therefore are they before the throne of God, and serve Him day and night in His temple: and He that sitteth on the throne shall dwell among them." (Revelation, chapter 7, verses 9-10 and 13-15)

Toward the end of the second half of Antichrist's reign, an alliance of nations will rally themselves against Antichrist and his armies. The battle will commence in the Middle East at a place called Armageddon. Antichrist will be sitting in the Jewish temple as god almighty. Armies opposing Antichrist will be attempting to dethrone him, and the armies supporting Antichrist will be defending his claim to divinity. The surviving Jews and the city of Jerusalem will be caught in the middle of the conflict. This final battle between humans orchestrated by Antichrist will be ended by the second coming of Jesus Christ:

"And I saw heaven opened, and behold a white horse; and He that sat upon him was called Faithful and True, and in righteousness He doth judge and make war. His eyes were as a flame of fire, and on His head were many crowns; and He had a name written, that no man knew, but He Himself. And He was clothed with a vesture dipped in blood: and His name is called The Word of God. And the armies which were in heaven followed Him upon white horses, clothed in fine linen, white and clean. And out of His mouth goeth a sharp sword, that with it He should smite the nations: and He shall rule them with a rod of iron: and He treadeth the wine press of the fierceness and wrath of Almighty God.......And the beast was taken, and with him the false prophet that wrought miracles before him, with which he deceived them that had received the mark of the beast, and them that worshiped his image. These both were cast alive into a lake of fire burning with brimstone. And the remnant were slain with the sword of Him that sat upon the horse, which sword proceeded out of His mouth (His spoken word): and all the fowls were filled with their flesh." (Revelation, chapter 19, verses 11-15; 20-21)

The battle of Armageddon is followed by the reign of Christ on Earth which will encompass a period of one thousand years. The beast and the false prophet are imprisoned within the lake of fire, but Satan, himself, is bound and powerless during this period known as the "millennium reign of Christ." Earth, as we know it, will not be destroyed until the millennium reign is over, and the promises God made to King David, to Abraham, and to faithful Christians have been fulfilled by Jesus Christ sitting upon the throne of David for a millennium. Thereafter, Satan will be loosed and allowed to wage his final battle against God:

"And I saw an angel come down from heaven, having the key of the bottomless pit and a great chain in his hand. And he laid hold on the dragon, that old serpent, which is the Devil, and Satan, and bound him a thousand years, and cast him into the bottomless pit, and shut him up, and set a seal over him, that he deceive the nations no more, till the thousand years should be fulfilled: and after that he must be loosed a little season. And I saw thrones, and they sat upon them, and judgment was given unto them: and I saw the souls of them that were beheaded for the witness of Jesus, and for the word of God, and which had not worshiped the beast, neither his image, neither had received his mark upon their foreheads, or in their hands; and they lived and reigned with Christ a thousand years. But the rest of the dead lived not again until the thousand years were finished. This is the first resurrection. Blessed and holy is he that hath part in the first resurrection: on such the second death hath no power, but they shall be priests of God and of Christ, and shall reign with Him a thousand years. And when the thousand years are expired, Satan shall be loosed out of his prison, and shall go out to deceive the nations which are in the four quarters of the earth, Gog and Magog, to gather them together to battle: the number of whom is as the sand of the sea. And they went up on the breadth of the earth, and encompassed the camp of the saints about, and the beloved city: and fire came down from God out of heaven and devoured them. And the devil who deceived them was cast into the lake of fire and brimstone, where the beast and the false prophet are, and shall be tormented day and night for ever and ever." (Revelation, chapter 20, verses 1-10; Patmos vision, 96 A.D.)

Who will participate in the millennium reign of Christ? The categories appear from Scripture to be as follows: Category one: those believers raptured prior to the reign of Anti-Christ (in their glorified bodies); Category two: the remnant of the nations surviving the battle of Armageddon (in their natural bodies); Category three: those aborted, or mentally incompetent, and those who died before the rapture but never heard the gospel (in their natural bodies).

The aborted and those who died without having a chance to accept Christ will probably be resurrected in their natural bodies. They will, along with the mentally incompetent, enter the millennium and accept or reject Christ in accordance with their free will. However, there will be no rebellion against Christ during His reign over earth and He will rule with a "rod of iron." The remnants of the nations that escaped the genocide campaigns of Anti-Christ and were not part of the armies exterminated by Christ when He ended the battle of Armageddon will also enter into the millennium in their natural bodies and will have an opportunity to accept or reject Christ as their sacrificial lamb in accordance with their free will but will be powerless to oppose Him.

Those participating in the millennium in their natural bodies will live long peaceful lives. An individual one hundred years old will be considered a mere child. However, physical death will still eventually occur and those in their natural bodies will marry and produce offspring spanning perhaps forty generations. The last human enemy to be destroyed by God is death and that destruction will occur after the millennium.

At the close of the millennium, Satan will be loosed from his spiritual prison and will raise a huge army from among the descendants of those who entered into the millennium in their natural bodies. Satan will lead his army against Jesus Christ and Satan's army will be cremated by fire issuing from God. Thus, Earth will be cleansed of all those choosing to follow Satan instead of Christ. Satan will be cast into the lake of fire prepared for him and his followers. Those who entered the millennium in their natural bodies and accepted Christ as their sacrificial lamb will be clothed with their glorified bodies.

The consignment of Satan to the lake of fire is followed by the "great white throne" judgment. The only individuals who appear at this judgment are those who steadfastly refused to accept God's forgiveness through the divine sacrifice of Jesus Christ including Satan's army cremated by God.

"And I saw a great white throne, and Him that sat on it, from Whose face the earth and the heaven fled away; and there was found no place for them. And I saw the dead, small and great stand before God; and the books were opened: and another book was opened, which is the book of life: and the dead were judged out of those things which were written in the books, according to their works. And the sea gave up the dead which were in it; and death and hell delivered up the dead which were in them: and they were judged every man according to their works. And death and hell were cast into the lake of fire. This is the second death. And whosoever was not found written in the book of life was cast into the lake of fire." (Revelation, chapter 20, verses 11-15)

This then is the death of all corrupted species upon the planet, Earth. The redeemed among all humanity will be in heaven with their redeemer, Jesus Christ. Those refusing redemption will be forever in the lake of fire with their spiritual father, Satan. Then will be brought to pass that which is written:

"Looking for and hasting unto the coming of the day of God, wherein the heavens being on fire shall be dissolved, and the elements shall melt with fervent heat......Nevertheless we, according to his promise, look for new heavens and a new earth, wherein dwelleth righteousness." (II Peter, chapter 3, verses 12-13)

"And I saw a new heaven and a new earth: for the first heaven and the first earth were passed away; and there was no more sea. And I, John, saw the holy city, new Jerusalem, coming down from God out of heaven, prepared as a bride adorned for her husband." (Revelation, chapter 21, verses 1-2)

So then, where has our search for truth taken us? We have examined the theory of evolution and found it to be a scientific impossibility, a laughable concept in view of our current understanding of microscopic life and irreducible levels of complexity. Even scientists who cling to evolution admit it is totally false, but they refuse for their own personal reasons to reject a known lie in favor of a divine Creator. We have considered all religions of the world with enough followers to be worth consideration and found only two concepts: reward for good works, and redemption through a divine sacrifice. Reward for good works usually takes the form of some better status in life upon reincarnation until one finally becomes one with the universe, or some similar cessation of endless cycles of reincarnation.

We discovered Islam to be a fairly recent bastardization of Christianity wherein good works are the key to eternal bliss in Allah's paradise strewn with brown-eyed virgins who cuddle with those who strike fear into the heart of the infidel. We reviewed Judaism as the forerunner of Christianity and found Judaism to be another religion based on works, keeping the law of Moses, or some variation thereof. Thus, Christianity is the only belief system that offers peace, joy, and eternal life totally apart from human works. The sacrifice of Jesus Christ makes possible the rebirth of the spirit wherein lust, pride and arrogance are replaced by love, humility, and forgiveness.

We challenged the veracity of the Holy Bible and found it to be unassailable. We traced the history of humanity through sixty centuries and found God to be gracious, merciful, forgiving and just; in addition to being long suffering, patient and loving beyond human comprehension. Sadly, we also had to acknowledge that the majority of every generation since Adam have chosen to worship Satan rather than God because humans love to wallow in lust, pride and arrogance just like their chosen spiritual father.

We looked for evidence of human existence upon Earth prior to 4,000 B.C. and found zero indication of such existence. We discovered solid evidence of dinosaurs within the same time window as humans. We reviewed evidence supporting a global flood and found it to be compelling. We tested the underlying assumptions for carbon-14 and radiometric dating and found such techniques to be totally unreliable. We also uncovered the fact that Charles Darwin did not believe in his own theories because the evolution of the human eye is admitted by Darwin to be totally absurd.

We had a good belly laugh from considering the gross stupidity of the "big bang" theory postulated by intellectuals who worship themselves. Thus, we found nothing except special creation by God to explain the existence of energy, matter, and living creatures upon Earth. Moreover, we found the word of God contained within the Holy Bible to be totally compatible with the sum total of human knowledge being accumulated from generation to generation. We see the "signs of the times" being broadcast around the globe via satellite into every nation, people and tongue.

Earth is filled with violence and every conceivable abomination, as it was in the days of Noah and in the days of Lot. We have butchered in America, within the womb, over fifty million of our children; and openly promoted sodomy and homosexuality on prime time television. We have spit in the face of God and ejected Him from our schools, courts, and daily lives. We cling to the mammon of evil and entrust our future to Satan, the destroyer. How do we weigh in the balance of divine justice and within the book of remembrance being compiled by the angels? The apostate Christians of today (the divine vomit, Revelation, chapter 3, verse 16) are occupied with satisfying the lust of the flesh rather than preparing for the rapture of faithful Christians.

Every single human, knowing right from wrong, and having heard the word of God expressed within the gospel of Jesus Christ, has made a decision either to follow Christ or to ignore him. There is no middle ground:

"Jesus said unto them, If God were your father, ye would love Me: for I proceeded forth and came from God; neither came I of Myself, but He sent Me. Why do ye not understand My speech? even because ye cannot hear My word. Ye are of your father, the devil, and the lusts of your father ye will do. He was a murderer from the beginning, and abode not in the truth, because there is no truth in him. When he speaketh a lie, he speaketh of his own: for he is a liar, and the father of it. And because I tell you the truth, ye believe Me not." (John, chapter 9, verses 42-45; Jesus Christ speaking)

All past the age of accountability have already chosen either Christ or Satan as spiritual father. No! No! you say, I have neither accepted nor rejected Christ. I haven't made up my mind on this issue. You are mouthing the lie of your father, Satan. When you refuse to accept the free gift extended to you by God, himself, you have made a decision to reject redemption by making lies your refuge and hiding under falsehood. What does the Scripture say?....."Today if ye will hear his voice, harden not your hearts, as in the provocation." (Hebrews, chapter 3, verse 15)

Aside from the rapture, we are all headed for the grave. It is only a matter of time and not of our choosing. What we can choose is our spiritual father. Will you serve Christ or Satan? There is no choice after physical death. Today is the day of salvation.....now is the accepted time. Choose this day whom you will serve.

Bibliography

Carbon-14 Dating, Radiometric Dating and Tree Ring Dating

[1] Plastino, W.; Kaih ola, L.; Bartolomei, P.; Bella, F. (2001). "Cosmic Background Reduction In The Radiocarbon Measurement By Scintillation Spectrometry At The Underground Laboratory Of Gran Sasso".

[2] Arnold, J. R.; Libby, W. F. (1949). "Age Determinations by Radiocarbon Content: Checks with Samples of Known Age". *Science* **110** (2869): 678–680. doi:10.1126/science.110.2869.678. PMID 15407879.

[3] Willard Frank Libby Münnich KO, Östlund HG, de Vries H (1958). "Carbon-14 Activity during the past 5,000 Years". *Nature* **182** (4647): 1432–3. doi:10.1038/1821432a0.

[4] Ramsey, C. Bronk (2008). "Radiocarbon dating: revolutions in understanding". *Archaeometry* **50** (2): 249-275.

doi:10.1111.2Fj.1475-4754.2008.00394.x. edit
[5] Scott, EM (2003). "The Fourth International
Radiocarbon Intercomparison (FIRI).".
Radiocarbon **45**: 135–285.

[6] "NOSAMS Radiocarbon Data and
Calculations". Woods Hole Oceanographic
Institution.
http://www.nosams.whoi.edu/clients/data.html.

[7] Stuiver M, Reimer PJ, Braziunas TF (1998).
"High-precision radiocarbon age calibration for
terrestrial and marine samples". *Radiocarbon* 40:
1127–51.
http://depts.washington.edu/qil/datasets/uwten98_
14c.txt.

[8] Suter M, Wölfli W (1994). "Systematic
investigation of uncertainties in radiocarbon
dating due to fluctuations in the calibration
curve". *Nuclear Instruments and Methods in
Physics Research* **92**: 194–200. doi:10.1016/0168-
583X(94)96004-6.

[9] Lerman, J. C.; Mook, W. G.; Vogel, J. C.; de
Waard, H. (1969). "Carbon-14 in Patagonian Tree
Rings". *Science* **165** (3898): 1123–1125.
doi:10.1126/science.165.3898.1123.

PMID 17779805.
[10] Kolchin BA, Shez YA (1972). *Absolute archaeological datings and their problems.* Moscow: Nauka.

[11] Beck JW; Richards, DA; Edwards, RL; Silverman, BW; Smart, PL; Donahue, DJ; Hererra-Osterheld, S; Burr, GS et al. (2001). "Extremely large variations of atmospheric C-14 concentration during the last glacial period.". *Science* **292** (5526): 2453–2458. doi:10.1126/science.1056649. PMID 11349137.

[12] Hoffmann DL; Beck, J. Warren; Richards, David A.; Smart, Peter L.; Singarayer, Joy S.; Ketchmark, Tricia; Hawkesworth, Chris J. (2010). "Towards radiocarbon calibration beyond 28 ka using speleothems from the Bahamas". *Earth and Planetary Science Letters* **289**: 1–10. Bibcode 2010E&PSL.289....1H. doi:10.1016/j.epsl.2009.10.004.

[13] Pennicott K (10 May 2001). "Carbon clock could show the wrong time". *PhysicsWeb.* http://physicsworld.com/cws/article/news/2676.

Big Bang Theory

[14] D. N. Spergel et al. (2007). "Three-Year Wilkinson Microwave Anisotropy Probe (WMAP) Observations: Implications for Cosmology". *Astrophysical Journal Supplement Series* **170** (2): 377–408. arXiv:astro-ph/0603449. Bibcode 2007ApJS..170..377S. Doi:10.1086/513700.

[15] Liddle, Andrew; David Lyth (2000). *Cosmological Inflation and Large-Scale Structure.* Cambridge. ISBN 0-521-57598-2.

[16] Edmund Bertschinger (1998). "Simulations of structure formation in the universe". *Annual Review of Astronomy and Astrophysics* **36** (1): 599–654. Bibcode 1998ARA&A..36..599B. doi:10.1146/annurev.astro.36.1.599.

[17] Harrison, E. R. (1970). "Fluctuations at the threshold of classical cosmology". *Phys. Rev.* **D1**: 2726. Bibcode 1970PhRvD...1.2726H. doi:10.1103/PhysRevD.1.2726.

[18] Peebles, P. J. E.; Yu, J. T. (1970). "Primeval adiabatic perturbation in an expanding universe". *Astrophysical Journal* **162**: 815. Bibcode 1970ApJ...162..815P. Doi:10.1086/150713.

[19] Ya; Zel'dovich, B. (1972). "A hypothesis, unifying the structure and entropy of the

universe". *Monthly Notices of the Royal Astronomical Society* 160. Bibcode 1972MNRAS.160P...1Z.

[20] R. A. Sunyaev, "Fluctuations of the microwave background radiation," in *Large Scale Structure of the Universe* ed. M. S. Longair and J. Einasto, 393. Dordrecht: Reidel 1978.

Quantum Mechanics

[21] "On the Law of Distribution of Energy in the Normal Spectrum". Francis Weston Sears (1958). *Mechanics, Wave Motion, and Heat*. Addison-Wesley. p. 537. http://books.google.com/books?hl=en&q= %22Mechanics%2C+Wave+Motion %2C+and+Heat%22+%22where+n+%3D+1%2C %22&btnG=Search+Books.

[22] Kragh, Helge (1 December 2000). "Max Planck: the reluctant revolutionary". PhysicsWorld.com. http://physicsworld.com/cws/article/print/373

[22] McEvoy, J. P.; Zarate, O. (2004). *Introducing Quantum Theory*. Totem Books. pp. 70–89, especially p. 89.

[23] Dicke and Wittke, *Introduction to Quantum Mechanics*, p. 10f.

Theory of Relativity

[24] Einstein A. (1916 (translation 1920)), *Relativity: The Special and General Theory*, New York: H. Holt and Company

[25] Miller, Arthur I. (1981), *Albert Einstein's special theory of relativity. Emergence (1905) and early interpretation (1905–1911)*, Reading: Addison–Wesley, ISBN 0-201-04679-2

[26] Will, Clifford M (August 1, 2010). "Space-Time Continuum". *Grolier Multimedia Encyclopedia.*

[27] Einstein's letter to the London Times in 1919.
  • Einstein Albert (Nov. 28, 1919). "What is the theory of relativity?"

The foregoing bibliography is not actually associated with direct quotes from the reference material, but rather was researched to comprehend the 21st century scientific disciplines indicated as opposed to the 20th century scientific literature on the same subject matter.

EXCERPTS FROM THE BOOK "FLIGHT FROM DEATH" BY DON ALEXANDER

Bishop Romas was both relieved and pleased that the Israeli people had voted to accept Natas' proposed compromise. He knew that Natas was aware of the acceptance although no comment had been forthcoming. Why? Did Natas secretly hope the Jews would defy the law and provide the excuse to attack them?   The memory of the bloody sword still made him queasy. He hoped the feeling didn't linger too long. Natas liked to hold conferences over lavish meals served in his private office where security was well established.

Romas checked his watch. The conference was still eight minutes away. He looked over his notes and tested his memory. Natas didn't like a briefing from notes. He expected his subjects to know the answers to questions without relying on props. Anyone could recite from notes. Natas showed respect for intelligence, not the ability to read. He had no patience with anyone who couldn't engage in an anticipated conference without cluttering up the table with written memory joggers.

They could review the Israeli situation over the brandy appetizer.   Then what?   Did Natas have something else to review with him? If not, why a dinner meeting? Natas never wasted time and seemed to be perpetually preoccupied with his own schemes. He never spent time with women or attended social activities that did not require his personal appearance. Maybe Natas was too taken with himself to feel desire for anyone else. He always felt inferior in Natas' presence, and the man frightened him. He seemed to read a person's secret thoughts as easily as reading a newspaper. That thought revived his nausea. He looked at his notes again.

The rapping of the guard's knuckles on the thick door of the executive lounge ended his short wait. The guard opened the door and looked inside. "He's waiting for you, Bishop." "Thank you, Hanzel. Lead the way." Romas got up and followed the guard. "Sure wish I could join you," Hanzel said. "Tonight's menu includes flame-broiled sirloin with all the trimmings. It's nice to dine with royalty. If the cook's too generous, save me a morsel," Hanzel said, trying to look agreeable. "I'll see to it," Romas promised.

Hanzel knocked on Natas' private door, paused and then opened the door. "Bishop Romas is here, Your Majesty." "Come in, Julius," Natas invited. "I'm sorry for the delay." Hanzel retreated and closed the door behind him. Natas rolled his chair back from his desk, stood up and greeted Romas with a firm handshake. "It's been a busy time. Sit down and join me in a little relaxation." Romas sat down in the guest chair to the left of the desk. "These are exciting times. The world owes you a lot. You have achieved the impossible."

Natas smiled as he reached inside his credenza for the brandy and snifters. "There is nothing that is truly impossible once fear and ignorance have been properly channeled. He poured the brandy and raised his snifter. "To my loyal subjects." Romas joined the toast. "To one law, one faith, and one ruler." He drank heartily, hoping the brandy would increase his confidence level. His armpits were damp again. Natas raised his snifter again. "And to the Children of Abraham. May they rest in peace." "Forever," Romas added. He drank the second toast with Natas. The remark did not really surprise him. He no longer had any doubt where the Jews stood with Natas. They were marked for extermination. Why? They were no longer a threat to world peace. What was Natas' true motive? Whatever the reason, Romas had made a conscious choice. He would be an accomplice in the murder of an entire nationality. A modest price to pay for Natas' trust and favor.

Natas poured more brandy. "Tell me, Julius. What did you think of the Israeli Prime Minister?" Romas arched his eyebrows and stroked his chin. "A tough negotiator with a hide like a rhino and stubborn as a mule." "Did he give you a history lesson?"

The question startled Romas. How did Natas know that! The Prime Minister had never met Natas and he, himself, had never told anyone about the negotiation dialogue. "Yes. As a matter of fact, he did ramble through a bit of ancient history. He thinks you're just another pharaoh who can't be persuaded to let the Hebrews prosper."

"Raamses only killed the newborn males." Natas chuckled. "A halfway measure that led to his ultimate demise. We shall be more thorough." The brandy gave Romas a false bravery. "Why is extermination the only solution?" A strange fire danced in Natas' eyes. "A legend does not die easily. Like a precious gem, it is handed down from generation to generation. To kill a legend, one must kill those who are succored by it. When Abraham's seed is extinct, the promises to his children are also extinguished."

Hanzel knocked on the door and opened it for the servants. "Dinner is ready, Your Majesty." Natas nodded and smiled at Romas. "We can continue our more serious business over dinner." He rose and led the way to the table which had been prepared before Romas' arrival. They seated themselves across from each other at the center of the table and spread their napkins. "I hope the brandy sparked your appetite," Natas remarked. "I ordered the sirloin thick, juicy and man-sized." "Hanzel offered to eat my leftovers," Romas replied. "I noticed that the corner guards are absent.....a change in security?" "More a question of privacy. The corner guards have been made unnecessary by beefed up security outside my office. A suggestion by Chief Wallace."

Their waitress arranged the fresh garden salads, spices, selection of dressings, baked potatoes, sour cream, butter and hot rolls. Another attendant brought in a red dinner wine for Natas to inspect and taste. Natas' eyes scanned the label and checked the integrity of the seal. "1967. . . was that a good year, Julius?"   "I was an young altar boy in 1967. Yes. As I recall, that was an excellent year."

The attendant broke the seal and poured a sample into Natas' glass. He swirled it, sniffed it, and swished it over his taste buds. "That will do just fine," he said. He looked back at Romas while the attendant filled their glasses. "What kind of reception are you getting around the kingdom, Julius?"   "More or less indifferent at this point, but the concept of one faith is more difficult to impose than one law and one ruler."   "Have you seen any evidence of significant resistance?"   Romas tasted his wine. It was very smooth and delightful. "What I see is blind adherence to tradition. Very few people can explain precisely what they believe or why they believe it. However, tradition is like a bad habit. People won't turn loose even though they know that death may result."

Natas spread chunky blue cheese dressing on his salad and buttered his potato, then smothered the potato with sour cream and chives while appearing to ponder Romas' statement. Romas now knew that Natas didn't need to ponder anything. He knew exactly what he was going to do regardless of what anyone said or did. He understood the human spirit and wanted his subjects to follow willingly. Romas sprinkled his salad with Italian dressing and garlic salt, then garnished his potato with heaping portions of butter and sour cream. He added salt and pepper and buttered a hot roll.

Natas tasted his salad and potato. "We need to strip the tradition away one layer at a time. It's much easier to skin a carcass from the outside than from the inside. First, we get rid of all religious books, writings, symbols and ornaments. Then, we destroy all religious shrines and convert places of worship into government property for rehabilitation. Next, we provide the public with an exhibition of your power to raise the dead. Finally, we seal the coffin by making it a crime to speak or write anything contrary to your spiritual guidance."

Romas forked his mouth full of salad to give himself time to think. Raise the dead? Is he serious? "I might fall a little short on my end. Raising the dead is a pretty tall order ......not something I do on a routine basis." "Do you believe in life after death, Julius? Do you believe that humans have an immortal soul?" Romas dabbed at his lips with his napkin. "I used to think so. That's why I became a priest. Now, I worry more about staying alive and enjoying the life that I have now."

Natas studied him pensively. "What disillusioned you?" "I suppose the lust of the flesh overcame my longing for immortality. I have never seen any evidence of life after death or witnessed any miracles outside of Hollywood productions." "Suppose you had witnessed someone raise the dead.   Would that have duly impressed you?"   Natas refilled their wine glasses. Romas became more and more uncomfortable.   Natas was testing his fickleness.   "It would have certainly captured my attention."   "Do you believe that Jesus raised Lazarus from the dead after Lazarus had lain in his tomb for four days?"   Romas' armpits were wet again.   "Isn't that the same as asking whether I believe in life after death?"   Natas' eyes became more intense and more piercing.   "That's not exactly what I had in mind. I'm more interested in whether you believe that it is possible to restore life to a dead body."

The waitress brought the steaks and gave Romas a breather.   His palms were now damp with nervousness. What was Natas driving at?   He knew he was beginning to appear inept and hypocritical.   Natas had earlier referred to a public display of his power.   What power? If this line of questioning continued, he would need assistance to get up from the table.   Did Natas really expect him to perform some sort of miracle as evidence of his competence to function in his assigned role?   His appetite was fading fast.

The steaks were broiled to perfection and garnished with steamed mushrooms. Natas applied a liberal layer of steak sauce and sliced into his sirloin. The outside was slightly charred and the center was pink and moist. He tasted the meaty flavor and grunted with approval. Romas dug into his steak and tried to come up with an intelligent response to Natas' last question.   Did he believe that it is possible to restore life to a dead body? Did he? No. He did not. He sliced off another bite of meat and answered: "Death is the absence of life. Whatever spiritual awareness follows physical life cannot be of the same quality. Physical life involves nurturing of the flesh, bones, organs and blood chemistry. In the absence of life, such nurturing ceases and the body undergoes irreversible corruption. No. I do not believe that a dead body can be restored to physical life after the brain and organs die for lack of oxygen."

Natas chewed his meat and gazed at Romas. "Where does that leave morality?" Romas locked eyes with Natas. "Morals are the product of environment and culture. Culture is the mixture of religious fables, man-made law, physical needs and social structuring while environment is the geographical boundaries separating mature cultures. In one society, it is moral to kill and eat other humans. In another social order, it is immoral to eat the flesh of hogs. Morality is whatever the majority of people within established social boundaries proclaim it to be. The norms become confused when diverse cultures are fused into a global society."

Natas was not impressed with Romas' attempt to evade the question. "What is morality for Julius Romas?" Romas reached for his wine glass. "To be cool in summer, warm in winter, work very little, eat and drink what pleases me, and to die at a ripe old age." "Then, what?" "Then, I am dead. Julius Romas no longer exists. I mix forever with the elements. My lovers and closest friends will soon forget that I ever lived and move on to new relationships."

Their waitress brought in an assortment of desserts and hot coffee. She poured the coffee into fragile china cups and removed the abandoned plates, side dishes and condiments. Natas helped himself to apple cobbler and vanilla ice cream. "You have just described the life of a sheltered stud. Does it really matter whether such an animal lives long enough to die of old age? How often must a living creature experience the same pleasures before life becomes meaningless and monotonous? If continuous enjoyment of carnal lusts is the essence of life, then wouldn't old age be a curse rather than a fervent hope?"

Romas had chosen strawberry pie and whipped cream. He savored the richness and sipped hot coffee. "Old men have the erotic desires of young stallions. Fantasies of eternal youth distort the true image in the mirror. Old men do not really see the wrinkled skin, the sagging flesh, and withered muscles. They see themselves being pursued by young virgins as they snort, paw the earth and display their masculine virility. Unlike the lower animals, humans have the capacity to believe themselves to be something that they are not. It is the pride of life that warms the breasts of old men."

Natas was tiring of Romas' human vanity. It was time to move on to thoughts more relevant to his purpose for entertaining Romas. "For the purpose of deeper meanings, let's assume that humans do have a spiritual existence that survives the physical body. In such an eternal state, would you prefer to serve in heaven or reign in hell?"

Romas' heart skipped and his hand trembled slightly. He set his cup down and lowered his hands below the table. "I have no firm concept of either habitation. I cannot choose between status levels of which I am ignorant." "Well said, Julius," Natas replied. "Where you profess your ignorance, I declare my specific knowledge. I have both served in heaven and reigned in hell. You need only to read my name backward to see that I speak with authority and experience. I have come from my everlasting habitation to save willing souls from the bondage of heaven. To that end, I shall bestow upon you the power to destroy your enemies with the flames of hell and to raise me from the dead."

Natas' declaration shook Romas to the very core of his being. He was beginning to understand the significance of the sudden appearance of Antiochus Epiphanes at the command of Natas. That display of power was a prelude to this revelation. A subtle sense of strength and calmness swept over him and he was no longer afraid of Natas. He resisted the urge to flatter him with praise. Natas perceived his change in comfort level. He watched as Romas moved his hands back into view and continued consuming his coffee and dessert.

"Do you wonder why your dread of me has vanished, Julius? A man always dreads what he doesn't understand. There is no dread when the inevitable is accepted. Your soul belongs to me. My mark is forever in your forehead. Heaven is eternally barred to you and hell awaits your coming. In the meanwhile, there is much to be accomplished. It is time to elevate your status in the eyes of all mankind."

"Is hell truly a reality?" Romas inquired. Natas flashed a devilish grin. "Hell was created as a temporary prison for those who rebel against heaven. The immortality of fallen humans is confined there until the great battle for human souls is ended. The full measure of Lucifer's struggle will be decided less than seven years from now. A great lake of fire has been created to swallow up hell and to imprison Lucifer and the fallen angels. Our task is to help Lucifer conquer human immortality."

Romas began to see the total picture. "We will share Lucifer's earthly kingdom and then join him in the lake of fire?" "Yes. And so will all humans who side with him. Thus, you can see why I must leave to prepare for the quantitative victory. Lucifer will succor you as he has been with me in the earth. He is in me and he shall be in you.

Oren Natas had an angry scowl on his face as he sat upon his throne thinking about the Children of Abraham. Wallace had failed him, and Romas had negotiated a peace pact that was more liberal than the original compromise. Everyone on earth now worshiped him except the defiant Jews and the remaining Christians still in hiding.

He gritted his teeth and cursed all Jews everywhere. Soon, he would go to Jerusalem, sit upon the Throne of David and force the seed of Abraham to worship him. Nothing that he had done impressed the Israelis, and the Jews that were deceived, both in Israel and around the world, despised him. The registered Israelis had taken his mark as part of the compromise provisions and for no other reason.

A foul taste fermented in his mouth and his head began to ache. One third of the Israelis had not yet registered, much less rendered any homage to him. The rest of Jewry only paid him lip service while looking upon his mark as just a necessary evil to be endured in order to be able to buy and sell. Since the miracle of his resurrection had little impact upon those ignoring him, total extermination of all who refused to worship his image was the only way to establish an undivided kingdom.

His security forces had been inept in their attempts to capture and execute the two witnesses who mocked him and continued to plague his kingdom. That would have to change immediately or else his followers might begin to suspect his divinity. Even the angels in heaven did not ridicule the adversary of God, and he certainly wasn't going to allow humans to abase him.

The Captain of the temple guards approached and bowed down before him. "The reporters are all assembled, Divine Majesty. Do you wish to receive them?"   "Have they been fully instructed concerning temple protocol?" "Yes, Divine Majesty."   "Very well. You may allow them to enter."

The media correspondents entered the temple in single file with six feet separating each reporter. One by one, they bowed down in front of Natas and then took seats from left to right in the witness gallery. They had been instructed to maintain complete silence except for two questions per correspondent beginning in the order in which they were seated.

Natas sat motionless with his feet flat on the throne platform and his arms resting on the elevated sides of the throne seat. His fingers curled comfortably in front of the arm supports. He wore a jewel studded royal robe woven from pure, white silk that fell around his kingly sandals made from pure gold and lined with diamonds and rubies. His head was adorned with a crown of gold encrusted with precious gems of all shapes and colors. He looked on passively while the assembly was properly accommodated. The only sounds that violated the complete silence were an occasional cough or sniffle. The first correspondent seated rose in front of her seat, bowed her head to Natas and began the round of questions: "Divine Majesty, now that you have cleansed our fresh water supplies, can you tell us if we will have to endure more plagues?"

Natas gazed at her with a blank expression. "There are opposing forces within the spiritual realm which struggle for dominance. Humans are positioned only above the animals in the order of living beings and cannot comprehend the nature of the upper hierarchy of life. There will possibly be more plagues while I do battle with the opposing forces on behalf of mankind. Should more evil befall us, it must be endured until such time that I can overcome the enemy."

"Divine Majesty, would you tell us something about your origin and why you have chosen not to reveal yourself unto us until now?" The corners of Natas' mouth crinkled into a wry smile. "The eternal beings who look down upon humans are not concerned with the number of times Earth rotates on its axis or circles the nearest star. Such calculations have meaning only to mortal creatures whose life span is fleeting. For eons of time, I have defended my kingdom against those who would usurp my power. I neither hunger nor thirst nor desire the treasures which delight the eyes of humans. I sit at the top of the hierarchy of life and do battle where and when it pleases me. You see me now because this planet has become a divine battleground. Your mortal minds are not capable of grasping my origin, and so I will only speak of those things which are within your understanding."

The matronly anchorwoman bowed to Natas again and sat down. The distinguished gentleman to her right rose and bowed to the throne. "Divine Majesty, would you tell us by what physical process the waters became blood and how this pollution was so suddenly reversed?"

Natas' expression became icy and his eyes appeared to darken. "Humans are filled with unjustified vanity and consider that only those things which they have literally experienced are within the natural order of the universe. Suppose that from the beginning of measured time, great hailstones fell upon the earth, or the waters periodically took on the chemistry of blood, or swarms of mutant locusts emerged from the bowels of the planet. Would you be concerned with the question you have posed? Or, would you merely accept such phenomena as natural events governed by immutable laws of chemistry and physics? You ask me elementary questions that encompass what you perceive as a great mystery only because of your limited life experiences. The history of mankind upon the planet, Earth, is but one heartbeat within the past and future eons of existence. Thus, you have witnessed but a single scene in the unending drama of immortality which is played out beyond the scope of human reasoning. Both water and blood are composed of the elements which spring from eternal energy that behaves in accordance with divine will."

"Divine Majesty, will you tell us the source of the energy which forms itself into the atoms which make up our periodic table of the elements as we attempt to describe such energy?"

Natas looked upon him with condescending tolerance. "The hierarchy of eternal life emanated from the unison of divine wills so that such life preceded the formation of the energy that fills the space perceived by humans as well as regions unknown to mortal beings. Energy radiates from the upper hierarchy of life and forms what you call gases, liquids and solids as a transitory phase within unmeasured eternity. The chemical composition and temporary appearance of gases, liquids and solids as interpreted by the mortal senses of seeing, hearing, smelling, tasting and touching are changeable whenever divine will counteracts what you erroneously believe to be unalterable laws of physics, biology and chemistry. Such laws have been postulated through your inability to recognize anything but your own life experiences and your lower position within the hierarchy of living beings. When divine tolerance allowed you to split the atom, you quickly acknowledged the destructive energy that constitutes what you call matter. Were you able to further divide particles of visible energy, you would find such particles continue to release inherent energy until the pure substance of motion, velocity and momentum is no longer discernible through your mortal senses. Since you cannot perceive the true nature of energy, it is your human vanity that causes you to ponder its origin."

The silver haired gentleman bowed to Natas and sat down again. To his right, an attractive redhead who rose to celebrity status by using her brain rather than her sex appeal stood and bowed her flaming locks. "Divine Majesty, would you tell us whether human beings perish at death like the lower animals, or do we possess immortal souls?" Natas studied her and wondered if she really cared. "There is a spark of human immortality which survives the death of your physical bodies. You may use whatever word you believe best expresses that eternal state of which you are truly ignorant. You worship me now and you shall forever remain with me in my everlasting habitation. You may come to question the value of your immortality when physical death opens the eyes of your so-called soul. In the meanwhile, you would be well advised to satisfy your carnal desires within the permissiveness of our global law."

"Divine Majesty, are there such eternal habitations as heaven and hell? And if so, what are they like?" Natas' eyes twinkled with amusement. "You have coined the word heaven to describe different concepts such as the planet's atmosphere, the space beyond that atmosphere, the visible sky, the outer regions of space filled with galaxies, the dwelling place of divine beings, and a state of perpetual bliss. I assume that you are not requesting that I comment on all those diverse concepts, so I will answer by assuring you that all of those references to heaven are well founded. Living beings do indeed occupy habitations beyond Earth; and hell describes one of those dwelling places where the eternal state is rebellious rather than blissfully contented."

The next reporter stood and bowed to the throne. "Divine Majesty, is this place we describe as hell a habitation of endless and fiery torment?" Again, Natas indicated his indulgence of human limitations with a tantalizing smile.

"Your comprehension is diluted by the imperfection of your mortal senses. Torment for immortal beings is a state of discontent and separation from fellowship with those enjoying blissful servitude. The smoke and fire of such torment are indeed everlasting."

"Divine Majesty, there are millions of people who are hiding out and refusing to join our new world society. They mock your authority and live as parasites off our natural resources. Do you plan to correct this problem?"

Natas' smile faded and his face turned to flint. "It is within the divine nature to be merciful and gracious. Hence, these dissenting vagabonds shall be given a final opportunity to come forth from hiding and voluntarily join my kingdom. Those who continue to rebel must be hunted down and executed. I have ordered Chief Malinsky to make this task his top priority and have further instructed him to assign sixty-six million of his men to a thorough and continuous search throughout zones one and two. I expect that the problem will soon be eliminated."

The next correspondent raised a similar question. "Divine Majesty, will you continue to allow the Jews inside Israel to worship another God? Will you honor the peace pact which Chief Malinsky and Bishop Romas were forced to negotiate because the Israelis refused to otherwise give up their military weapons?"

Natas masked his rage with an expression of

benevolence. "Jerusalem must cease to be a burdensome stone and a yoke around the neck of law abiding citizens. To that end, I will personally go to Israel and bring about global harmony."

"Divine Majesty, how is it that these self-proclaimed prophets, which some call witnesses, seem able to appear at any place of their choosing and yet elude the police?" Natas rose from his throne indicating that the audience was being terminated. "They are protected by the spirit world that opposes my kingdom, but are not invincible. They are mere humans that will be sought out and executed. Anyone who harbors them, or has knowledge of their location and fails to report that information, will share their fate." Natas sat down again upon his throne while the correspondents stood, filed past the throne, bowed to him and headed toward the exit arch.

David Solomon traced the rim of his wine glass with his right index finger while listening with reservation to Aaron Hartstein. The old general was crafty, but sometimes overly cautious. David wanted to act more quickly before Natas launched an organized genocide campaign against the Jews. "If we wait too long, we will box ourselves in even more," he insisted. Hartstein placed his palms flat on his reading table and eased his weary body out of the cushioned leather chair. He circled his library and ended up at the liquor cabinet as David said nothing to permit Hartstein to ponder what had already been said. Such prolonged pauses were customary during their discussions, and David knew that his courtesy was deeply appreciated by his old friend.

Hartstein took another bottle of sherry from the cabinet, refilled their glasses, set the bottle on the table and sat down again while looking at David with squinted eyes and furrowed forehead. "We should do nothing that provides Natas with an excuse to attack us immediately. The world is aware of the peace agreement, and fear of adverse public reaction will hold Natas at bay for awhile. Regardless of how the general population feels about the existence of the agreement, they would lose respect for Natas if he unilaterally breaches the peace."

"Flight From Death" in both novel and screenplay formats as well as Don Alexander's other thirteen books and two screenplays are available at Amazon.com on the internet. At Don's website livingbreadnpinc.com on the page entitled "Gift of God" all previous books and the two screenplays are listed with a brief synopsis and a direct link to Amazon.com for purchase. The books and screenplays are also available on Kindle E-book readers.

Reader's Notes